IMAGES
of America

FINNS OF MICHIGAN'S UPPER PENINSULA

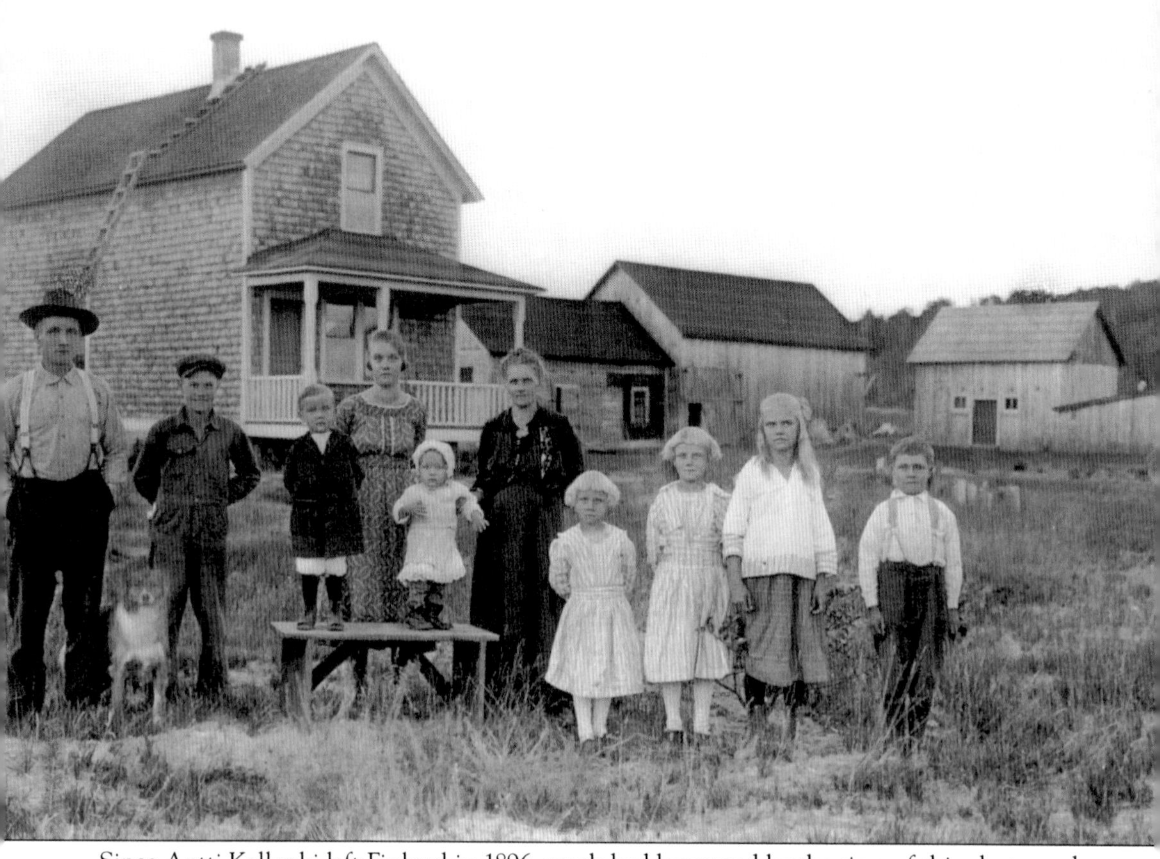

Since Antti Kallunki left Finland in 1896, much had happened by the time of this photograph taken in Tapiola, Michigan, in 1921. He was married with eight children, with another on the way. Behind stands the home and outbuildings he built on his own land, purchased by frugally saving his wages from working in the copper mines of Calumet. Photographs such as these assured relatives back in Finland their American loved ones were doing well. (James Kurtti.)

On the Cover: The work never ends for old or young. Rauha Koski helps her immigrant grandmother Marie Hakola haul firewood in Newberry in the 1940s. Rauha went on to have a long career in nursing, becoming an instructor and head nurse at the Yale University Psychiatric Clinic, and married Suomi Synod pastor Alex Koski. (Finlandia University's Finnish American Heritage Center and Historical Archive.)

IMAGES
of America

FINNS OF MICHIGAN'S UPPER PENINSULA

The Finnish American Heritage Center
Foreword by Kay Seppälä

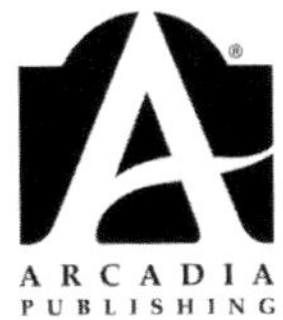

ISBN 978-1-4671-2978-7

Published by Arcadia Publishing
Charleston, South Carolina

Printed in the United States of America

Library of Congress Control Number: 2018935229

For all general information, please contact Arcadia Publishing:
Telephone 843-853-2070
Fax 843-853-0044
E-mail sales@arcadiapublishing.com
For customer service and orders:
Toll-Free 1-888-313-2665

Visit us on the Internet at www.arcadiapublishing.com

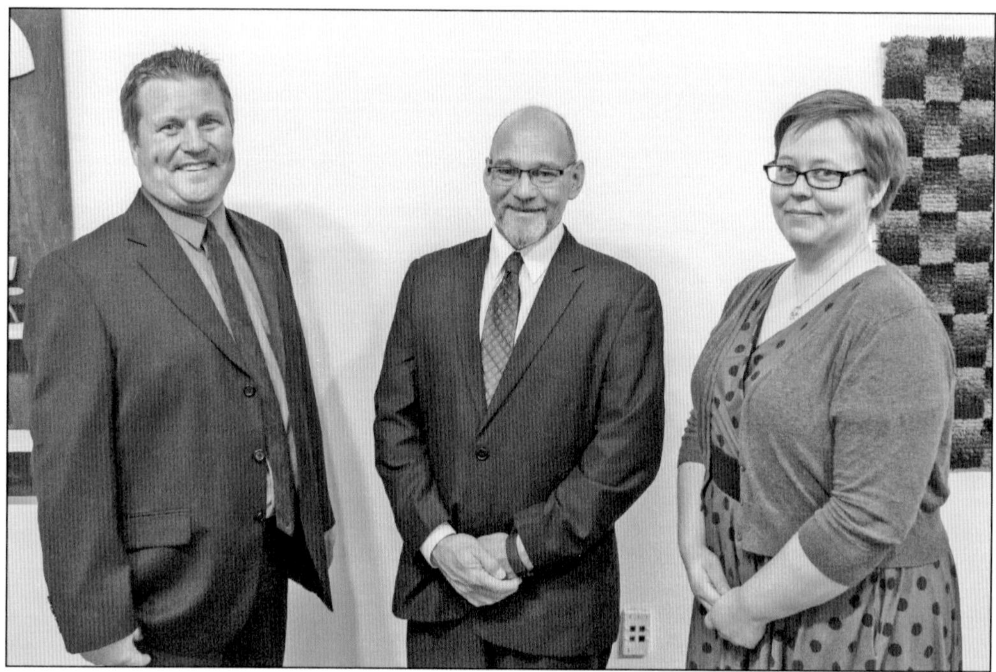

David Maki (left) is the assistant editor of the *Finnish American Reporter*; James Kurtti (center) is the director of the Finnish American Heritage Center, editor of the *Finnish American Reporter*, and honorary consul for Finland in the Upper Peninsula; and Joanna Chopp (right) is the archivist at the Finnish American Heritage Center and Historical Archives. (Finnish American Heritage Center and Historical Archive.)

Contents

Foreword

It was not until I moved away that I realized how Finnish American I was. Growing up in Ontonagon, a small town in the western Upper Peninsula (UP), I thought everybody went to Saturday night sauna, danced the Raatikkoon at wedding dances, watched *Suomi Kutsuu* while getting ready for church on Sunday morning, and ate *pannukakku* every other week. When I returned to the UP 20 years ago, I was pleased to discover the Finnish American Heritage Center with its dedicated staff, who work to preserve this slice of Finnish American life that I had grown to cherish. Indeed, the Heritage Center has supported me in creating and directing the children's Finnish folk dance group, the Kivajat Dancers, as well as enabled me to organize and lead the Ilon Kaiku Kantele Ensemble.

The archive at the Heritage Center has been collecting materials since the 1930s and has an amazing wealth of Finnish American manuscripts, books, records, and artifacts. I am delighted to see this pictorial history book created from their extensive collection, for it is a great way to preserve and treasure our Finnish heritage as well as encourage other ethnic groups to embrace their heritage too. Why preserve this cultural heritage? Singer John McCutcheon, in his song "Water From Another Time" says it well: "It don't take much, but you gotta have some / The old ways help the new ways come / Just leave a little extra for the next in line / they're gonna need a little water from another time."

It is my pleasure to introduce this little gem to you. Enjoy.

—Kay (Marttinen) Seppälä

Acknowledgments

The Finnish American community across the Upper Peninsula maintains a strong bond with its heritage. It is because of this pride that Finlandia University's Finnish American Heritage Center exists—to preserve our shared history and culture. Unless otherwise noted, all images appear courtesy of the Finnish American Heritage Center (FAHC) and Historical Archive collections.

Special thanks to our three Finnish National Agency for Education interns who worked on various stages of this book during their time at the FAHC: Emppu Siltaloppi, Mika Tompuri, and Pauliina Lehto. Our thanks also to the American Scandinavian Foundation for sponsoring these vital internships.

Our sincere appreciation to the small army of individuals and organizations that contributed their knowledge or photographs: John Backman, Kristin Cohen, Christine Evans, Amy Goodman, Rebecca Hoekstra, Martin Johnson, Ron Kaminen, Jeremiah Mason, Dan Necas, Alana Nolan, Norma Nominelli, Betty Petroski, Kay Seppälä, Dale Skogman, Luanne Skrenes, Bror Träskbacka, Kristin Ojaniemi, Chassell Historical Organization, Central Upper Peninsula and Northern Michigan University Archive, Delta County Historical Society, *Finnish American Reporter*, Gallen-Kallela Museo, Gentlemen's Choice Barbershop, Immigration History Research Center Archive, Iron County Historical Society, Keweenaw National Historical Park Archive, US Ski and Snowboard Hall of Fame, Quincy Mine Hoist Association, Zion Lutheran Church, and the patient people at Arcadia Publishing.

INTRODUCTION

Everyone in Michigan's Upper Peninsula (affectionately known as the UP) knows how to correctly pronounce the word "sauna," Finland's only offering to international dictionaries. But to credit the Finns with bringing sauna culture to the UP only begins to scratch the surface of how Finnish immigrants and their descendants have shaped the UP's unique culture.

Finns have a long history in North America. While Finland was yet ruled by Sweden, many Finns helped establish and settle the New Sweden Colony along the Delaware River between 1638 and 1655, before it was absorbed by other colonial powers. These Finnish settlers are credited with bringing log cabin construction to North America, and the oldest such structure still in existence, the Nothnagle Log House in New Jersey, shows tell-tale signs of Finnish construction methods.

However, it was another tumultuous time in US history that was instrumental in bringing the first Finns to Michigan's Upper Peninsula: the first great mineral rush. At the time of the US Civil War, copper from the UP was a vital part of the Northern war machine, but the mines faced a lack of able workers as young men were conscripted into the military. The Quincy Mining Company sent agents to Finnmark, the far northeastern province of Norway, where many Finns had migrated looking for work in the copper and silver mines, after years of bad crops and famine back home. The promise of work in America coupled with the possibility of land ownership was a siren song to many. Many left Finland with plans of one day returning, but only a few ever did.

It is said that the first Finns arrived in the UP, landing in Hancock—then no more than a small and meager mining village—on midsummer eve in 1865. From the docks they climbed the steep hills to the copper mine site and were surprised to find they were expected to begin work in the bowels of the earth the next day, a day they regarded as ordained by God and consequently a day of rest and religious observance. As the copper industry continued to flourish, the growing number of Finnish immigrants branched out into other industries as well. Some who became tired of the dangerous life of a miner bought the cheaper cutover land, or "stump farms," left after the virgin forests were razed. Besides mining and farming, Finns were also famously adept at fishing and lumbering in the early days.

By 1930 nearly 30,000 Finns lived in the UP, roughly a quarter of all residents, making it the most densely Finnish enclave in the United States. Many UP communities had large Finnish populations and Finnish churches, halls, cooperative stores, temperance societies, and the like. Ishpeming and Hancock, especially, were important nationally as significant Finnish cultural centers in the New World.

Nowadays, only about 16 percent of the overall population of the UP claims Finnish ancestry, but the six counties on the western end of Lake Superior's shore represent the only counties in the country where Finnish Americans are the largest ethnic group.

Often accused of being clannish, bull-headed, and distant, Finns, particularly those living in rural areas, have retained their language and customs well beyond the expected time. But they have struck a balance between faithfulness to their ancestral roots and fully embracing all that it means to be American.

Yes, folks in what some call "the Sauna Belt," still see smoke rising from humble, small buildings (saunas), sometimes perched on lake shores or otherwise positioned for a quick dip or roll in the snow. Sauna is more than breaking a sweat; it is an ancient social relationship between family and neighbors, as well as nature.

Country roads bear the surnames of early settlers; in the case of Hancock, the main streets proudly bear bilingual names, such as Kukkulakatu and Koulukatu. Hancock is also the home of Finlandia University, formerly Suomi College—the only existing school of higher learning founded by Finns.

Because of Finlandia University's inextricable connections to Finnish American and Finnish culture, the Finnish American Heritage Center and Historical Archive was opened in 1990, representing the largest collection of Finnish-American archival materials found anywhere. The center provides a variety of community classes, including Finnish language, folk dance, and *kantele* instruction, and publishes the leading newspaper for Finns in North America, the *Finnish American Reporter.* The archive's vast collection of photographs was the source of the bulk of the images found within these pages, with the FAHC staff providing historical provenance for each picture.

These photographs were selected to offer at least a glimpse of how significant the Finns' impact on Upper Michigan culture and life has been. Besides being milkmaids and loggers, Finnish women and men also became college presidents and political activists; but no matter which task they undertook, they always did so with undeniable *sisu*. And when not working, Finns also knew how to have fun.

From Ironwood to Sault Ste. Marie, from Copper Harbor to Escanaba, the Finn has made as much an impression on the UP as mosquitoes and snow. Within these pages, we have provided a variety of photographs from those different spheres of life, hopefully evoking memories and personal family stories, as well as providing some new information relative to the characters, events, and institutions represented in this book.

We invite you to allow us to share these photographs and anecdotes with you as we reexamine the story of Finns in the Upper Peninsula of Michigan.

One

Scratching Out a Living

The Finns were rather late in coming to the United States when compared to other Nordic countries, but much like the others, they were largely unskilled immigrants from the countryside. They did not speak English, and American ways were unfamiliar to them. Consequently, they took what work they could, beginning at the bottom of the social ladder. In the Upper Peninsula copper mines, the men began as trammers, pushing the ore cars for long hours.

Even in the boardinghouses, the English-speaking miners were served meals first; the Finnish and Eastern European trammers were served last. However, being employed by a mine did not necessarily mean a career spent pushing ore cars. Mines needed carpenters, machinists, timbermen, teamsters, miners, firemen, and general laborers as well. As immigrants learned English and other skills, it was possible to move up the ladder.

Some found work in the iron mines of Ironwood and Iron Mountain, as well as Marquette County. Still other men became loggers, including many Swedish-speaking Finns, and yet others began at what they were already familiar with, such as commercial fishing, and as soon as they were able, purchased 40 or 80 acre "stump farms" from cutover lands. It was not uncommon for a man to tend to his farm during the short UP growing season and spend the winter working in a remote logging camp.

Single women became domestics, either in large mine captains' homes or humble workers' homes, filled with children or boarders or sometimes both. Women were also employed as lumber camp cooks, nurses, store clerks, and teachers, as well as being vital to the running of family farms and small businesses, and child rearing.

As the primary industries of the Upper Peninsula began to decline, more and more people looked for work outside the area, in particular, finding jobs in the Lower Peninsula's burgeoning auto industry. The hardships and uncertainty of the Great Depression even led many to Russian Karelia in hopes of creating a worker's paradise.

Whatever employment they found, the Finns gained a reputation for hard work and honesty, as well as sometimes radical political views. Religious or secular, radical or traditional, Finns lived as they worked—with strong resolve.

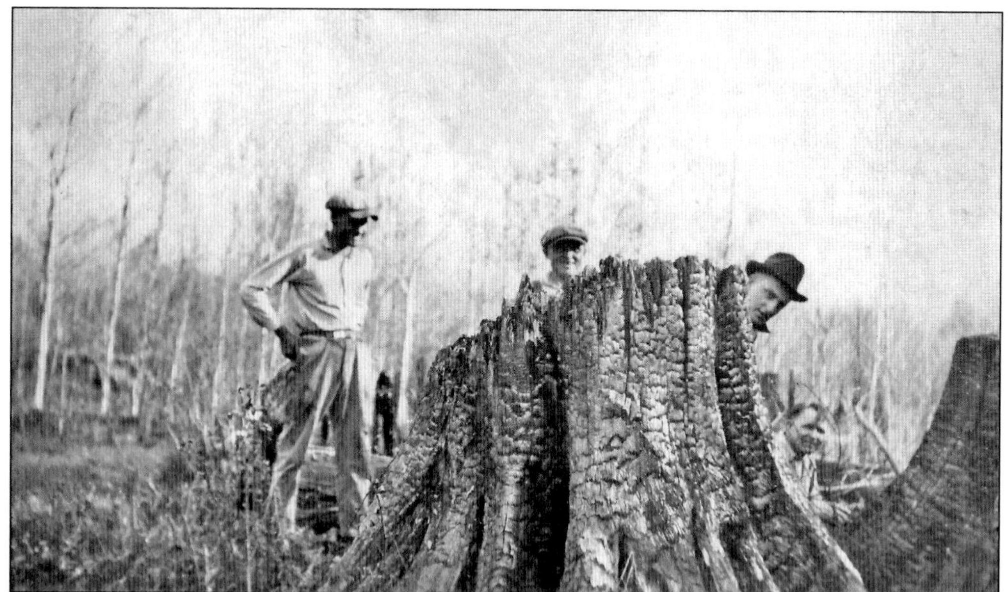

Finnish immigrant "stump farmers" saw the potential in cutover land and bought 40- or 80-acre parcels with the plan of clearing the land to build a home. First the stumps had to be removed with bare hands, brute strength, and occasionally, a bit of explosive. It was often said that the stumps themselves only understood Finnish. (James Kurtti.)

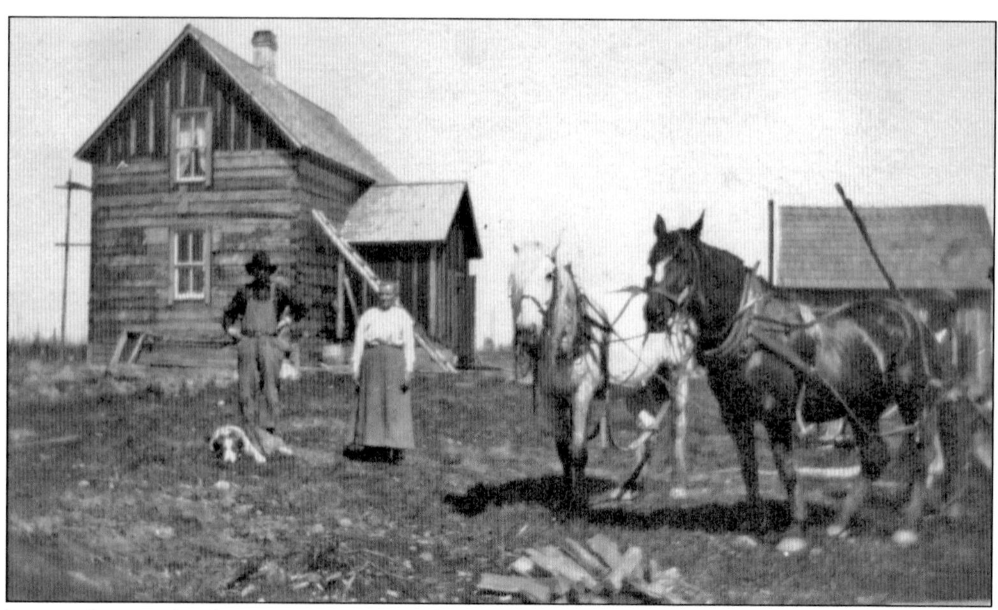

It was a long and arduous journey across the Atlantic Ocean for Finnish immigrants headed for America, one that many hoped to make again—in reverse—as soon as possible. Whether they intended to stay only a few years or start an entirely new life, these immigrants were proud of their parcels of land and made sure they reflected the pride they took in themselves and their work.

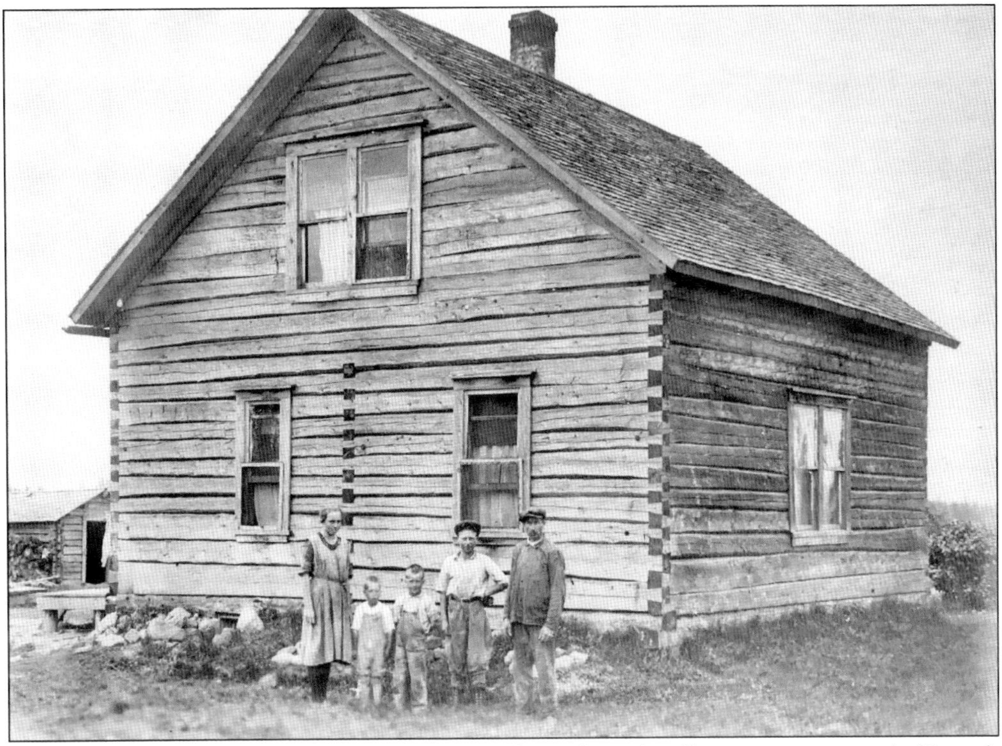

Tight, clean corners and symmetrical lines were the trademarks of home construction by Finnish immigrants to the UP. The logs themselves were hand-hewn, each crafted to match any natural curvature the neighboring logs might contain, creating an unparalleled tight fit without chinking. Much like their owners, the immigrants' homes were humble but filled with a sense of pride. (Ron Kaminen.)

One of the first Finnish-built houses in Wakefield, in Gogebic County, was built by Jonas Autio; Armas Laukkala and his wife, Miina, lived here for decades. This photograph was taken shortly after World War I. Finns called Wakefield home since 1886, and as recently as the early 1960s, there were numerous businesses that were owned and operated by the descendants of immigrants.

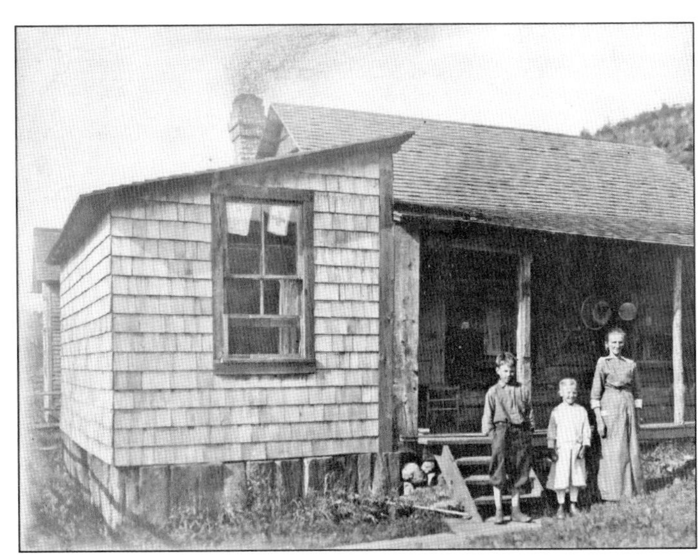

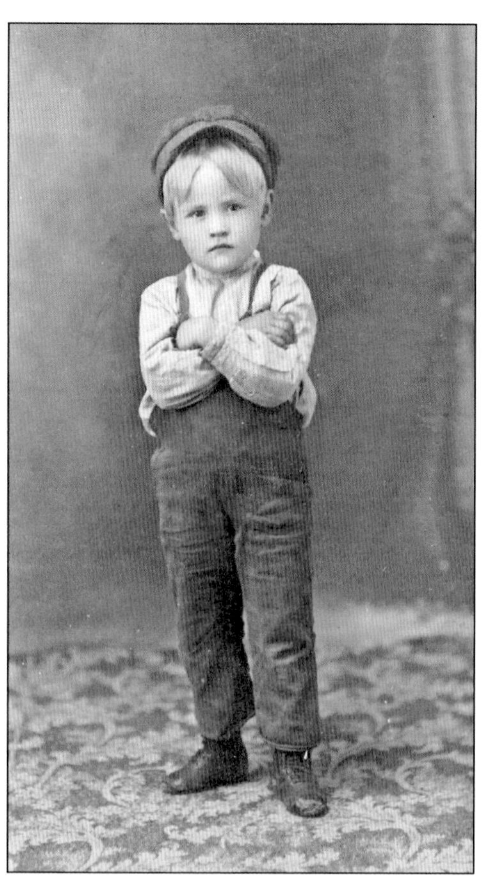

William Ruona (1903–1984) moved from the Houghton County village of Baltic in the early 1900s with his parents to the hardwoods area of Pelkie, where his father hewed out a farm and eventually built a general store. A studio photographer captured young William dressed for the type of work that led to his long and storied career as a logger and forester.

When renowned UP photographer J.W. Nara happened by this group of young people who were out enjoying an afternoon of recreation in the Keweenaw County location of Fulton and asked to take a photograph, "We ran into the house and put on our best Sunday clothes," Emma Simonen recalled. (James Kurtti.)

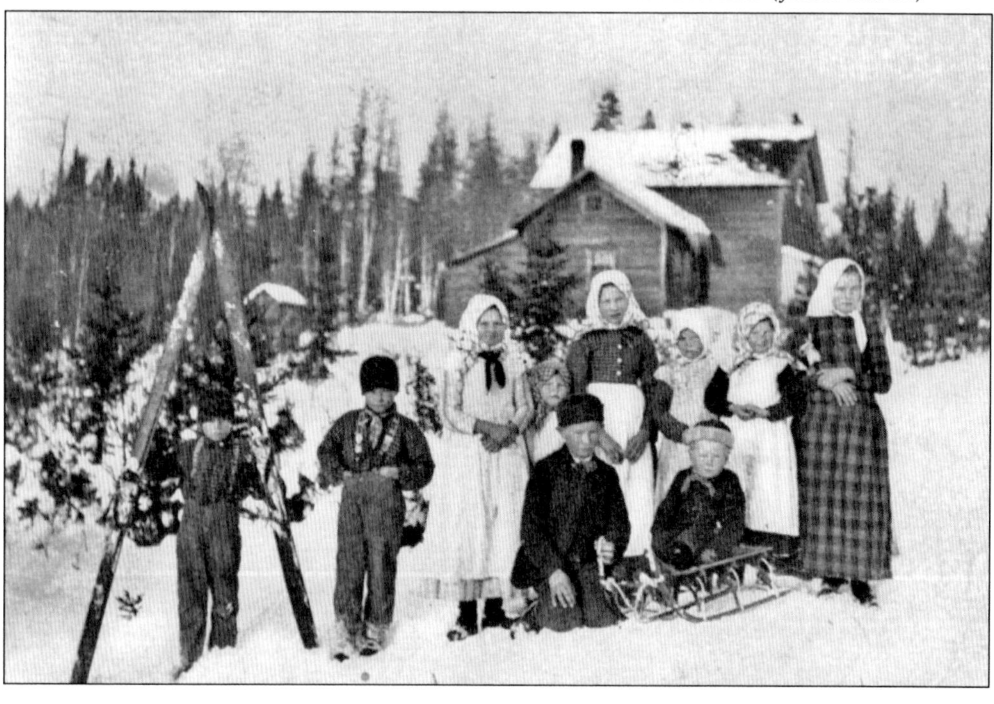

Mrs. Koski of Rudyard, like many women of her generation, had a spinning wheel in her home and put it to use regularly. Skill in the fiber arts was a necessity in the early years to create or mend the family's clothing and linens. While it served a practical purpose, spinning also served as a method of relaxation for many women.

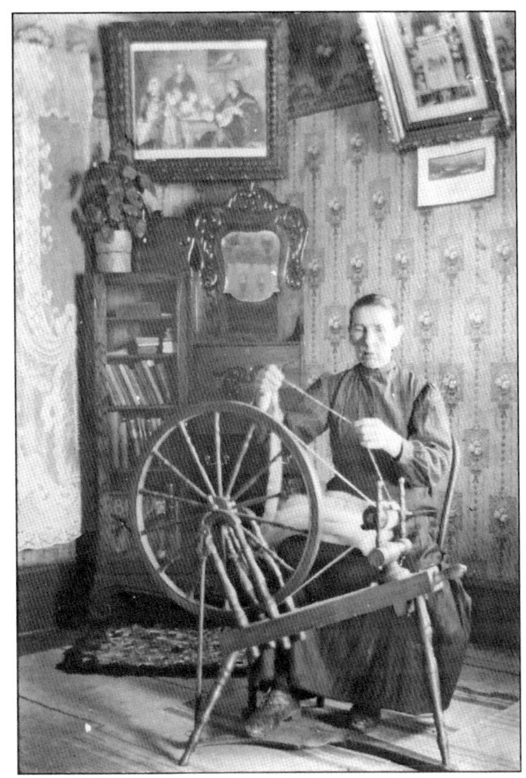

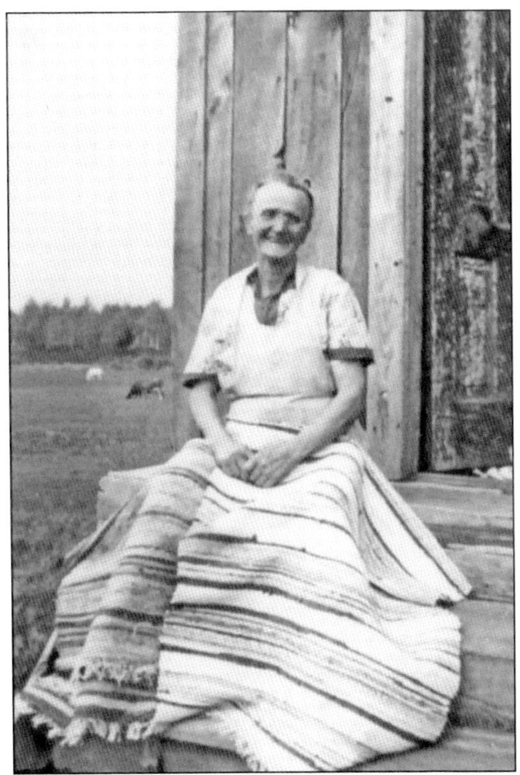

Times were tough, and for immigrants like Johanna Kallunki of Tapiola, nothing could go to waste. They recycled and reused whatever they could. The rugs draped over her lap were woven from rags. While the process was created out of necessity, it turns out these families were ahead of their time with the recycling and reuse movements of today. (Luanne Skrenes.)

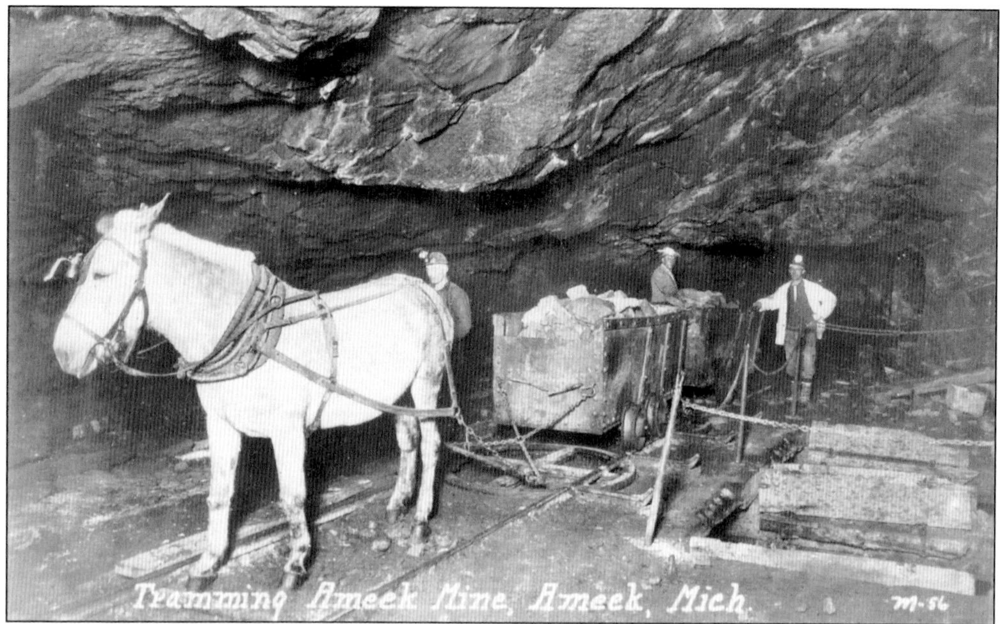

Before advances in technology improved the process of tramming, mines like the Ahmeek Mine (misspelled on this image) in Keweenaw County depended on "horsepower" to extract the ore. It was said that mine bosses valued draft animals, like this mule, more than their men, because replacing an animal mandated a purchase, while a man could be replaced by the next immigrant who was waiting eagerly for a chance to earn a wage.

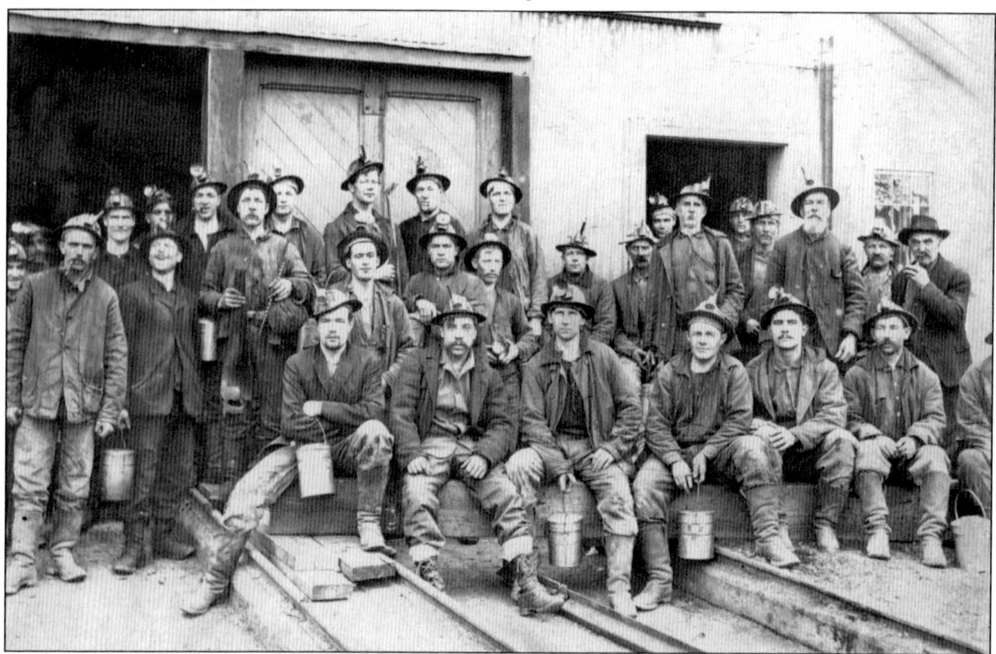

It could be a matter of life or death in a mine, so many miners from other ethnic backgrounds learned Finnish before they learned English so they could communicate with their coworkers. The bond carried over after the shift ended, as they would wash each other's backs after each shift, since the job made it so many men could not bend their arms to complete the task themselves.

It was cramped, dark, and dirty, not to mention life-threatening and back-breaking, but for men like (from left to right) Charles and Armas Torro, Andrew Wanhala, and Waino Kaiponen, who labored in the Painesdale Mine in 1930, it had to be done to feed the family. Progress like headlamps and one-man drills improved the process, but family members above ground prayed each day that their loved ones would return from their shift safely.

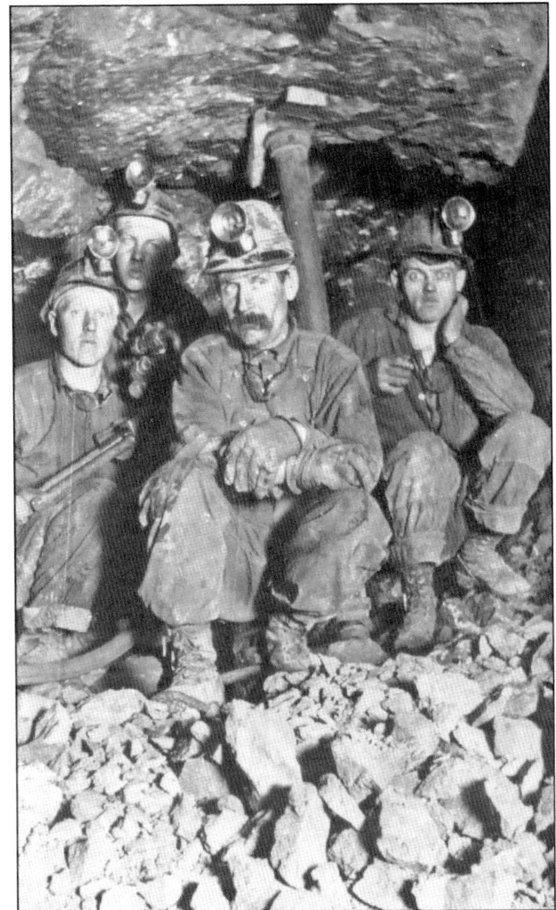

Bruno Nordberg, a Finnish immigrant from the Swedish-speaking part of the country, arrived in America in 1879 and is well known for his designs of mining equipment. In 1917, Nordberg designed and built the world's largest steam hoist, bought by Quincy Mining Company for its copper mine near Hancock. It was installed and running in November 1920 and was used for 11 years. (Quincy Mine Hoist Association.)

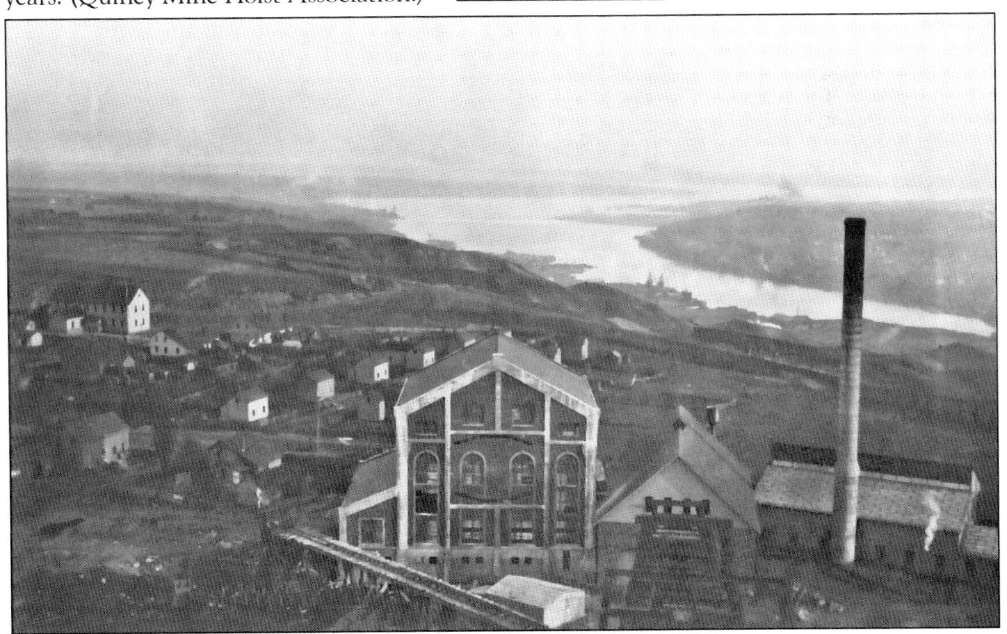

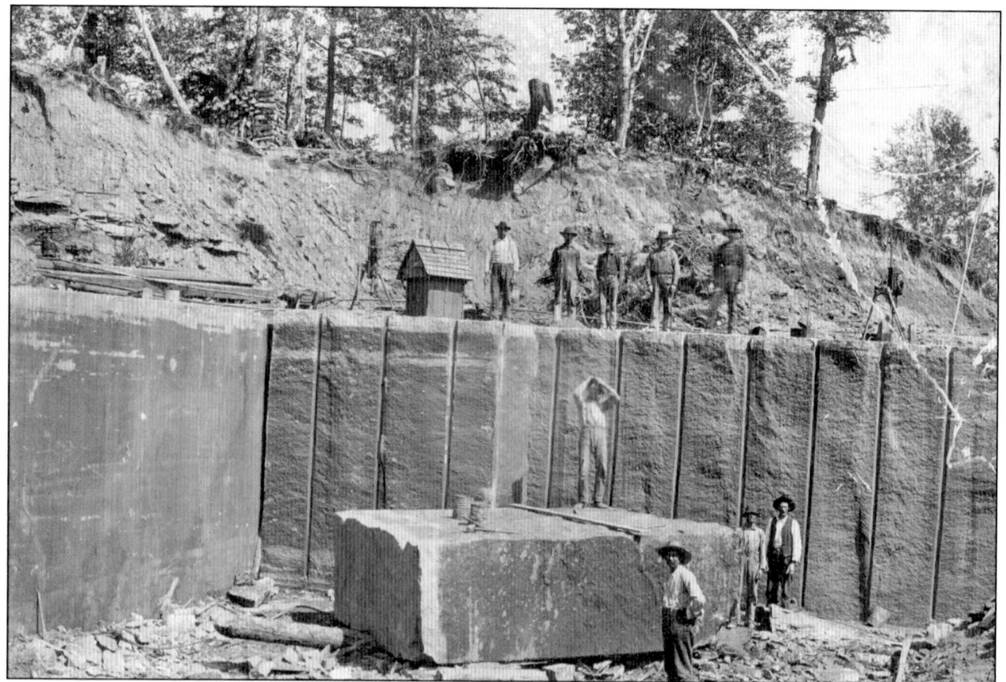

Jacobsville sandstone was desired for its durability and aesthetics but was dangerous and physically demanding to quarry. This distinct red material, which came from 32 quarries across the UP, was used to construct some of the most significant buildings that line the UP's streets even today, a testament to the sandstone's quality.

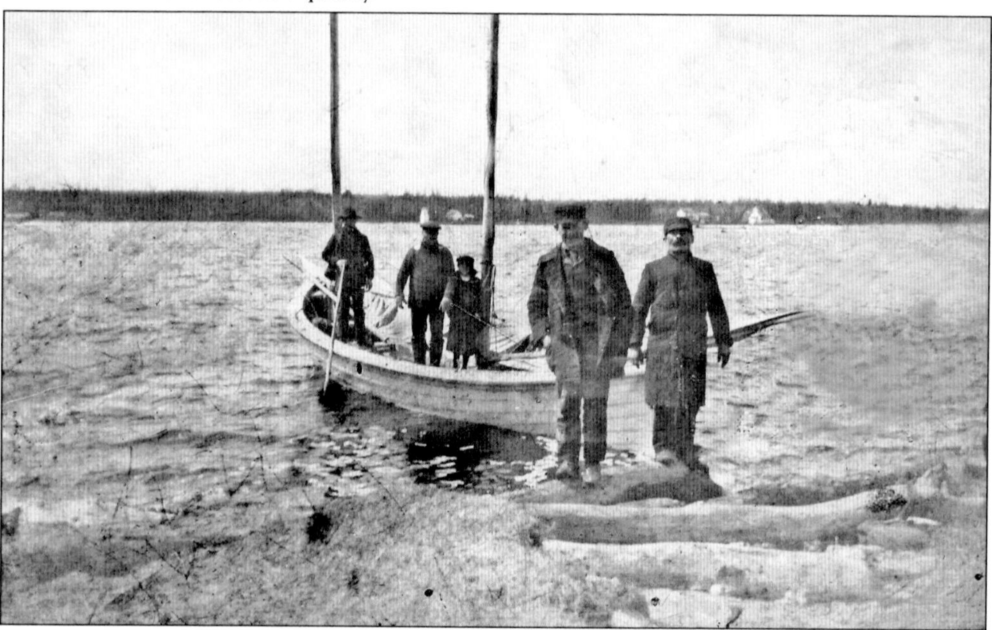

An early Finnish fishing boat is pictured on the shore of Finlander Bay, south of Portage Entry near Chassell on Lake Superior in 1900. In the foreground are boat captain Jaakko Karppi and sailor Kalle Wuornos. Commercial fishing was the primary source of income for many Finnish American families who settled along or near the shores of the Great Lakes.

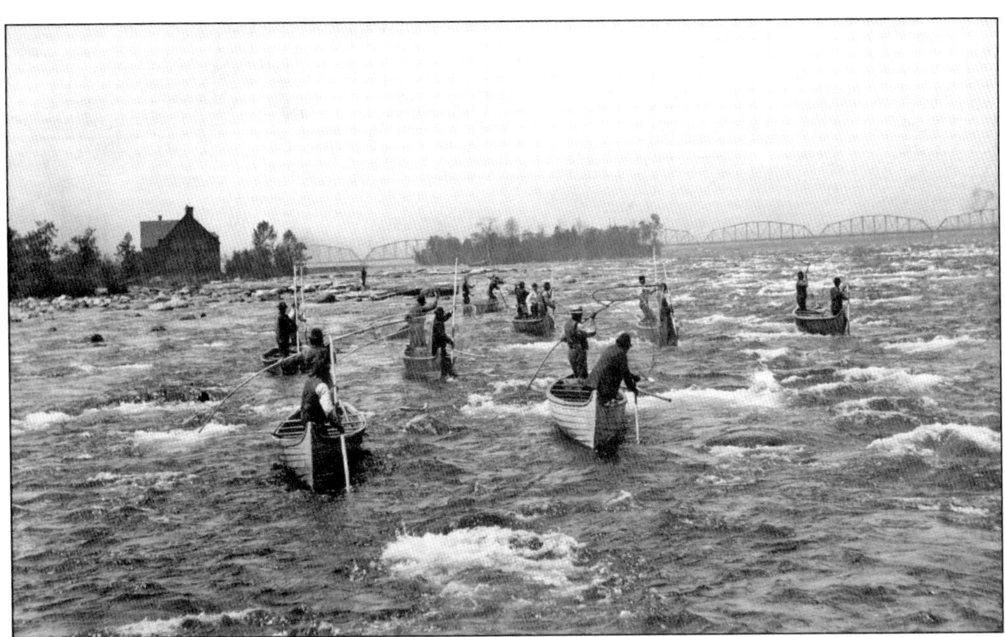

The rapids of the St. Mary's River, just below the river's exit from Lake Superior near Sault Ste. Marie, have been prime fishing ground for generations. These intrepid Finnish American fishermen used the now-defunct technique of dip netting to bring home the prized catch of the area, whitefish, in an area aptly named Whitefish Bay. Commonly, a single canoe could bring home several hundred pounds of whitefish from an excursion.

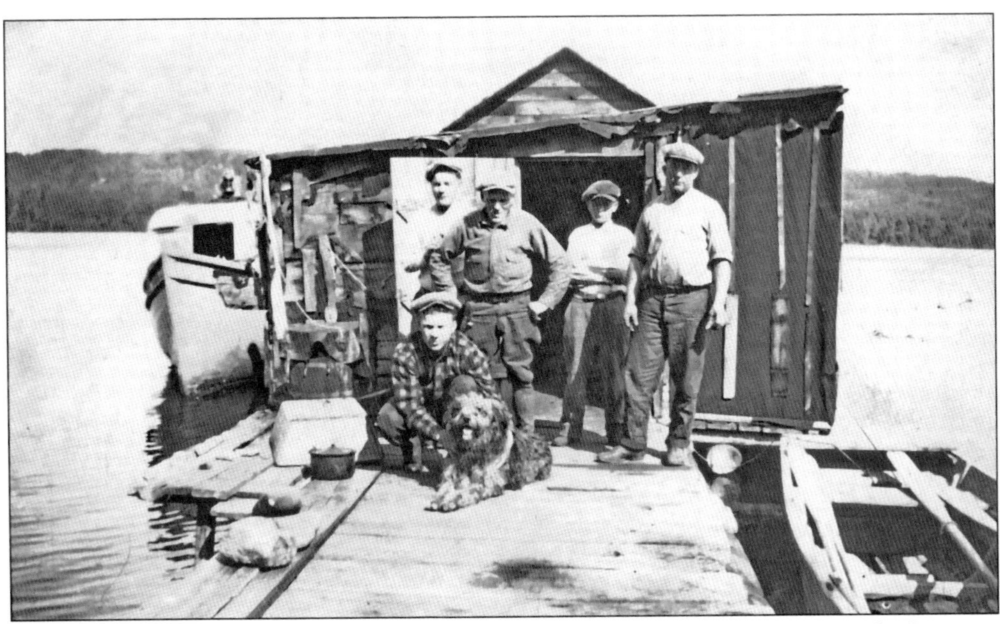

Small operations or large, Finns dominated the commercial fishing business on Lake Superior, such as this one on the Portage Lake Shipping Canal near Oskar. This photograph includes Emil Heltunen, second from left. Fishermen sometimes headed as far as Huron Island; Manitou Island, at the tip of the Keweenaw; "Kaukapakki," northeast of the Keweenaw somewhere near the Canadian border; and Isle Royale. (James Kurtti.)

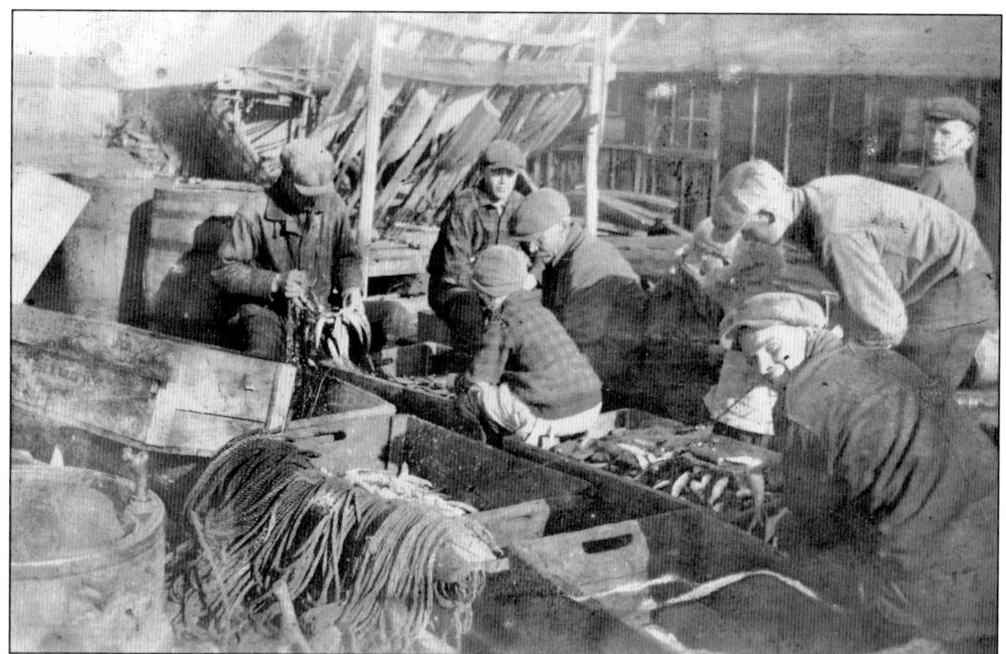

In this Chassell Fisheries photograph, fishermen pick herring out of their nets near Chassell. The Finnish fishing village that was situated at the south entry of the Portage Canal to Lake Superior was moved, houses and all, from the east shore of the canal to the west. (Chassell Historical Organization.)

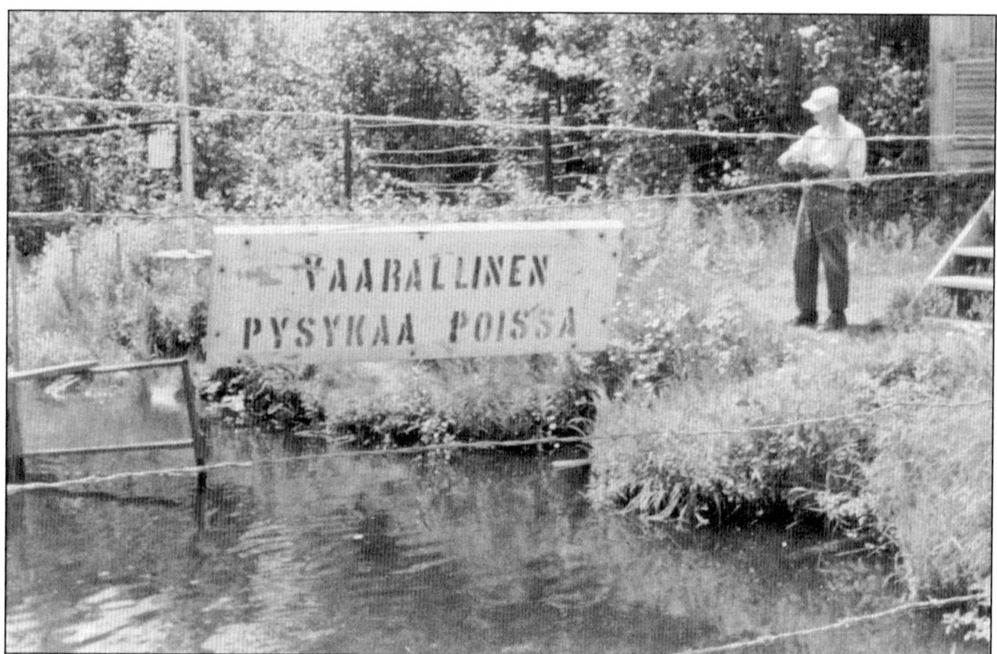

"Dangerous—Stay Away" reads the warning sign posted near the electrified lamprey trap in the water near Big Traverse in Keweenaw County. Those who posted the warning were clearly well aware of the ethnicity and language of the people who frequented the area.

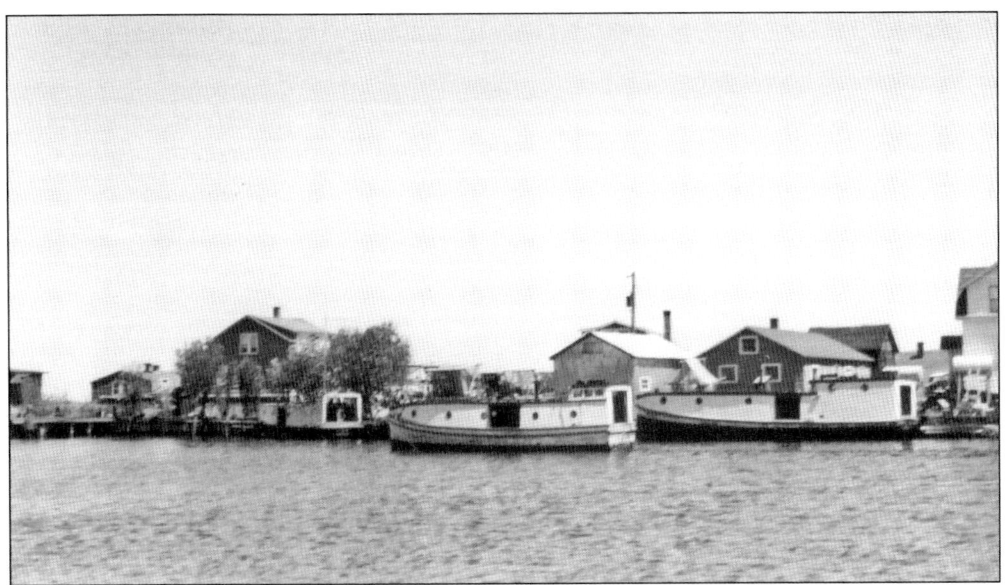

One of several Finnish fishing villages to sprout up along the shores of mighty Lake Superior was Big Traverse, near where Houghton and Keweenaw Counties share a border. Given its vast size, Lake Superior's currents and wave action are similar to an ocean and often presented life-threatening challenges to these intrepid anglers.

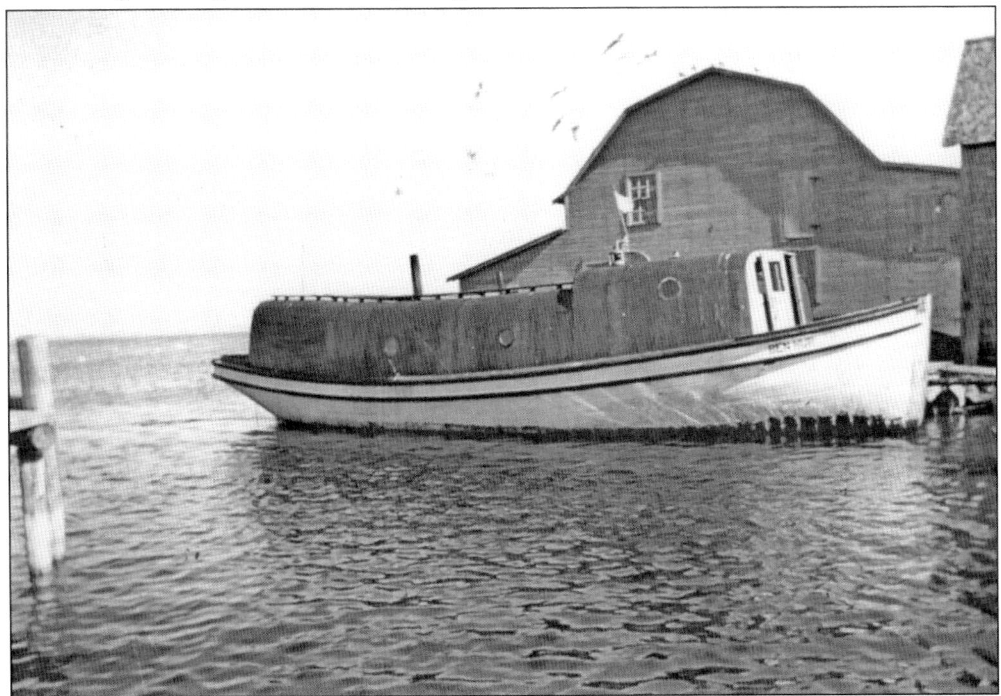

The Wiinikka Boat Works of Chassell, begun by Waino Wiinikka Sr., was the preferred boat builder of fishermen across the region. From the 1910s until about 1940, they crafted wooden fishing tugs for Lake Superior fishermen. They also built "reefboats," which were about 30 feet long and had a shallow draft, which made them ideal for working nets close to the shores of the rocky Keweenaw Peninsula. (Chassell Historical Organization.)

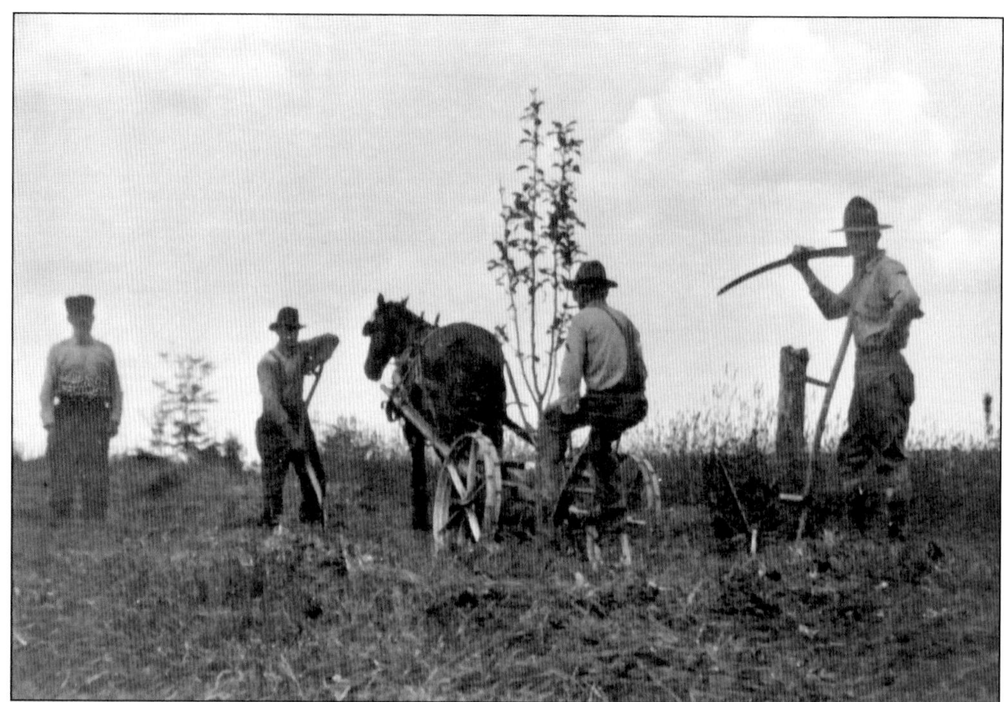

Those who knew these farmers readily identified them by their familiar hats. Herman Hakala (far left) was easy to identify, as he and his family and neighbors began a harvest on the farm near the Baraga County location Askel. In this 1920 image, Job Hiltunen is seated atop the mower, his son Peter is next to the horse, and "Uncle Matt" is leaning on the scythe.

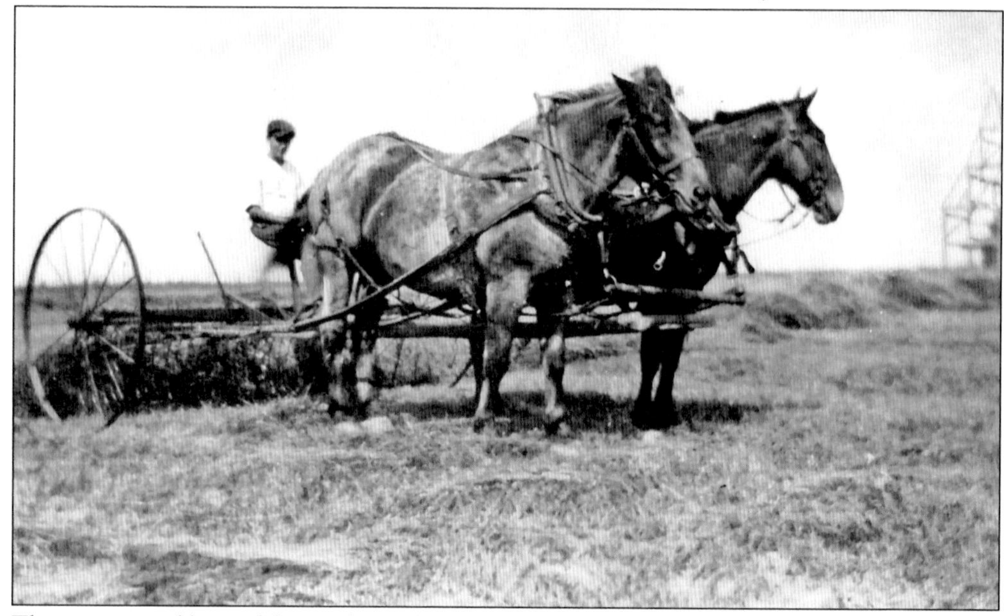

The symmetrical lines of the windrows that resulted from a day spent with the rake behind a horse team at Birch Noll Farm in Sault Ste. Marie served as a gratifying reassurance to the farmer just how much he was able to accomplish in a single day's work, even though he knew that when he woke up the next morning, he would be back at it again.

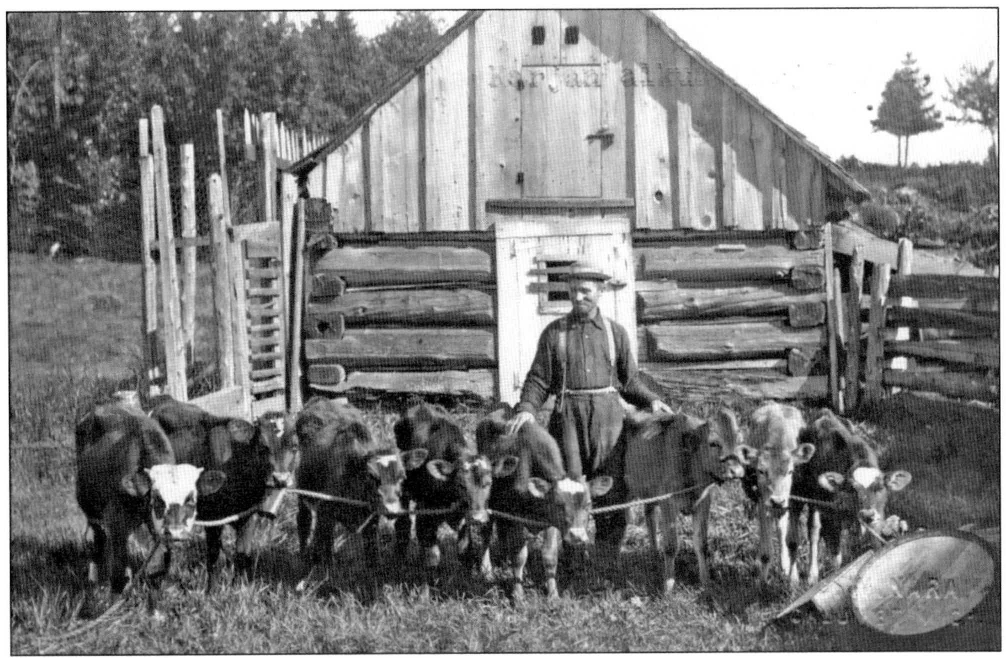

Photographer J.W. Nara captured the pride of the immigrant farmer, with his cows and calves, in an area the Finns call Karjala (Finnish for Karelia, the area of land ceded to the Russians after the Winter War), southeast of Lake Linden in the northern part of Houghton County.

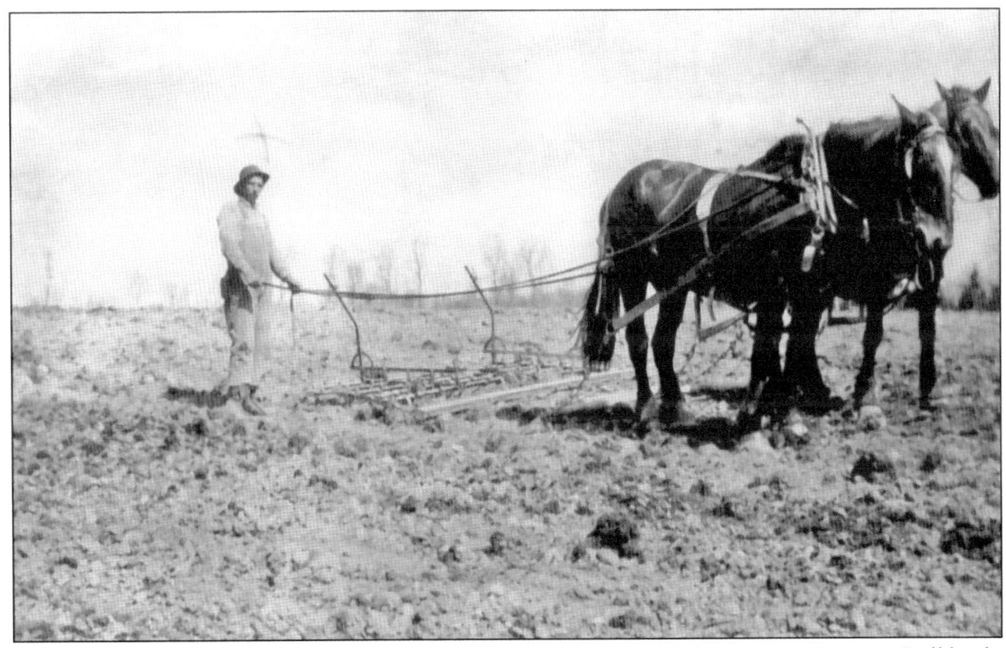

Pioneer Matti Mukari rakes his fields near Bruce Crossing in rural Ontonagon County. Still backbreaking work, it is a far cry from his earlier days when he and other Finnish American immigrant farmers either removed the stumps or planted around them. (James Kurtti.)

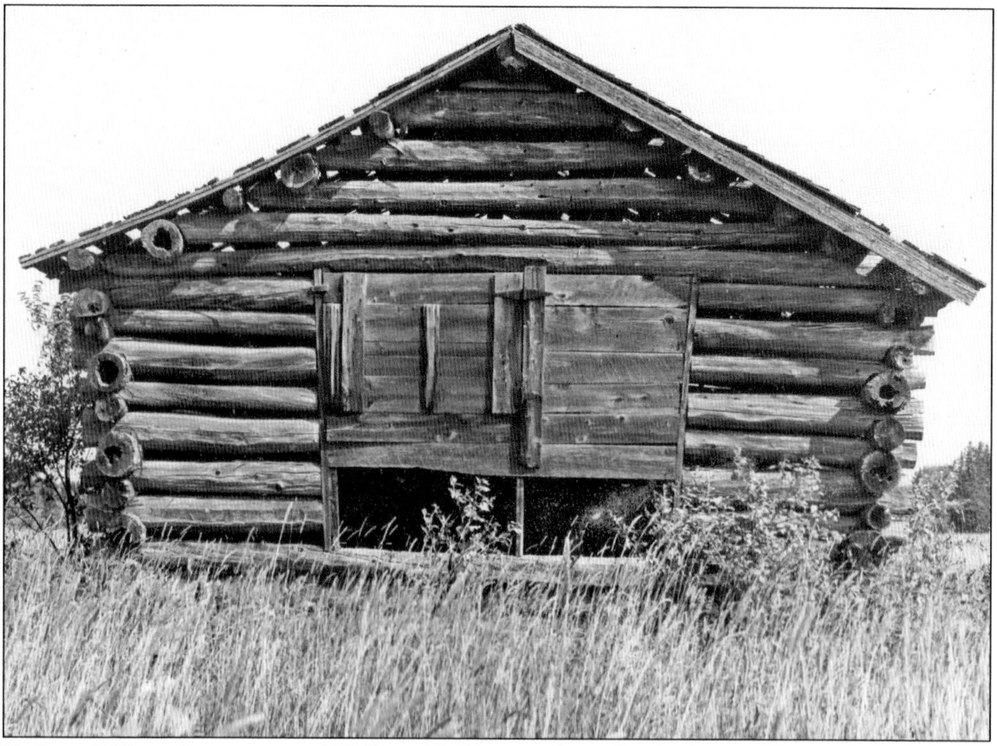

Built in 1905 on the property of William Heikkinen of Nisula, this hay barn exemplifies Finnish ingenuity. It was built in the field, with a wide doorway for ease of putting the hay inside, gaps between logs to ensure ventilation, and walls pitched outward to prevent roof runoff from seeping into the structure, so the hay—used in the winter—would remain as dry as possible.

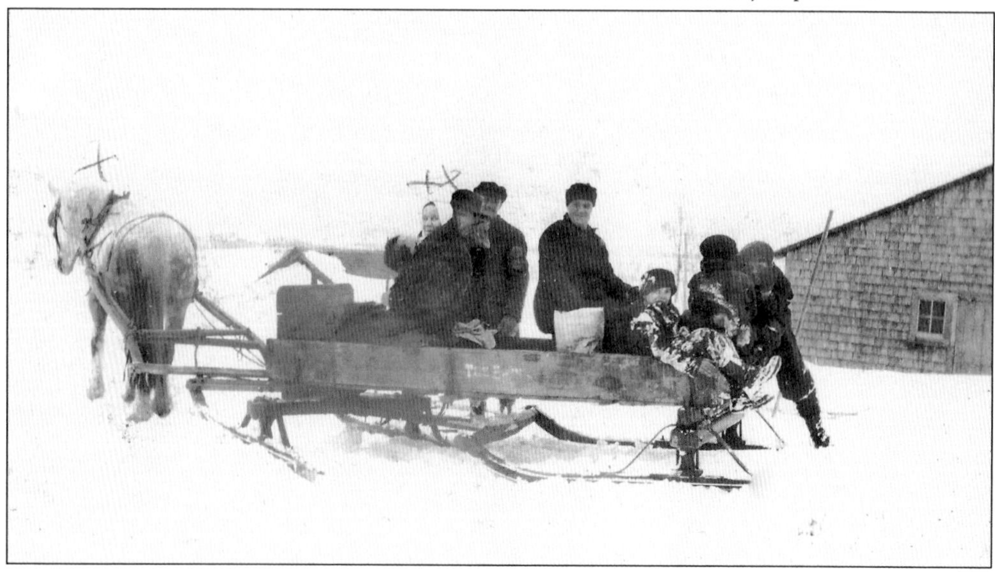

No matter the season, a horse was essential to Finnish American farms in the early 20th century. These beautiful and powerful creatures were treated with care and affection, and they humbly returned the favor by laboring without hesitation or fuss, pulling wagons, sleighs, plows, and stone boats. (James Kurtti.)

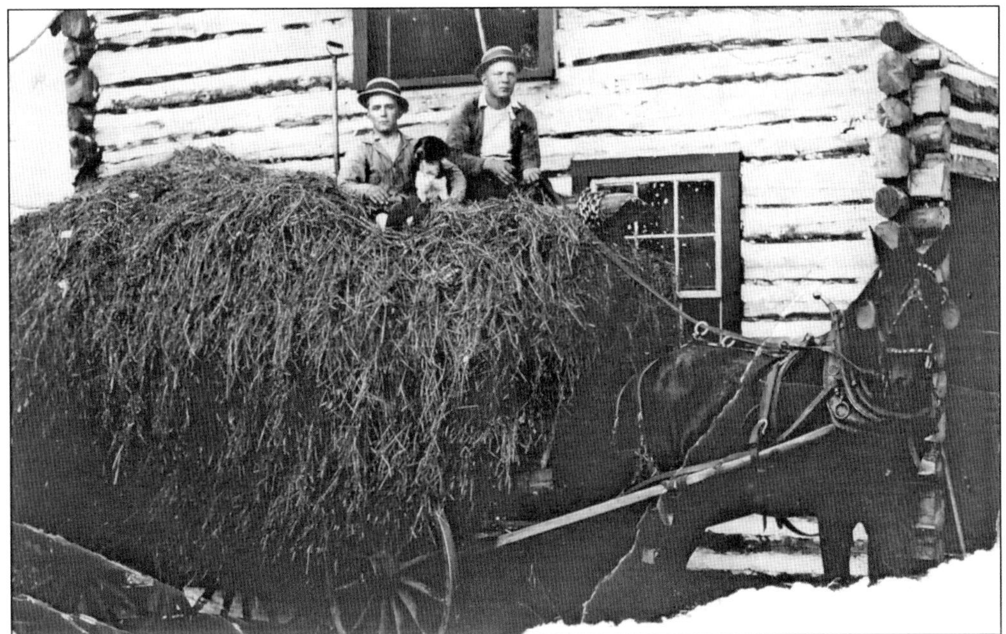

Young men briefly stop to pose after bringing in a load of hay; the ride atop the heap was the lone bit of respite in this arduous process that took place under the hot summer sun. When the wagon arrived at the barn, it was forks in hand, as the hay had to be pitched up into the mow of the barn.

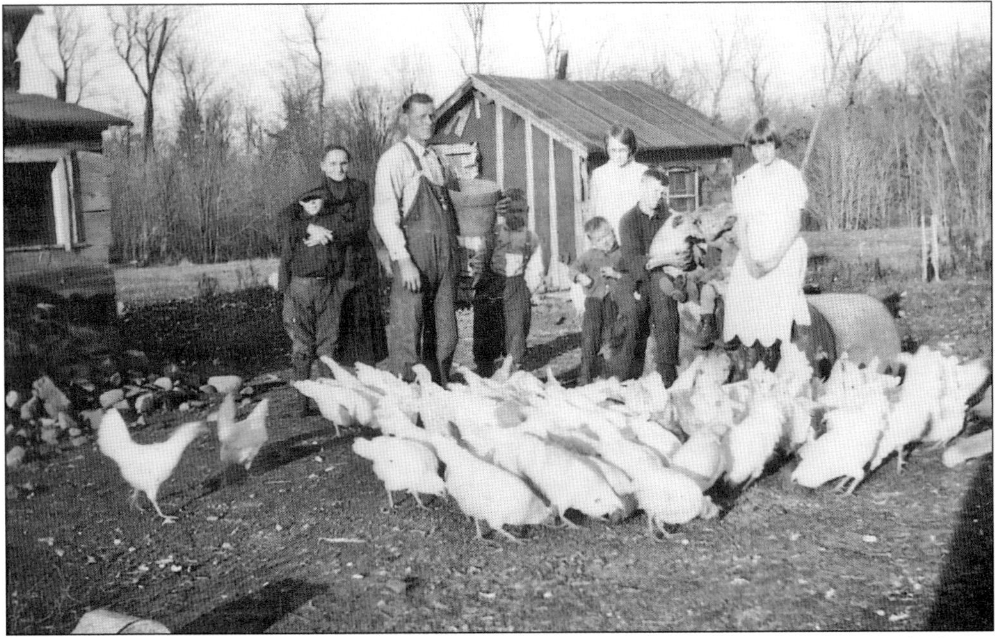

When immigrant farms like the Mattila farm of Toivola (seen here in 1930) added chickens, they did so to make eggs more readily available for cooking and baking. Only when a member of the flock stopped being a productive layer was she butchered and eaten; the Finns were not predisposed to consuming poultry as part of their diet. (Rebecca Hoekstra.)

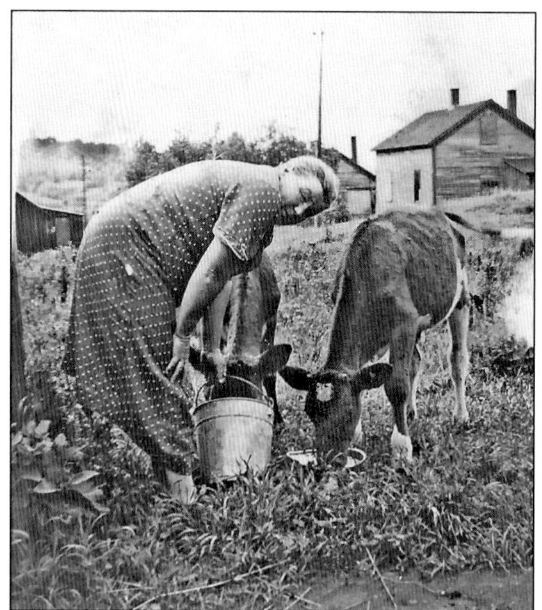

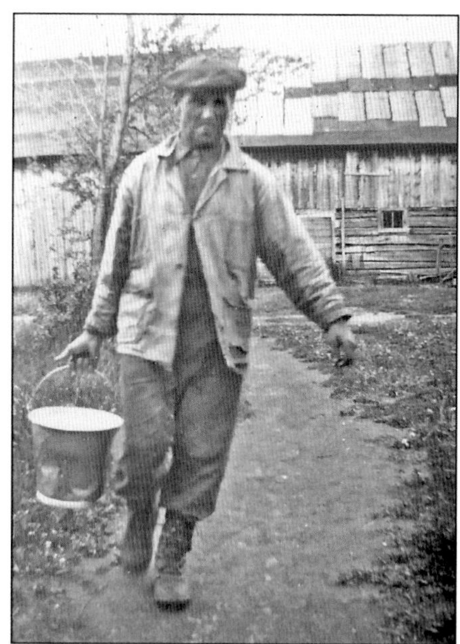

Lena Räisänen of Redridge, a mining town in Houghton County, tended to the livestock as part of her regular daily chores. Mine employee housing included a small barn on each home's parcel, and cows grazed freely in the community. It was essential that townspeople, when returning home after dark, be cautious to avoid tripping over a resting cow—or something else. It was difficult to focus on fast-moving farmer Eeseri Lahti of Tapiola, whose posture reveals the weight of his burden as he hurries from the barn with a pail of fresh milk, perhaps to be made into *leipäjuusto* (squeaky cheese), the tasty treat immigrant Finns introduced to the UP. (Left, James Kurtti.)

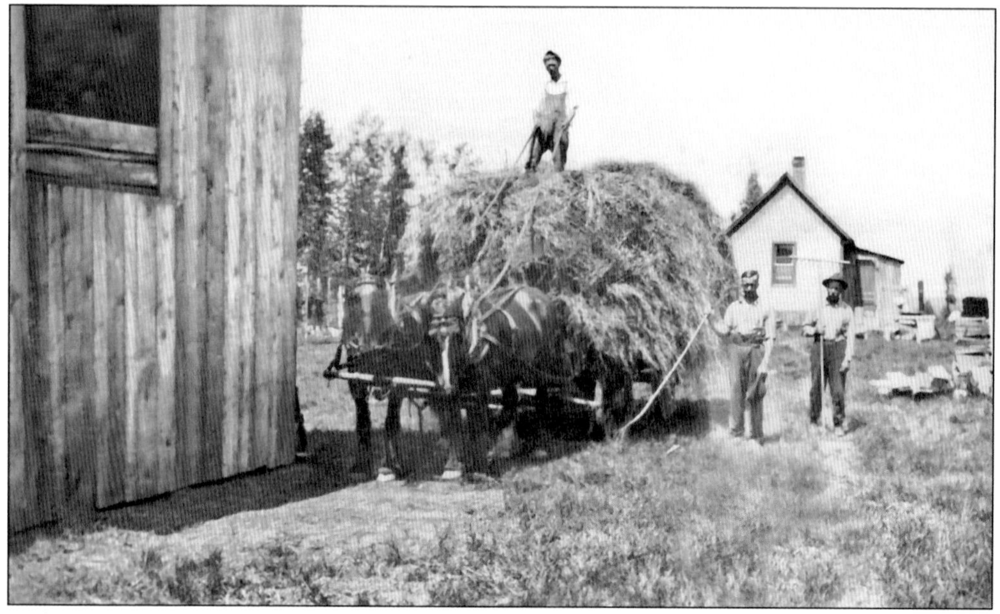

At haymaking season, it was all hands on deck. Relatives, friends, and neighbors came from "town," and those who moved to the cities came back to help families like the Lelvises bring in the summer's most important crop. Ultimately, the experience was a social activity as much as a necessary project, with a hot sauna for the haymakers every night. (James Kurtti.)

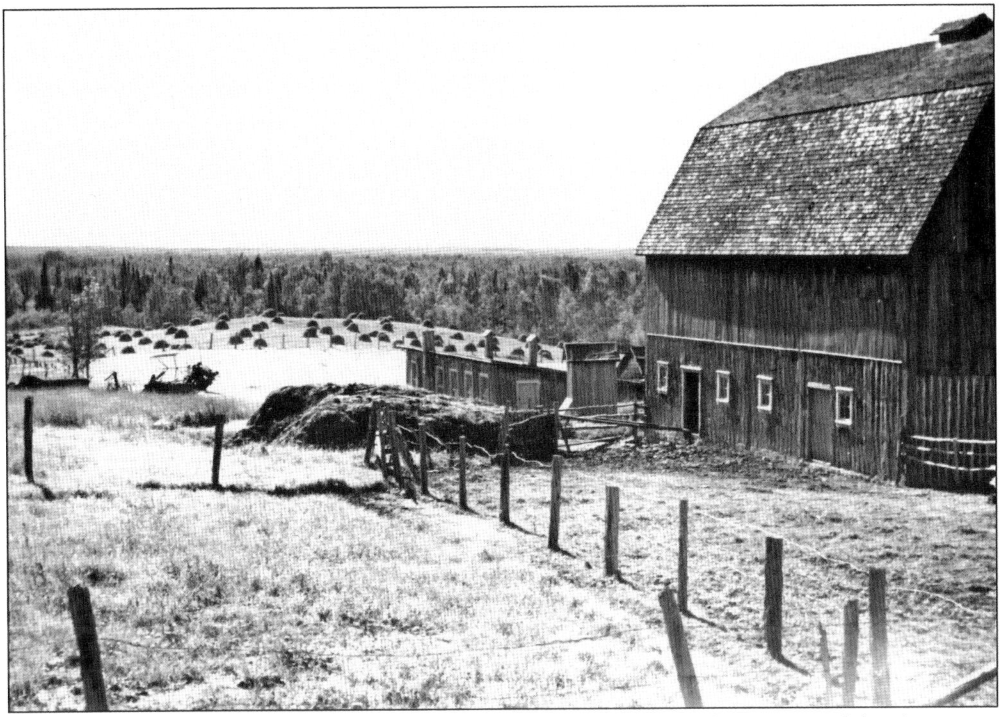

A clean and orderly farm was a testament to immigrant farmers' achievement of the American Dream, as represented by the Emil Ojennus farm in Bruce Crossing, a village in southern Ontonagon County. From stately, handsome barns to well-groomed fields, a well-maintained farm even became a tourist attraction for camera-toting passersby.

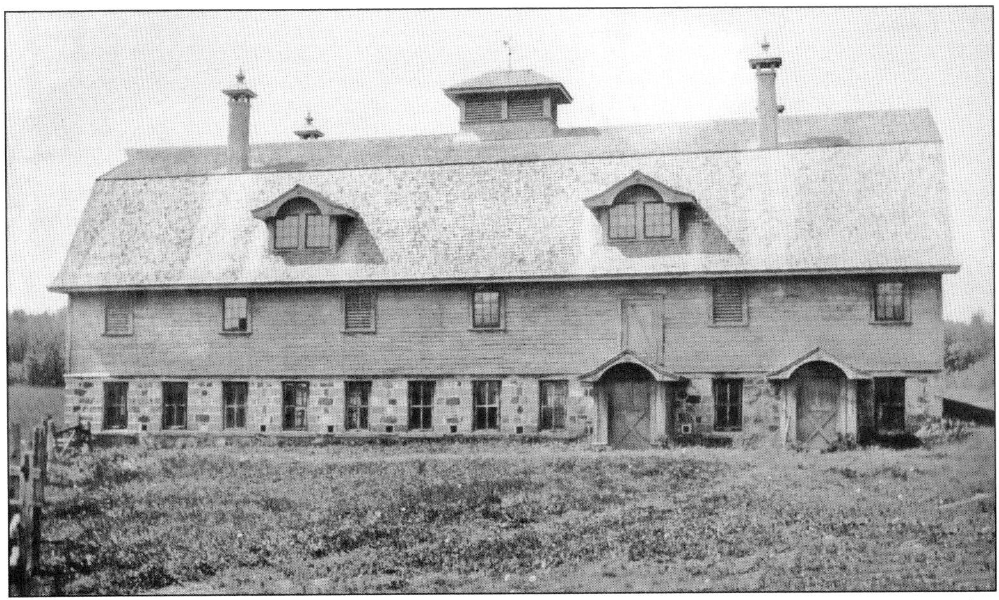

Although most UP Finnish farms were rather small and the buildings unadorned, the John Haanpää farm between Trout Creek and Bruce Crossing in southern Ontonagon County had decorative exterior elements and housed vast tubs and other equipment, making it a top-of-the-line dairy barn. (James Kurtti.)

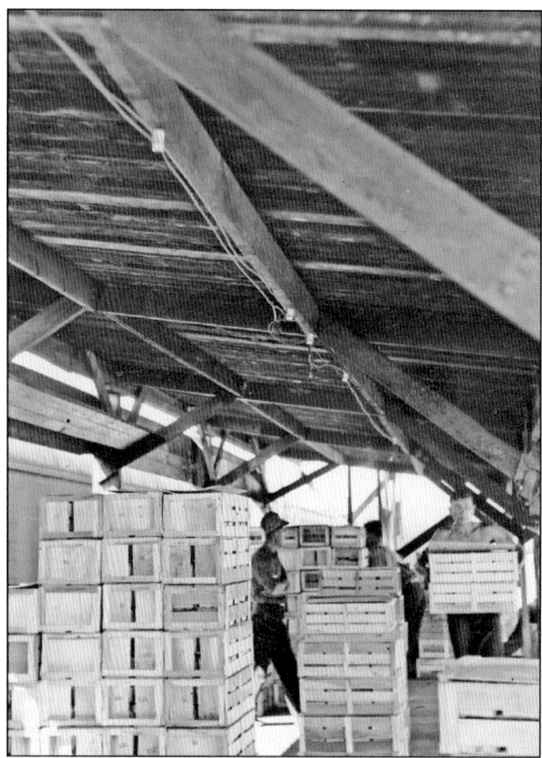

A US Department of Agriculture (USDA) study determined that the Copper Country's growing season and soil types are ideal for strawberries. Many farms, especially in the Houghton County village of Chassell, took on this cash crop with great success, as the juicy red fruit was enjoyed locally and in cities across the country. To this day, the community hosts an annual festival celebrating its signature crop. (Chassell Historical Organization.)

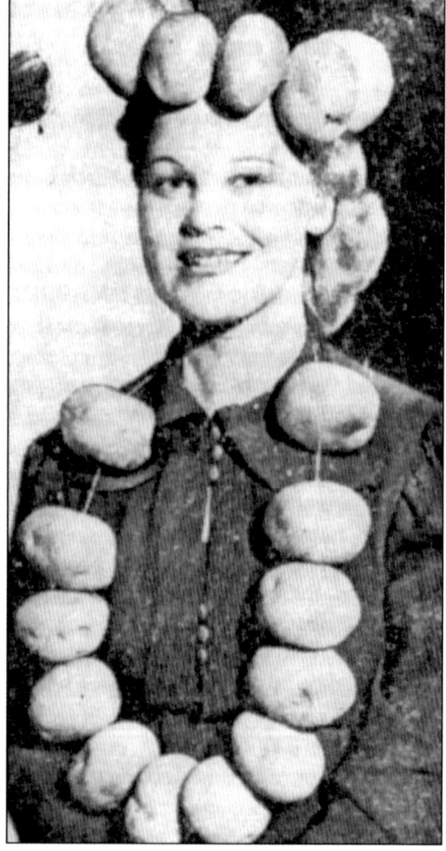

The smile on the face of 22-year-old Ellen Harkonen of Pelkie reveals her joy in being crowned Michigan's Potato Queen for 1936. The honor was bestowed on the young Yooper during a celebration that marked a banner year of potato growing across the state. A USDA study determined that the tuber would grow well in the UP, and many Finnish American farms opted to produce what became a stellar cash crop.

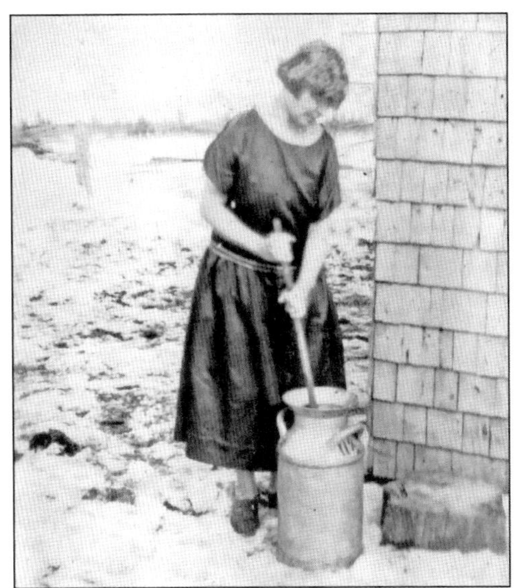

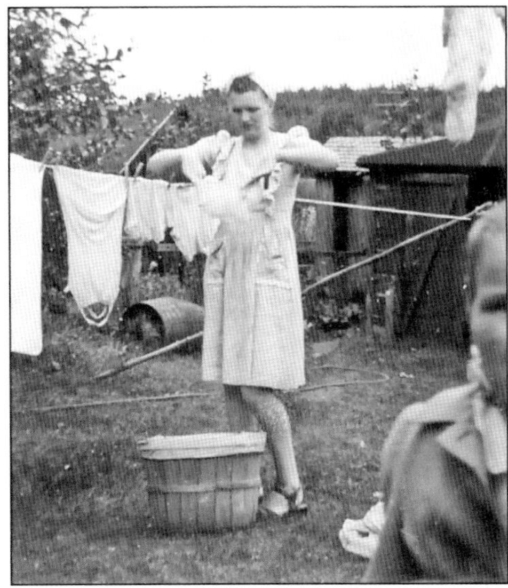

Several small Finnish American farming communities emerged south of Sault Ste. Marie in Chippewa County, especially in Dafter and Kinross, where a photographer spotted this woman churning butter as part of her busy day on the family farm. Early Finnish settlers in Kinross came from locations such as Siikainen and Kangasniemi, Piippola, and Kauhava. After sweating over a stove to prep wash water, then going elbow deep into a tub to scrub the stains away, it was a reprieve to step outside and hang laundry on a breezy summer afternoon, especially compared to completing the same task in winter, when the woman's chafed hands would pin the clothing to the line in a brisk wind and retrieve the frozen-stiff apparel later that day. (Right, James Kurtti.)

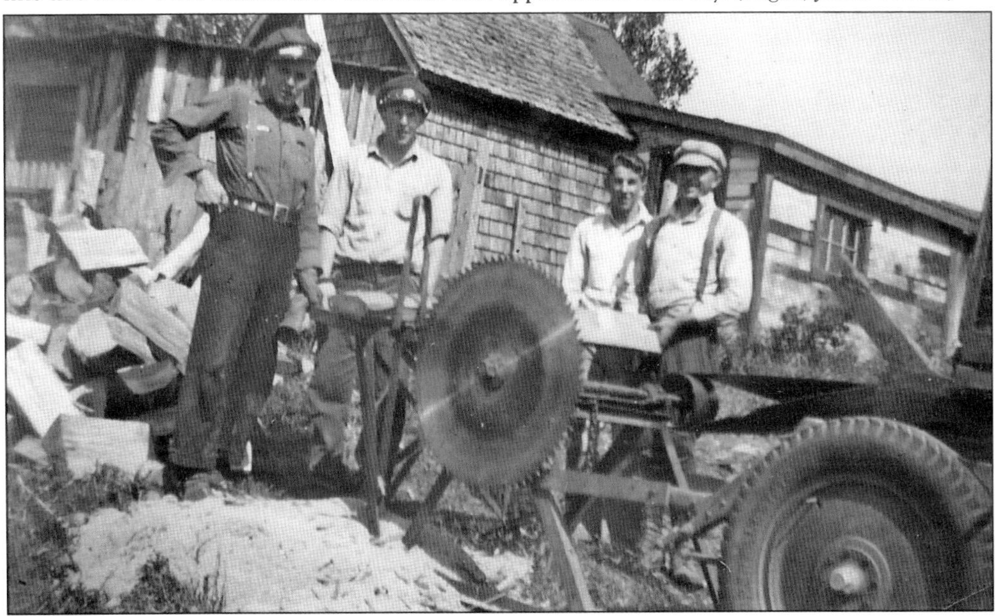

Those who "make wood" are warmed twice by the process—once when cutting the blocks in the summer or fall and again when burning them in the stove throughout the winter. Though still physically demanding, the process was made easier when creative folks like these Redridge residents powered a buzz saw with a tractor, or *jokeri*, a *fingliska* (Finnish-English) term for a truck or car repurposed for farm use. (James Kurtti.)

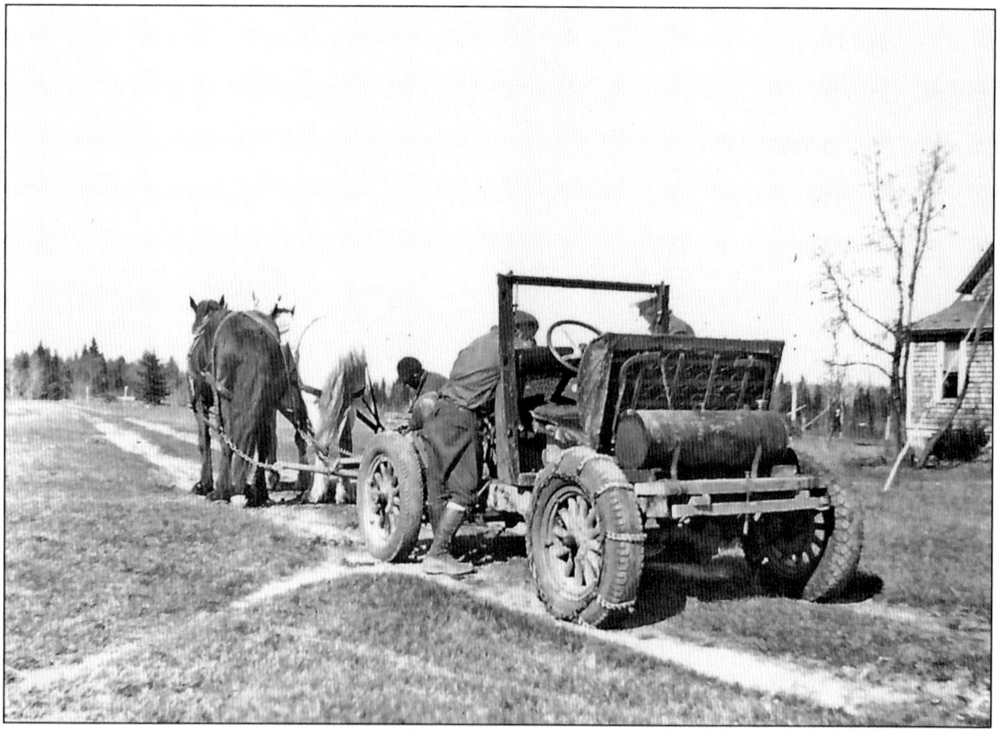

It was no laughing matter when the "joker" broke down, as it was counted on for helping to complete many chores. Urho Törrö and Ed Tiistola illustrate how every farmer needed to be a mechanic, inventor, and engineer.

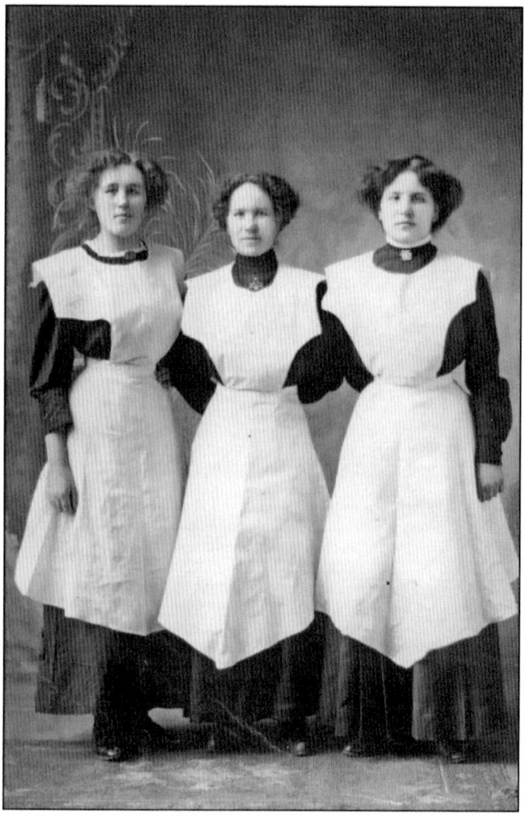

In Finnish, they were called *piika*. Their American neighbors called them maids. The women themselves called it earning a living. Many immigrant women were hired to help with the cooking, cleaning, and other necessary domestic work for not only the wealthy, but often new mothers, those who were sick, or others who simply needed extra hands in the house.

Single women needed to earn their own livings outside the home, so they worked tirelessly for minimal wages and even less recognition at hospitals like C.J. Sorsen Hospital, a Finnish hospital in Laurium, to nurse their patients back to health. Surgeon Charles Sorsen owned and lived in the building that housed the hospital. It closed in 1930 and was torn down in the following decade.

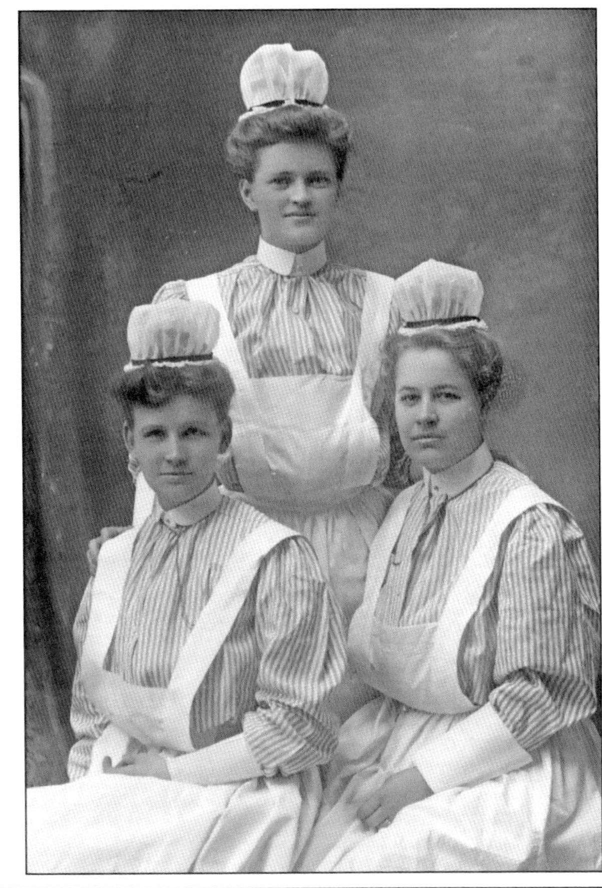

Many a grateful Finn earned his daily bread through the Works Progress Administration and similar public works programs during the Great Depression. Despite the back-breaking work, these four men still stand straight and tall on a road they have nearly completed near the Houghton County Finnish enclave of Tapiola.

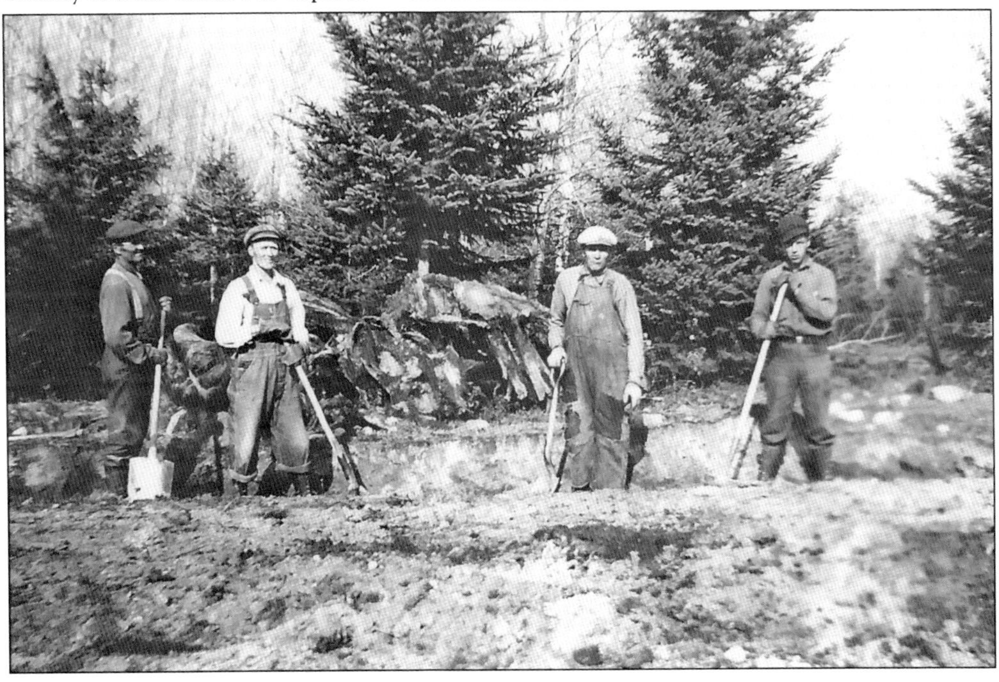

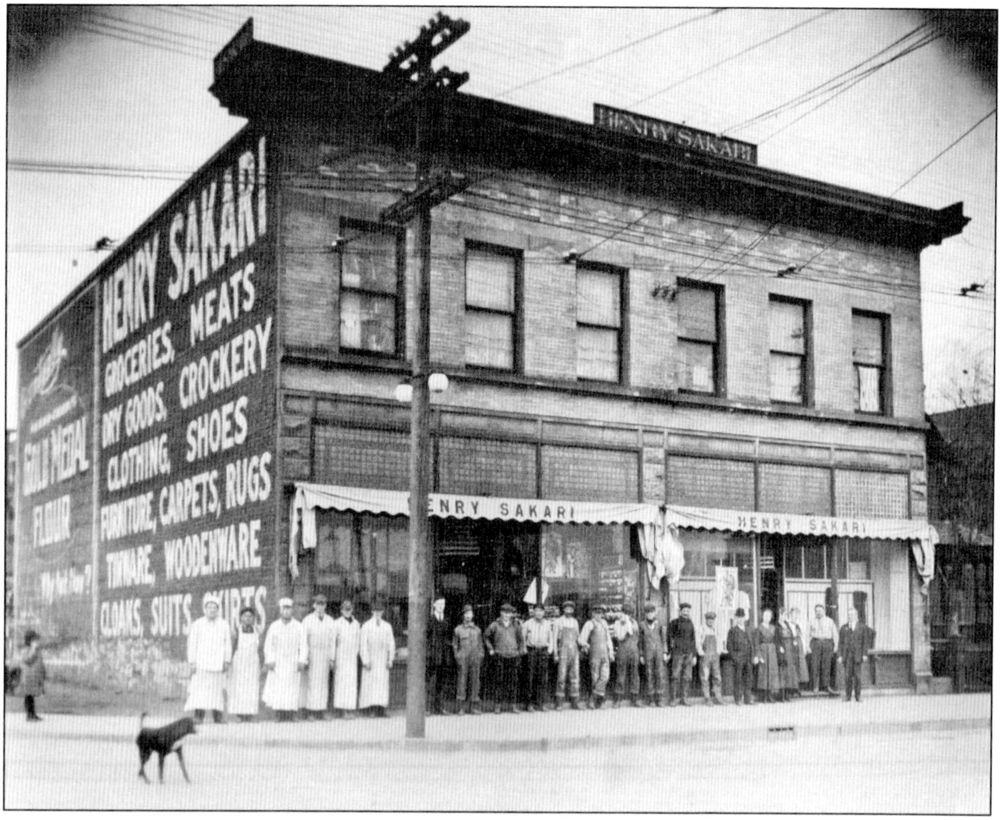

Henry Sakari peddled household goods prior to opening a small meat market. His success led to this larger store, opened around 1907 on Quincy Street in Hancock. Sakari immigrated to the Copper Country in 1887, operated several businesses in the community, including a slaughterhouse, and served as a mentor for many business-minded Finnish Americans of the area.

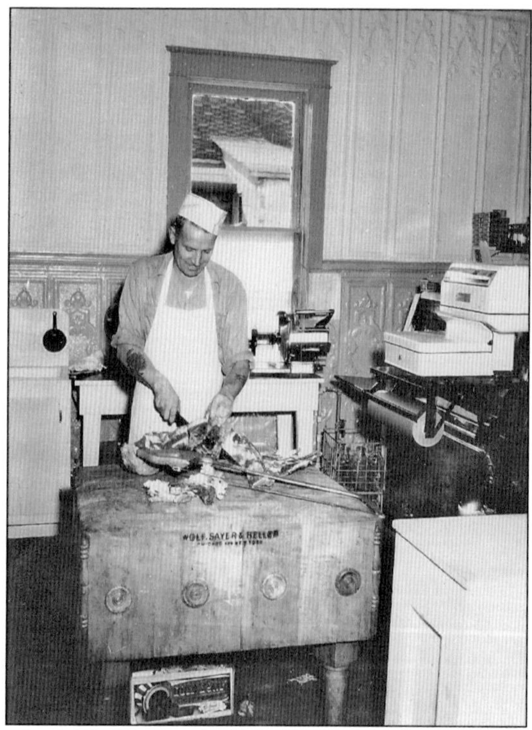

In the early days, butchers began with whole sides of beef. As shown here, the final cuts were performed on the other side of the meat case, where butchers, such as at the Settlers Co-op in Bruce Crossing, showcased their well-honed skills.

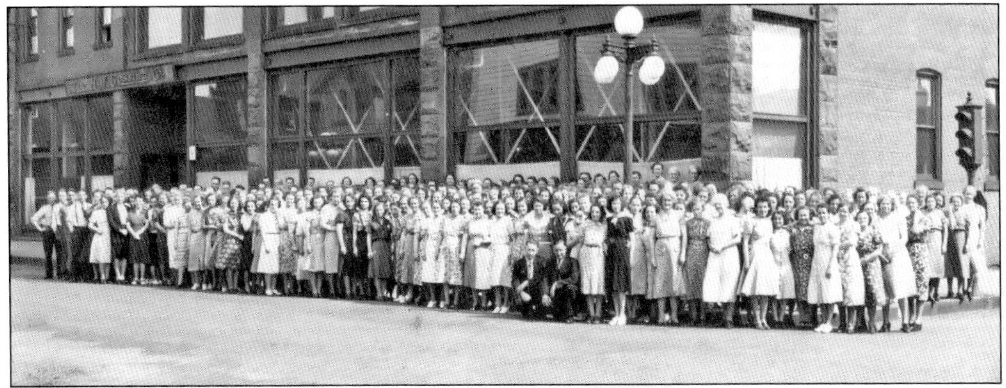

The Braastad-Gossard Building was erected in 1888 and expanded in 1903–1904 for Frederick Braastad for his department store, then remodeled and modernized in 1948 to house the H.W. Gossard factory, where hundreds of Finnish American women were employed. This was the site of a strike in 1949 that is remembered for the leading role played by women in beginning and carrying out the strike.

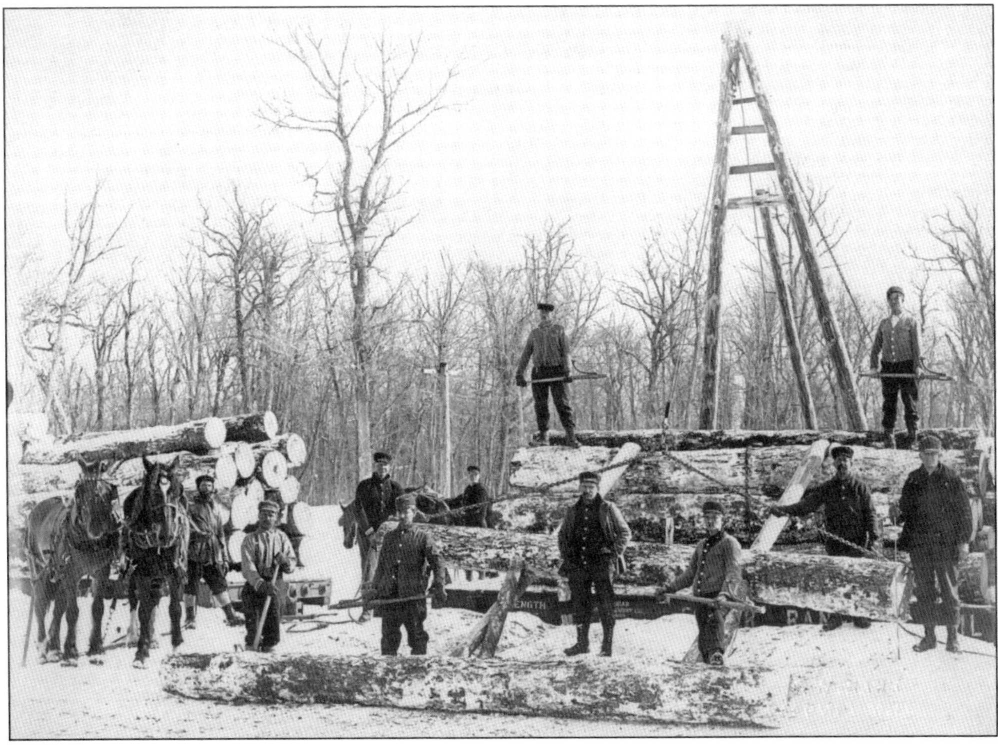

Word of mouth through letters back to the Old Country was important in bringing immigrants to the UP. Financial and community connections explain why so many Swedish-speaking Finns ended up in the logging industry, while Finnish speakers often began in the copper and iron mines. Over time, Finnish speakers too were felling trees, working the sawmills, and otherwise engaged in harvesting the UP's forests of white pine and maple.

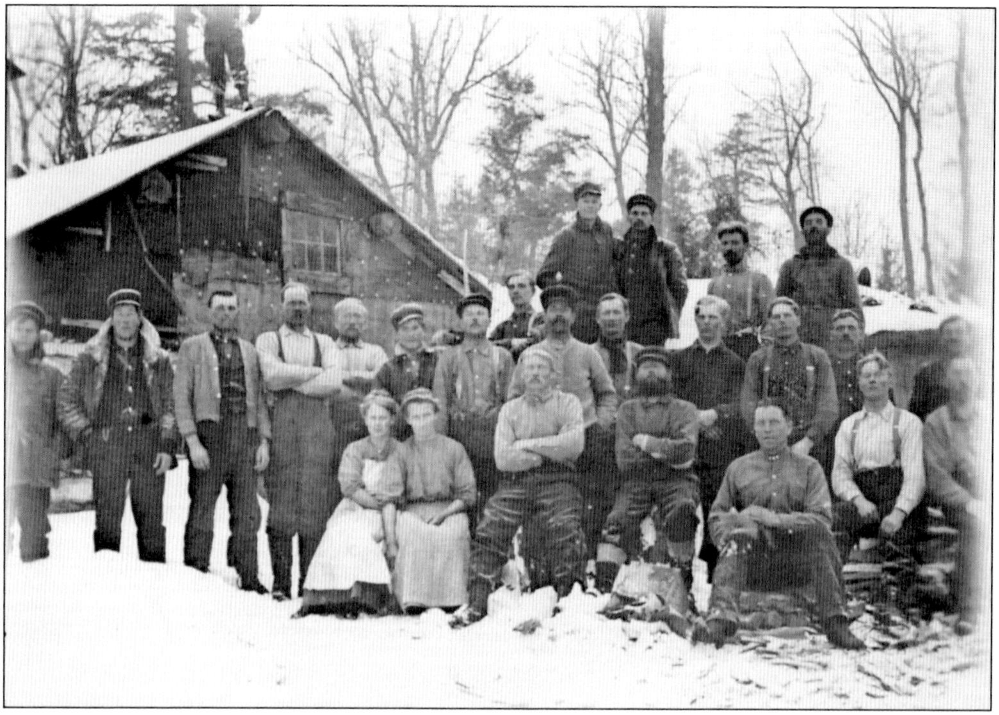

Logging camps were set up to bring the workers closer to the timber they were harvesting, and the men (and women who served as camp domestics) spent weeks at a time in relative isolation in the woods. They would return to town only periodically to get their mail, use the public sauna, and perhaps support a local watering hole with their hard-earned wages.

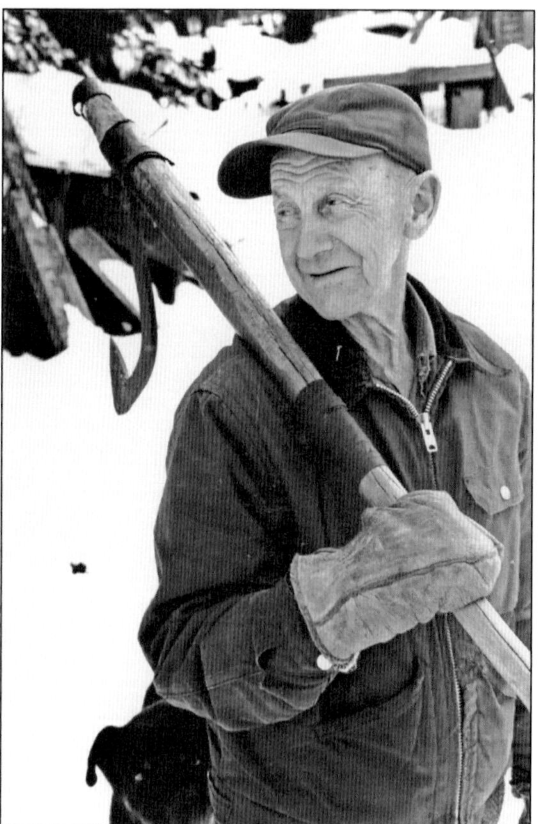

With a cant hook swung over his shoulder, Art Erickson of Pelkie knew what to wear to stay warm and efficient when working with some timber near his hometown in Baraga County. Every Upper Michigan logger learned the importance of a durable coat, *sarkka houssut* (heavy wool pants) and the lined buckskin mitts that are affectionately known as "choppers" in the UP.

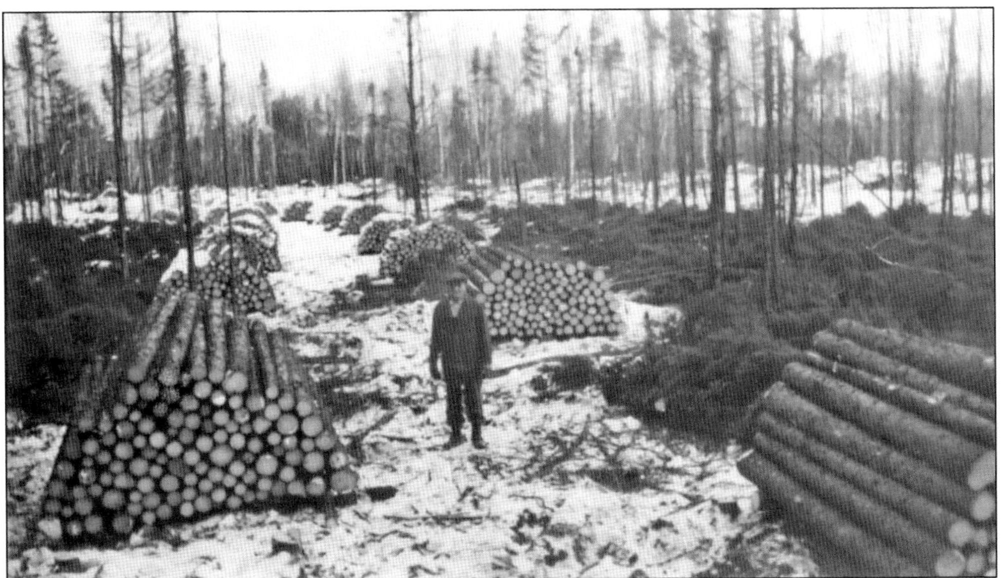

Matti Nurmela was 68 years old when he felled these trees in a Watton forest in the spring of 1942. While many logging operations were undertaken to harvest trees for lumber, other logs were harvested to provide material for the pulp and paper industry, which provided stable employment in the UP for decades.

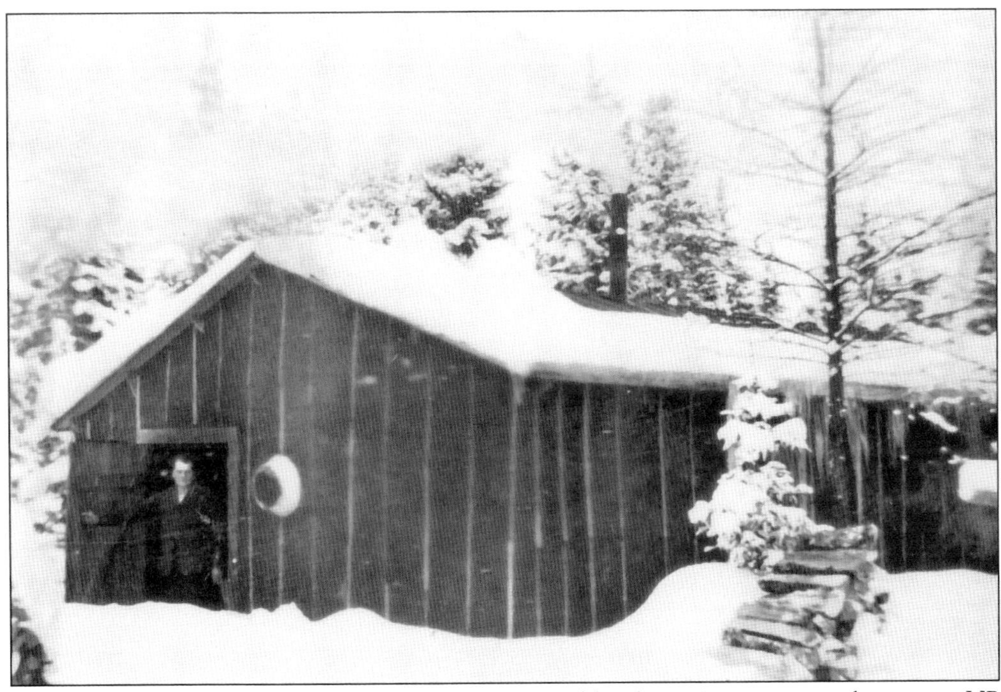

Nestled in the forests of Upper Michigan in locations like this 1924 camp near the eastern UP village of Kinross, hundreds of roughly made buildings dotted the vast forests but were abandoned as the lumberjacks moved on, leaving the camps to return to the wilderness.

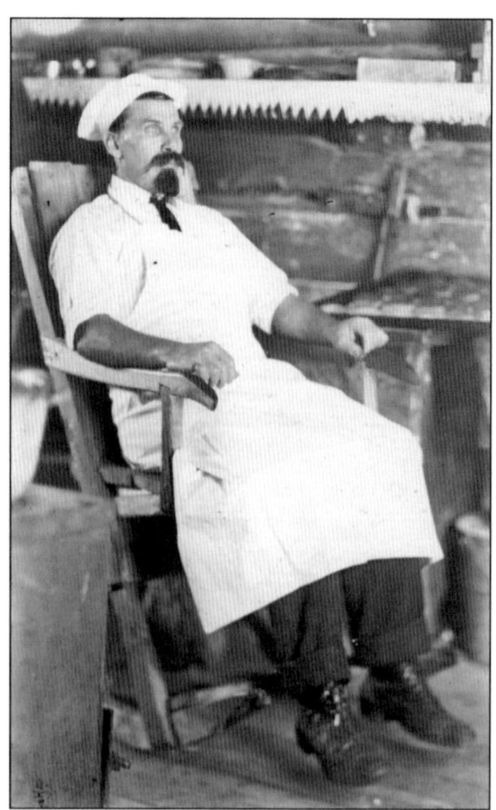

The most popular and most essential member of any logging camp crew was, without a doubt, the camp cook. It was entirely his burden to ensure the men of the camp had enough internal fuel to endure a full day of harvesting timber in the remote forests of Upper Michigan.

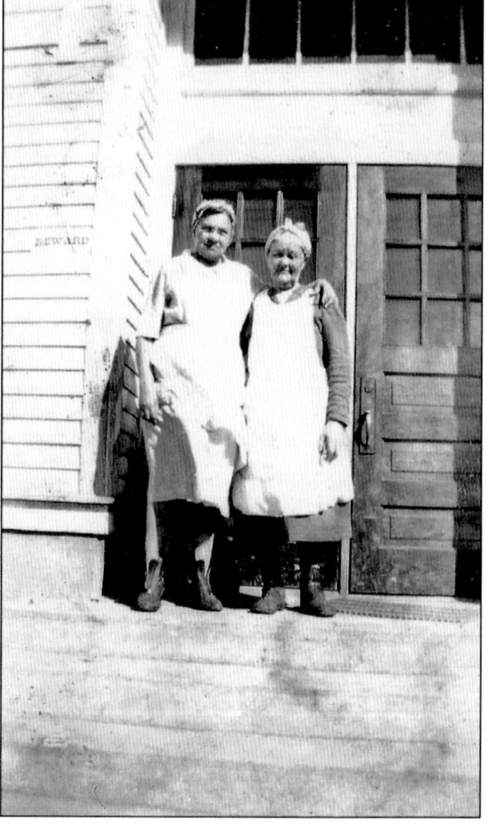

At the Bruce Crossing school, the students were nourished each day by the food prepared by Laura Uusimaa and Ottelia Mäkikangas, who labored for hours in the school kitchen and cafeteria preparing the day's meal for dozens of children. These women were among the many who had to enter the workforce as older adults after being widowed and otherwise lacking family income. (James Kurtti.)

Two

BUILDING FOUNDATIONS

It has been said that if you have three Finns, there will be a co-op store, a hall, and a church, with one Finn not wanting to get involved. In the spirit of *talkoo* (working together) and blessed with a very high percentage of literacy, the Finnish very quickly established churches, labor and temperance halls, and cooperatives of all sorts working for the common good. In 1879, the first Finnish language newspaper in the United States, *Amerikan Suomalainen Lehti*, was founded in Hancock, as was the second, along with numerous other newspapers and publications.

Centered around Suomi Opisto (Suomi College) was the Finnish American Printing Company, which published Finnish primers and religious materials. The Finnish temperance societies, as well as the Finnish leftists, the Knights and Ladies of Kaleva, and the Order of Runeberg (Swedish-speaking Finns) creating lodges and halls in every Finnish community. Likewise, Finnish Lutherans—Evangelical Lutherans, National Lutherans, various branches of Apostolic Lutherans—as well as Finnish-speaking Methodists, Pentecostals, and Baptists, established congregations and mission stations.

Finnish-language libraries were established in many of these halls and churches, with very ample amounts of literature friendly to their particular political and spirituals beliefs. Miners and maids, dead tired from long days of work, spent endless hours rehearsing their plays, memorizing poetry, and practicing their parts for brass bands, orchestras, and choral pieces.

Farmers and laborers walked miles to their country halls for talkoots, as well as dances and plays, sometimes with food and beverage, or perhaps an accordion strapped to their backs, only to trudge home again after hours of dancing or working.

As some old Finns would say, "You don't have to eat, but you have to work." It was that attitude with which their foundations of cultural life were built.

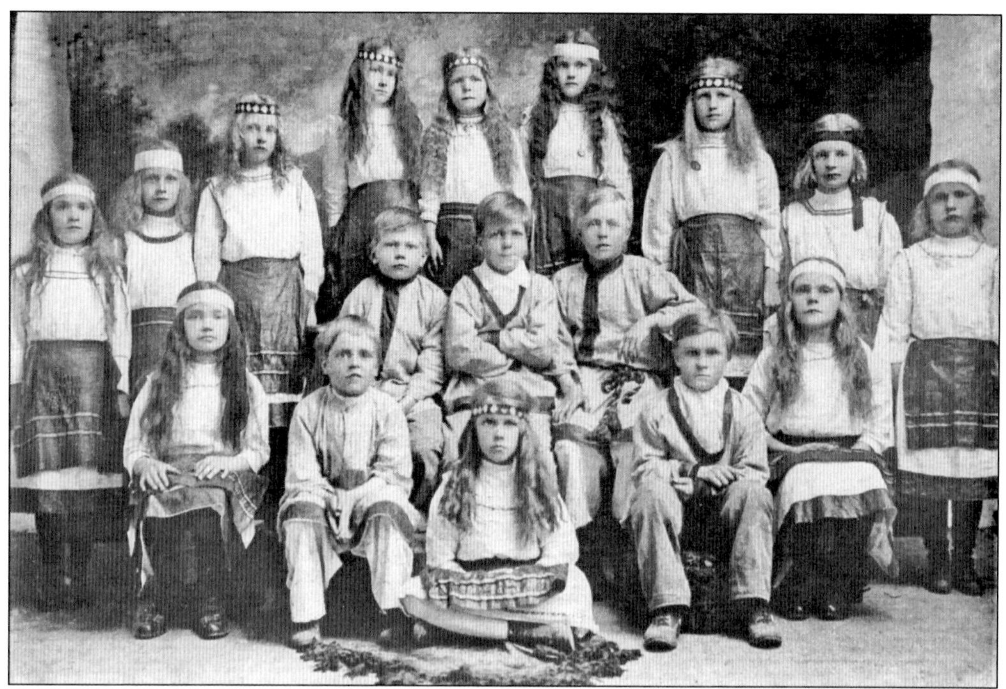

Finnish national identity was still in its infancy when many immigrants arrived in Upper Michigan. Following the lead from Finland (which was not independent until 1917) via newspapers and other correspondence, the UP Finns developed their identity through national dress and other means.

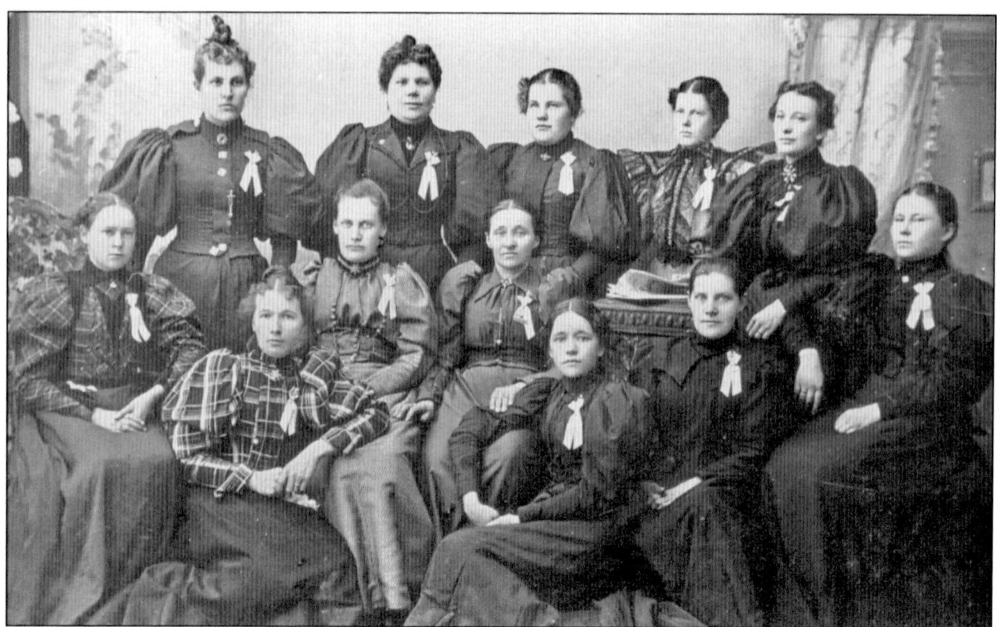

Finnish women were at the forefront in organizing congregations, temperance societies, theater groups, and educational programs, as well as promoting the ideals of suffrage. In Calumet, the Calumetin Suomalainen Naisyhdistys (Calumet Women's Society) came well armed as, in 1917, Finland was the first country in the world to grant women full suffrage.

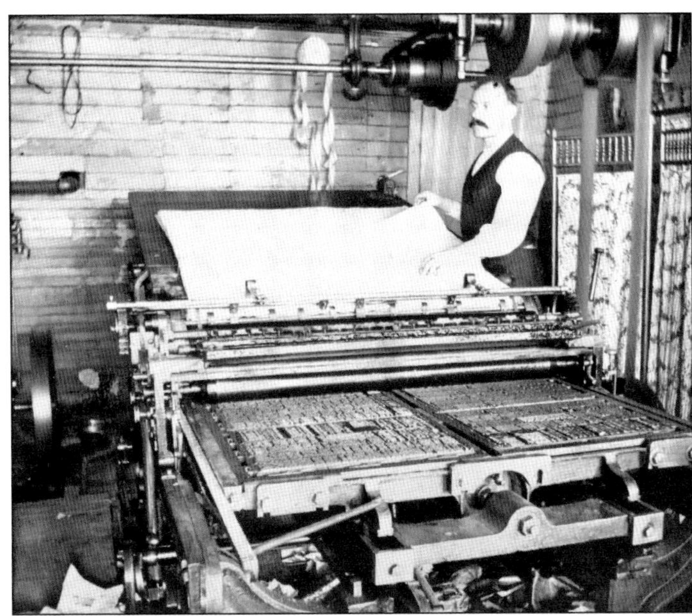

The first Finnish newspaper in the United States, *Amerikan Suomalainen Lehti*, was begun in Hancock in 1876 by A.J. Muikku, and from that humble beginning sprouted countless publications, many focused on supporting a particular political or religious affiliation. In this 1898 photograph, Victor Burman prepares a page of *Amerikan Suomalainen*, which was also produced in Hancock.

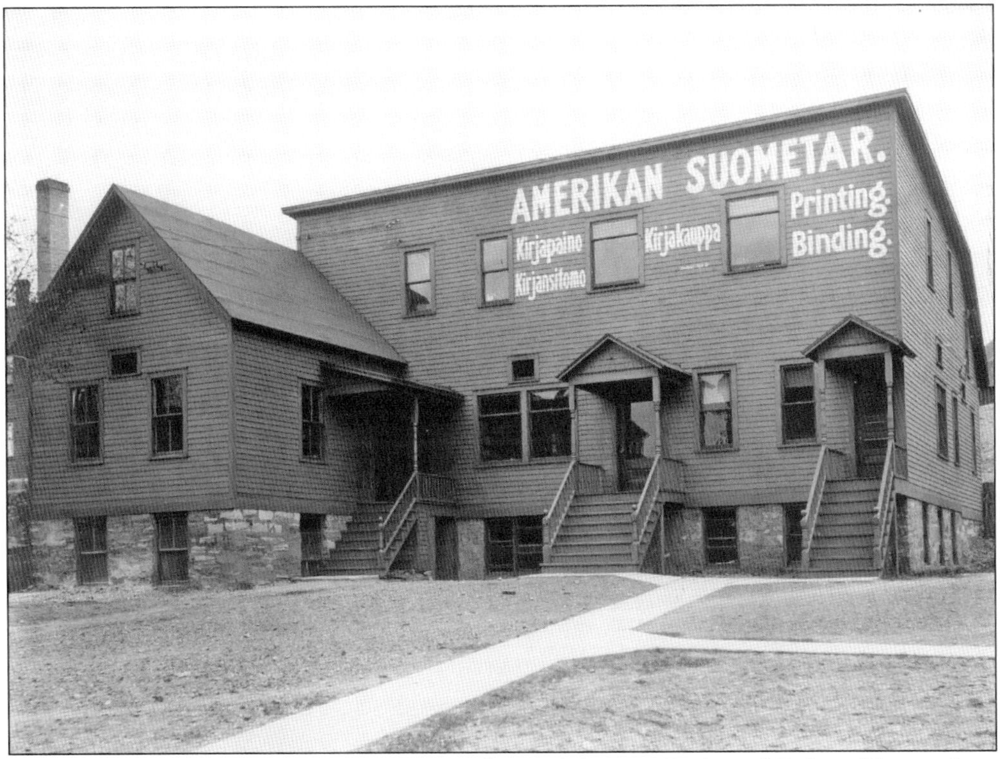

Founded by Pastors J.K. Nikander, Kaarlo Tolonen, Johannes Bäck, and Robert Ylönen along with three laymen in 1899, the Amerikan Suometar Publishing Company of Hancock formed to produce the newspaper of the same name and other printed material. Operating from a building near the Suomi College campus, the print house became the most significant part of Finnish American church life. The paper closed in the 1960s, and the building was razed in the early 21st century.

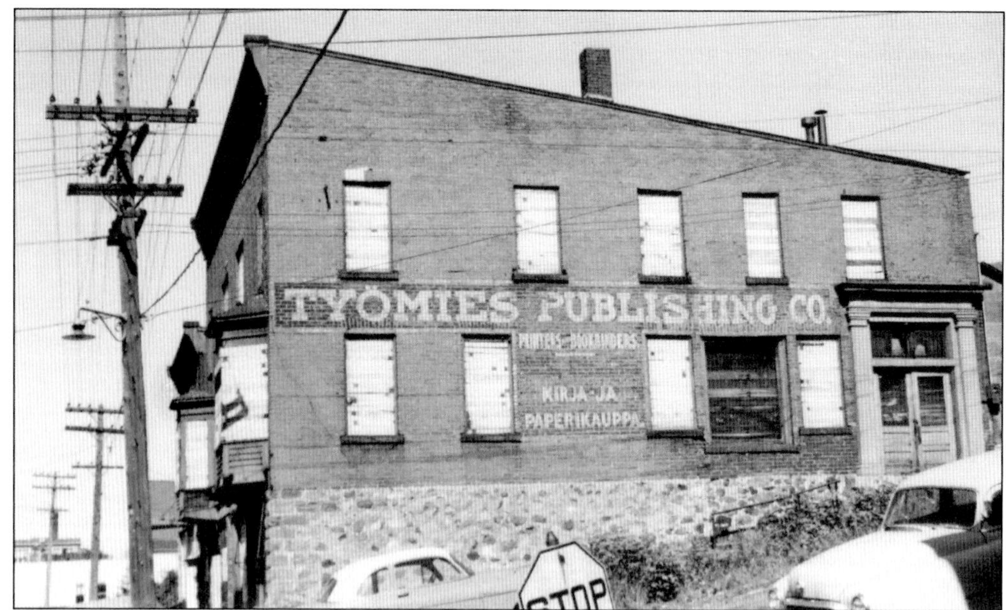

The foundation of Työmies Publishing Company (seen here in 1959) was the newspaper of the same name, which was established in Worcester, Massachusetts, in 1903. A year later, based on feedback from an ad salesman amazed by the level of labor-related activity, it relocated to Hancock and then, in 1914, to Superior, Wisconsin, where conditions were more favorable to businesses connected to the labor movement. A key factor for the move was the copper strike of 1913–1914.

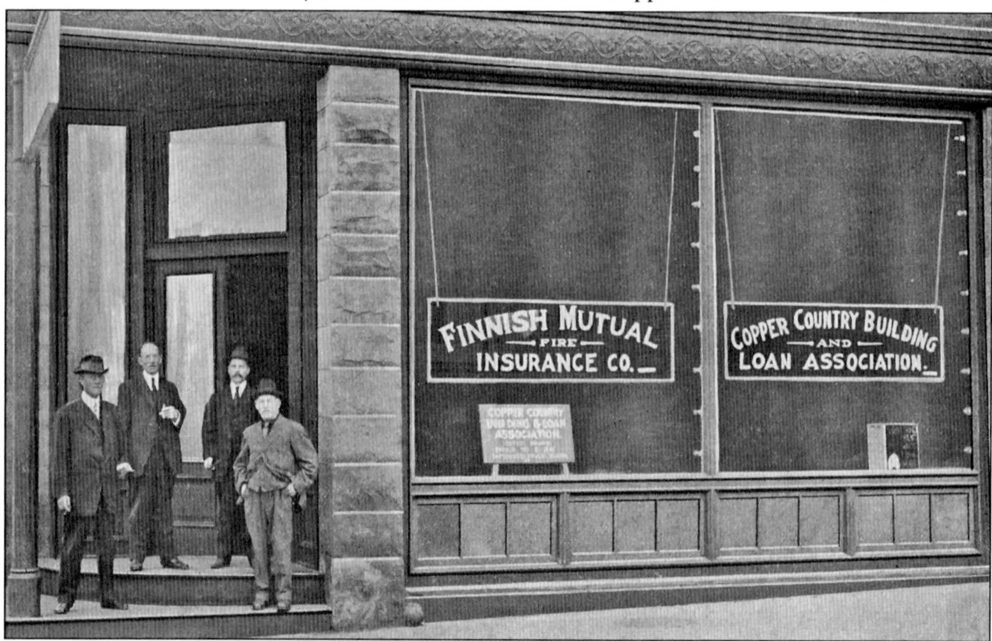

In 1889, Erick Käkelä, a farmer from Calumet, set out to form a mutual fire insurance company. Forty prominent citizens of Calumet signed the articles of incorporation in October 1889. The founders' heritage led them to name the company Suomalaisten Keskinäinen Palovakuutus–Yhtiö, which translates to Finnish Mutual Fire Insurance Company. The company was Finnish Mutual until 1990, when the name changed to Northern Mutual Insurance Company.

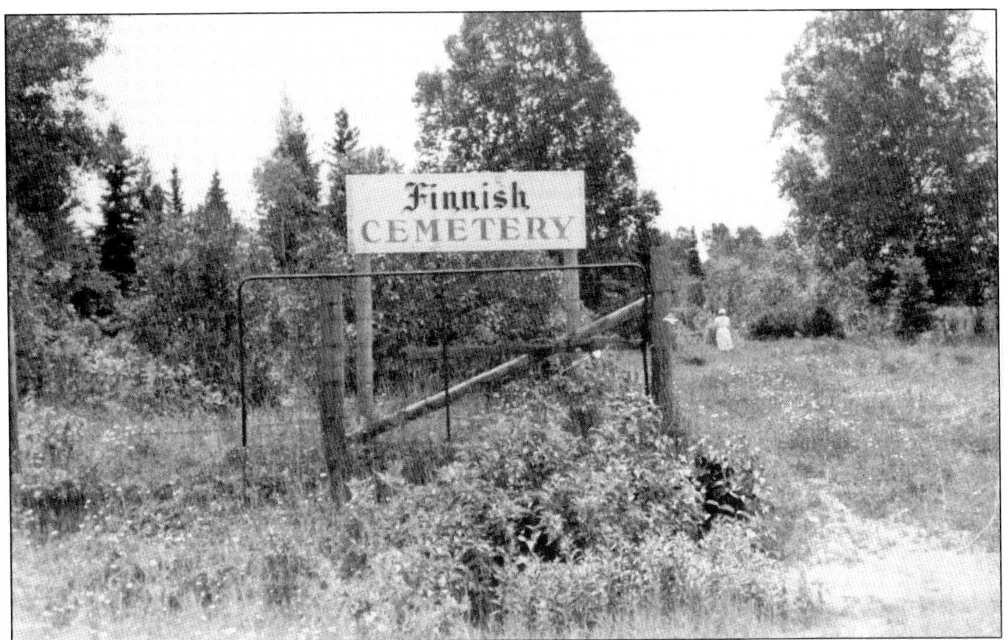

The Finnish cemetery on Drummond Island in Chippewa County was established in 1908. The cemetery, which was built on land donated by resident Jaakko Heikkinen, was dubbed Hautuumaa by the locals. The concept of ethnicity-based cemeteries was mirrored by other Finnish American communities across the peninsula.

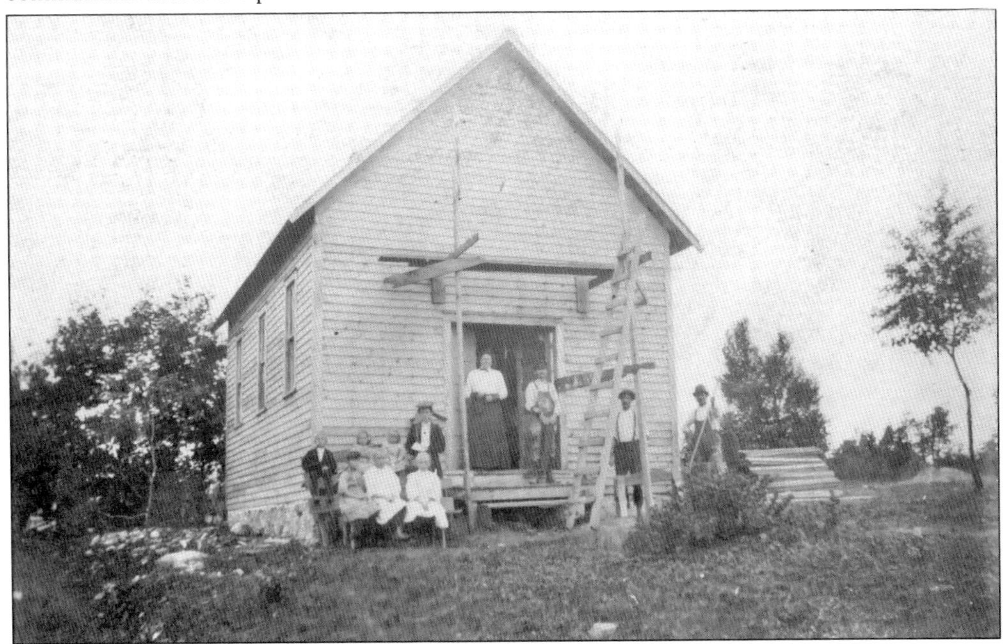

Margareeta Johanna Kontra Niiranen, also known as Maggie Walz, immigrated to Calumet, but made her mark across the UP. In 1903, she became the federal land agent for Drummond Island and founded a utopian Finnish colony there in 1905 based on the ideals of temperance, cooperative capitalism, and Christianity. However, she disassociated herself from the colony after a socialist takeover in 1914 and returned to Calumet.

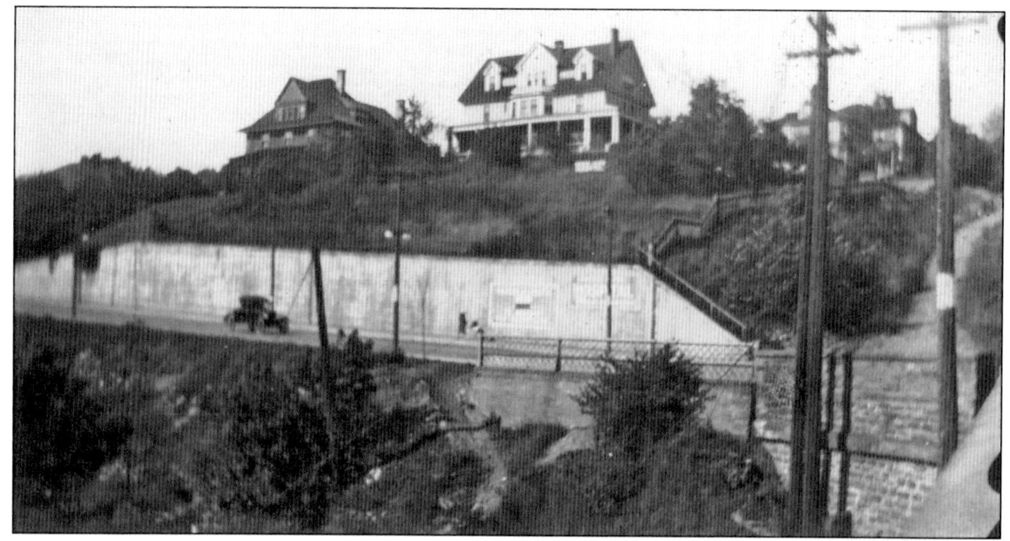

Dr. Henry Holm, a close friend of famed Finnish artist Akseli Gallen-Kallela, traveled from Ishpeming to Hancock in the early 1920s to provide services for the Finnish population of the Copper Country. He moved to Hancock in 1923 and established a clinic, and his reputation as a top-notch surgeon drew patients to his practice from as far away as Canada.

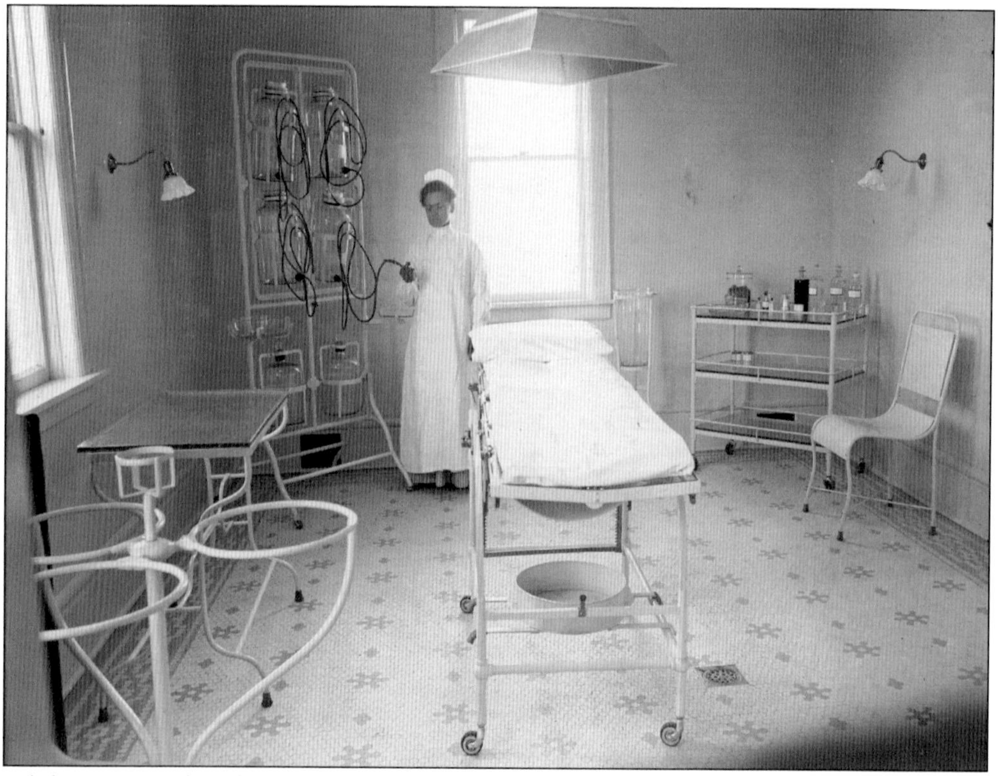

While many people today would consider it to be the middle of nowhere, UP mining towns drew people of many occupations who came to hang out their shingle. Dr. Charles Sorsen opened a private Finnish hospital in Laurium, catering to the medical needs of his fellow Finns. Shown here is one of the nurses inside the operating room in 1902.

The Hotel Salo, on Tezcuco Street in Hancock, was where many recently arrived immigrants spent their first nights on American soil. With room for 60 guests, it was the most ample lodging site in the city, known as a major "nesting place" (*pesäpaikka*) of Finnish America, since many immigrants' journeys to the United States funneled through Hancock.

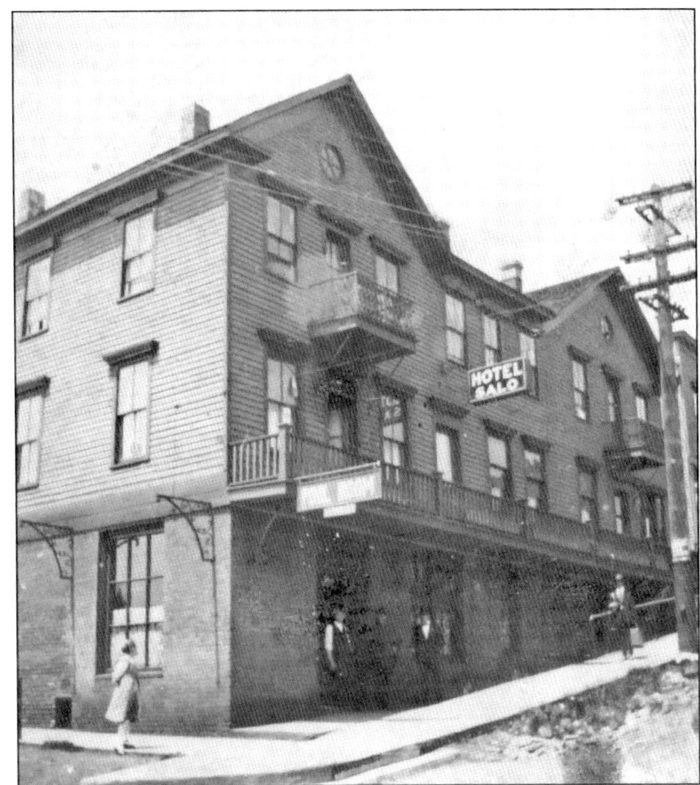

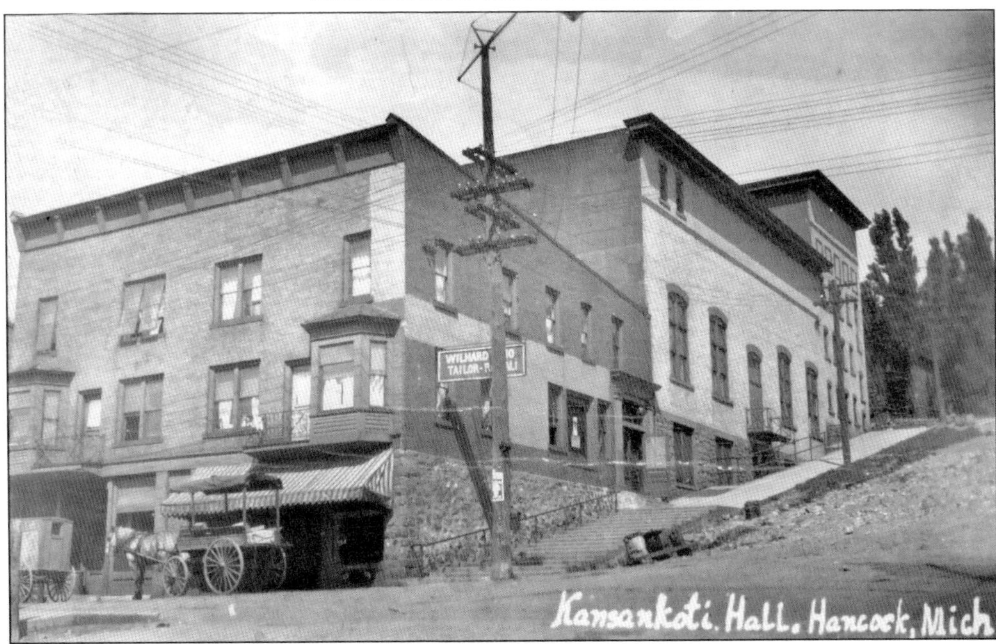

Built in 1910 and located at 201 Franklin Street in Hancock, Kansankoti Hall (Peoples' Home) was adjacent to and worked closely with the Työmies Publishing Company and was a social gathering place, as well as the headquarters for strikers during the 1913 strike and epicenter for labor organizers in the Copper Country.

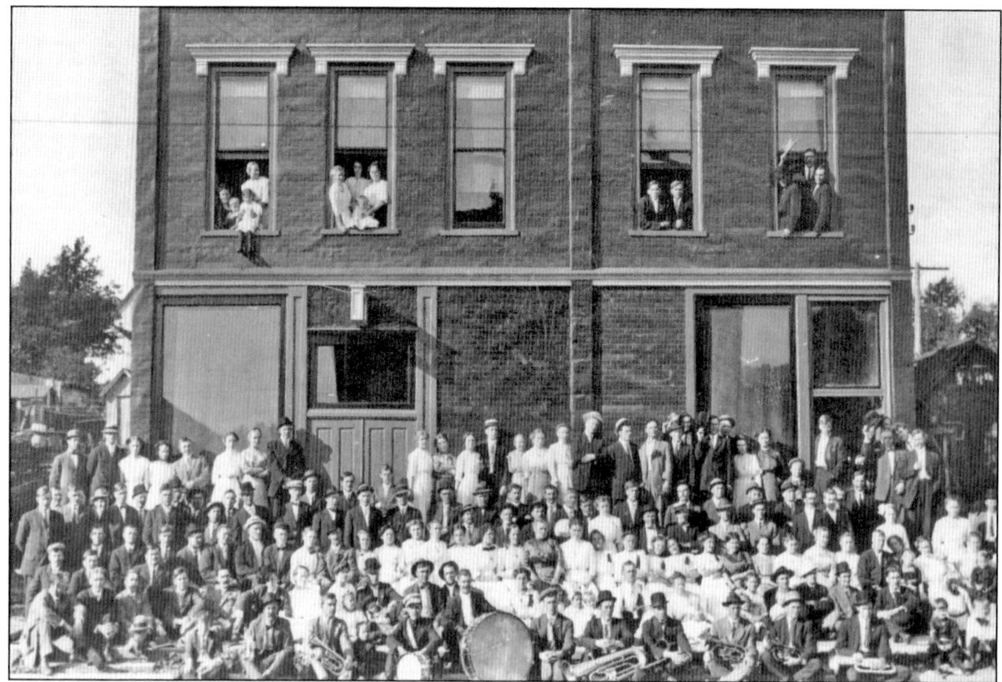

Liberty Hall was one of two Finnish halls in the city of Marquette. It opened with a gala celebration on Labor Day 1912. The Liberty Hall Band, under the direction of Thomas Tiihonen, had regular practices and performed concerts and dances at the hall, which was in the downtown area of the city.

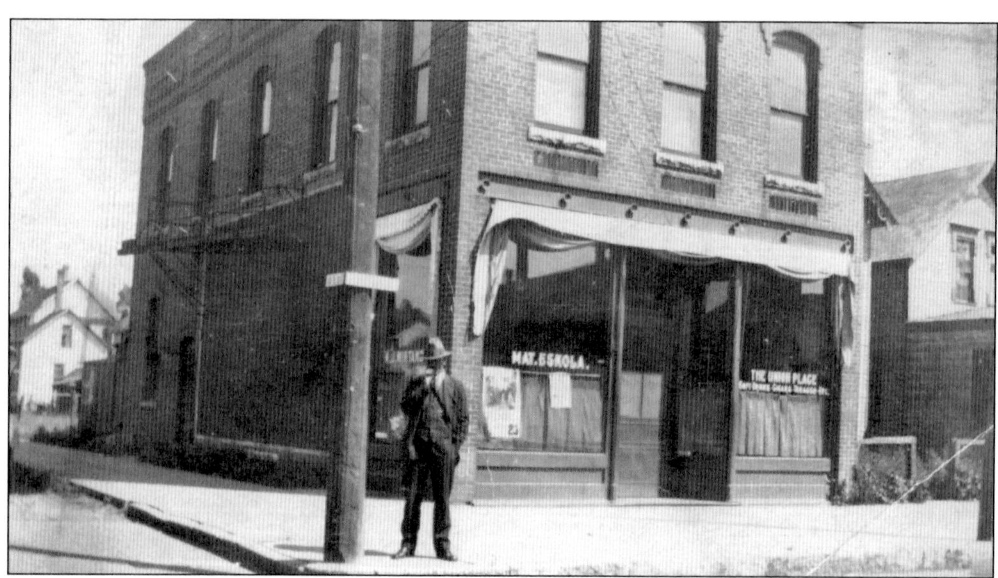

Escanaba's first Finnish store was opened in 1918 and operated by Matt Eskola and J.K. Wirtanen. This Delta County city was settled by Finns as early as the 1880s, attracted by the availability of jobs in the logging and mining industries of the region.

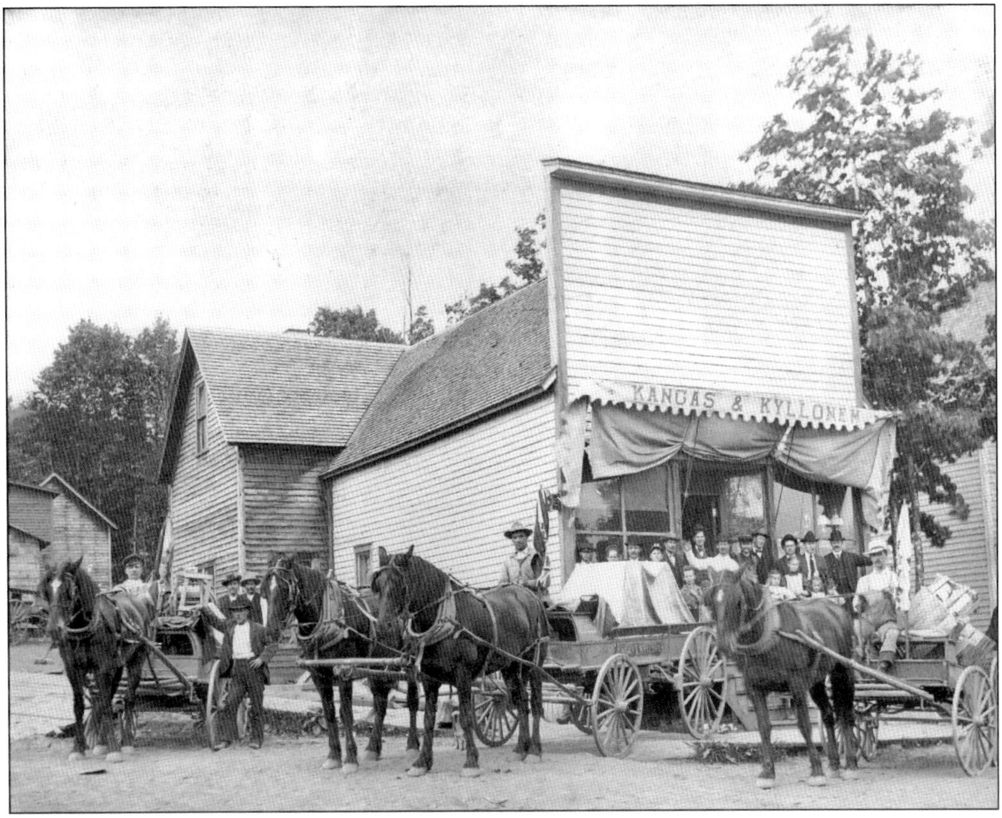

Mass City in Ontonagon County formed around the mining activity in the area, and like many hardscrabble communities across the UP, intrepid businessmen like Andrew Kangas and Matt Kyllonen filled the need for a retail center in the village and operated a market that provided the essentials for community members; it was one of numerous Finnish American owned shops in the village.

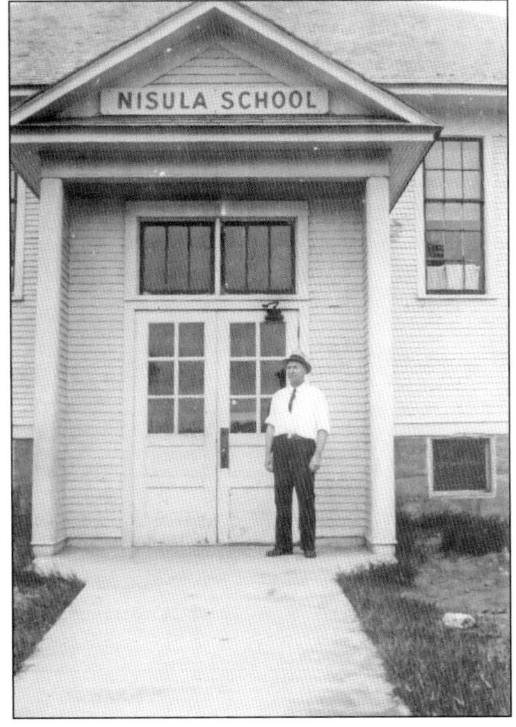

Education has always been a priority for the Finns. Though farming communities led to a wider geographic spread among settlers, they established schools in rural areas. These buildings quickly became multipurpose facilities, hosting church services and meetings, and when they closed, they were bought by Finnish congregations to become churches. This example of a rural school stood in Nisula, where Emil Heikkinen stands proudly at the front door.

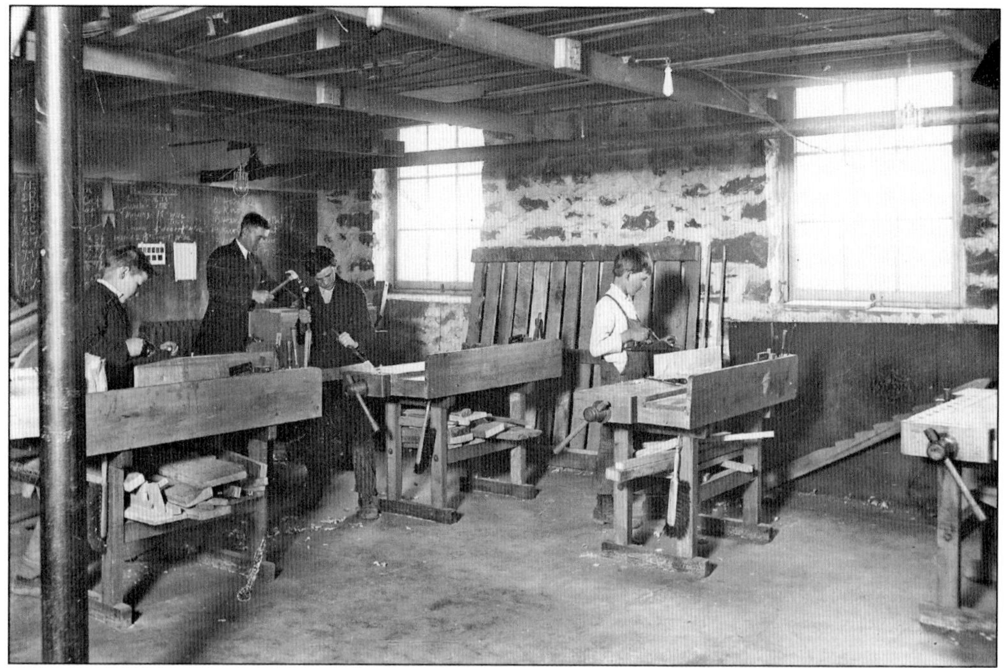

Though they understood the value of the three R's in education, rural schools such as the Doelle School in Tapiola recognized the importance of vocational training as well. Even in early grades, boys were introduced to the tools and techniques of woodworking. (James Kurtti.)

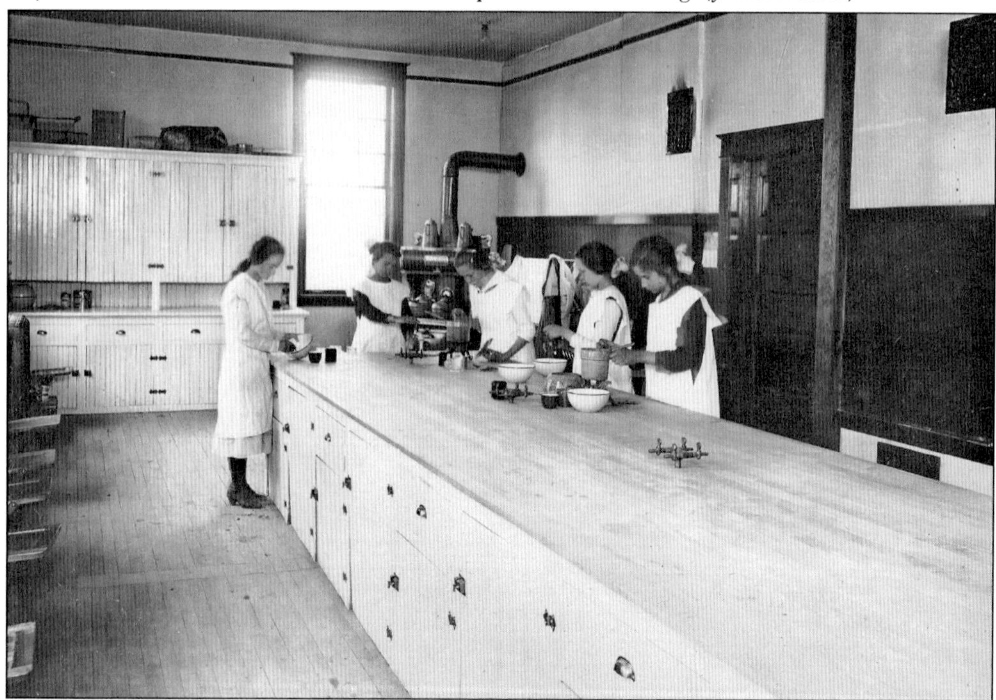

The girls at the same school—like many across the peninsula—were taught the skills necessary to be comfortable and competent in the kitchen. The Doelle School was established as an agricultural school, with a distinct focus on practical courses in addition to academic work. (James Kurtti.)

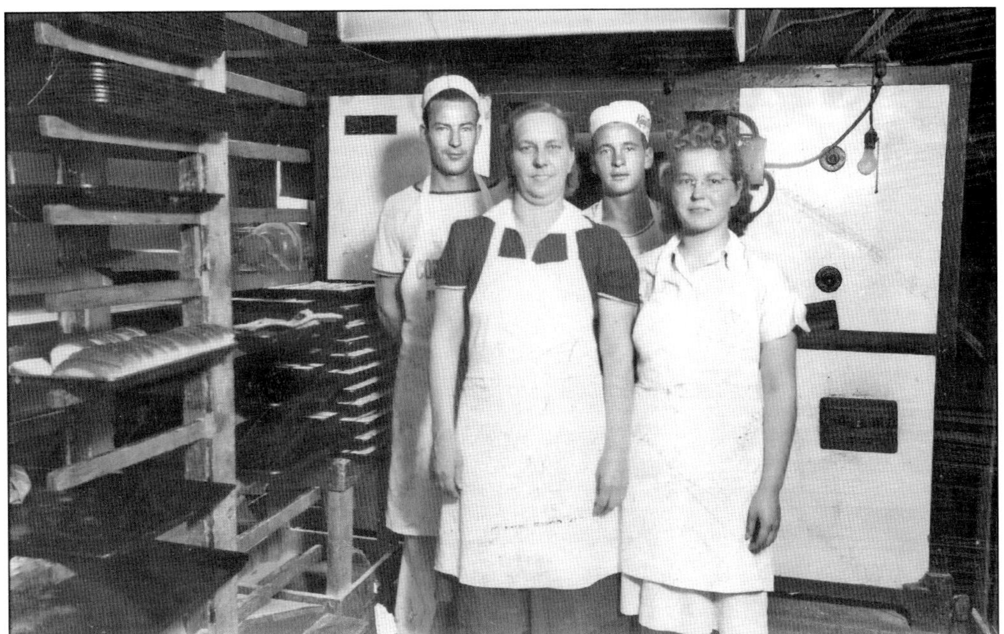

From left to right, Reino Laine, Saima Jussila, Ed Waananen, and Kate Aalto enjoyed their work at the Trenary Home Bakery in central Marquette County. How could they not? They were surrounded by the mouthwatering aromas of fine baked goods, most notably their famed *korppu*, dubbed Trenary Toast, the crisp cinnamon hard toast popular with coffee "dunkers" served across the UP to this day.

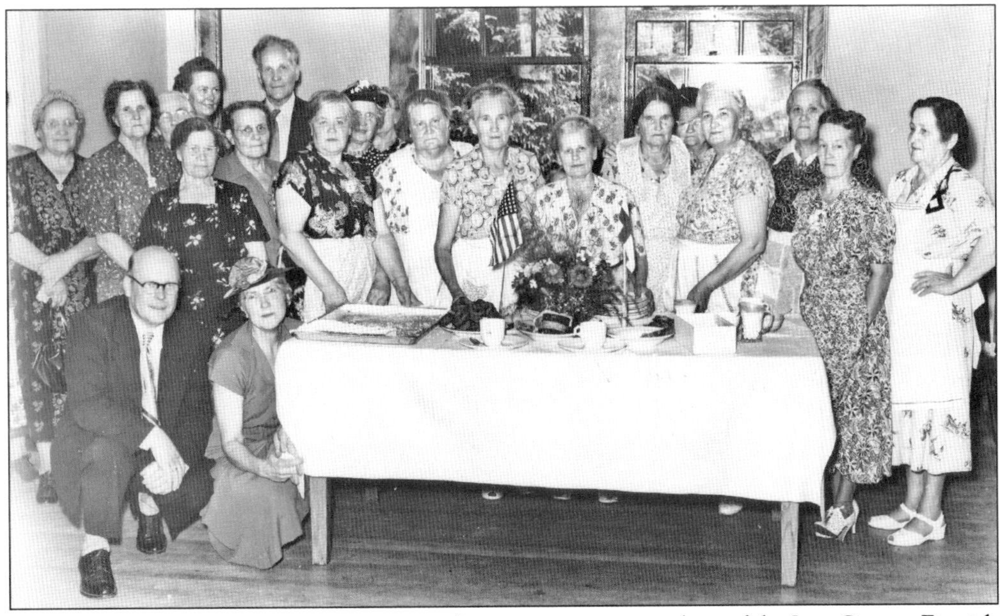

Good food and good company were among the many reasons members of the Iron County Finnish Historical Society came together at a Crystal Falls restaurant to celebrate their heritage in 1950. Keen to remember where they came from, many Finns across the UP formed historical societies devoted to preserving the stories of immigration to the United States and of the culture those immigrants left behind.

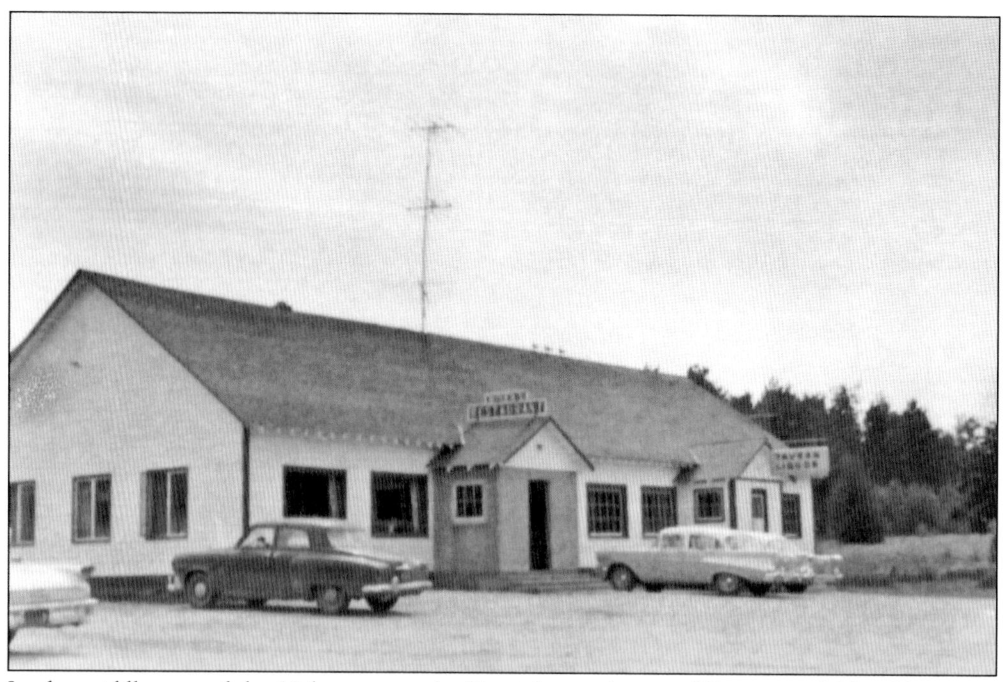

In the middle part of the 20th century, the Finnish population of Drummond Island began to dwindle. Most of the men who remained on the island were employed by the limestone quarry, which produced some two million tons per year. The tourism industry was another source of income for islanders; Hilkka Restaurant and Tavern supported both locals and visitors.

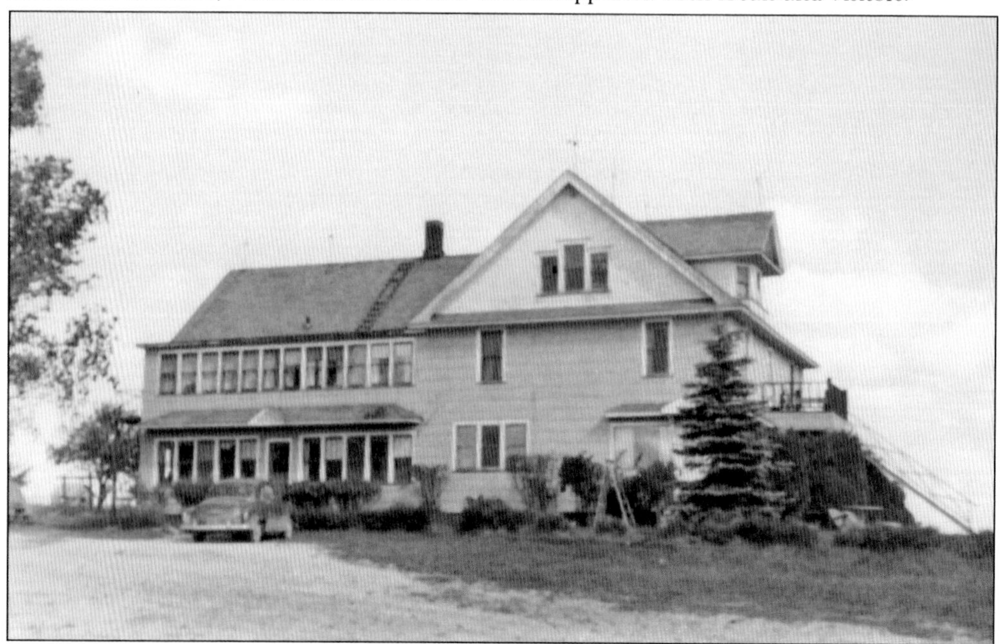

One of Covington's earliest settlers was August Huttula, who cleared some 300 acres for cultivation upon his arrival in 1899. The main building on his farmstead, which was constructed during the area's lumber boom, was used as a rest home for the older residents of the area, including famed entertainer and political activist Rosa Lemberg, who is buried in the Covington cemetery.

Sarepta Rest Home in the central Marquette County village of Republic was formed in June 1934 when Rosa Laine sold her home to Pastor K.V. Myykänen so he could establish a home for the aged. In the following decade, the demand for rooms in the rest home grew, necessitating the purchase of the larger building seen here.

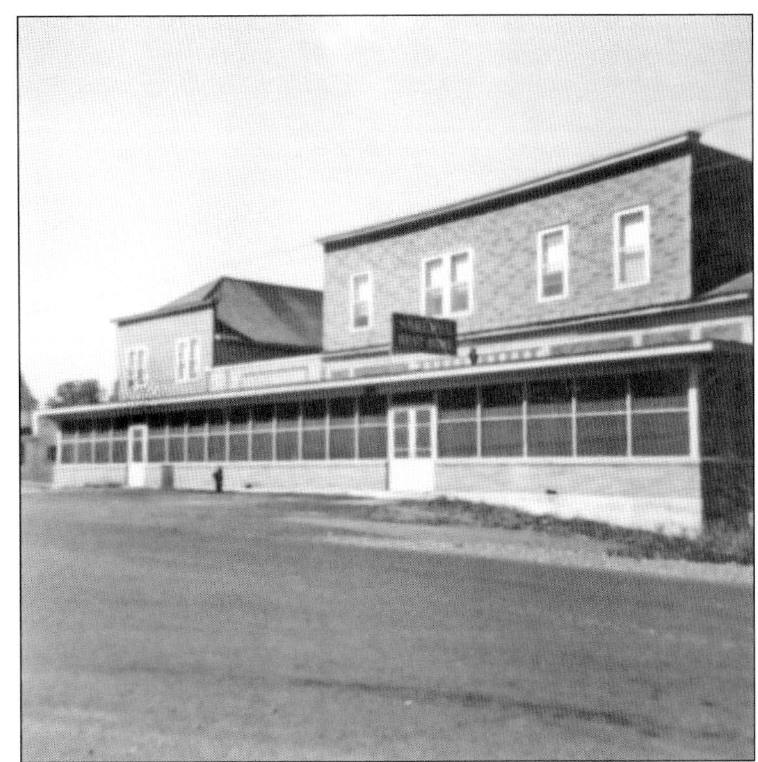

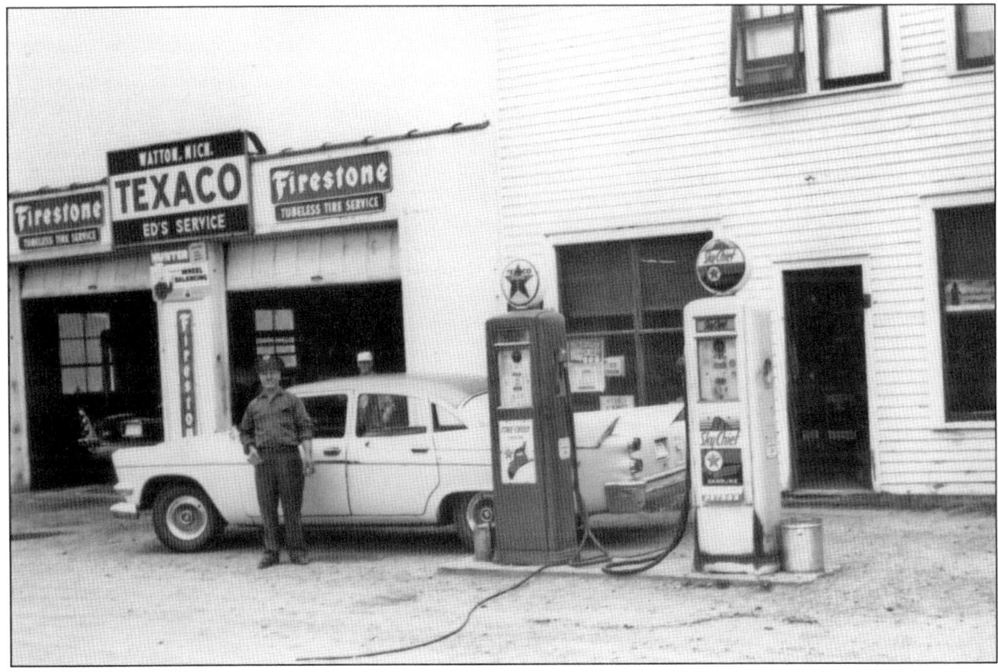

When folks would venture out for a summer day's drive around the UP, they could rest assured they were never too far from a well-equipped service station with an attendant fluent in both Finnish and English, should the need arise. Ed's Service of Watton, seen here in a July 1962 snapshot, exemplified the welcoming nature of station owners across the UP.

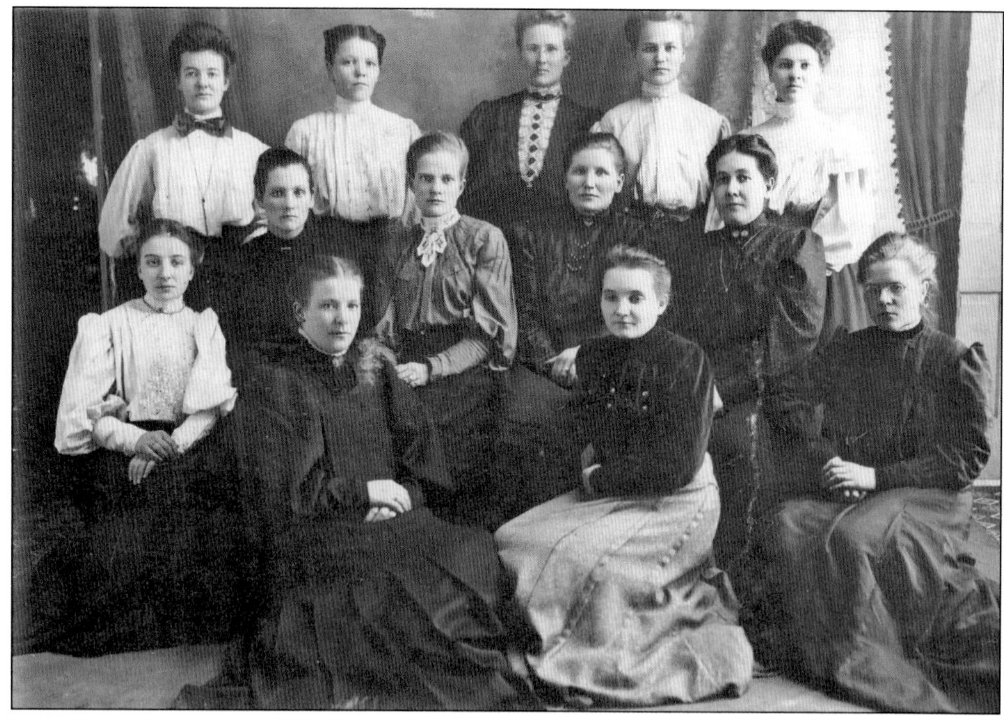

Kyllikin Tupa in Ironwood, whose founders are pictured here, was organized February 2, 1906. The Tupa was instrumental in organizing the Wakefield Ladies of Kaleva, a lodge at Crystal Falls, and one at Rolla, North Dakota. The national convention has its meetings every other year; it was held in Ironwood in 1914 and 1932.

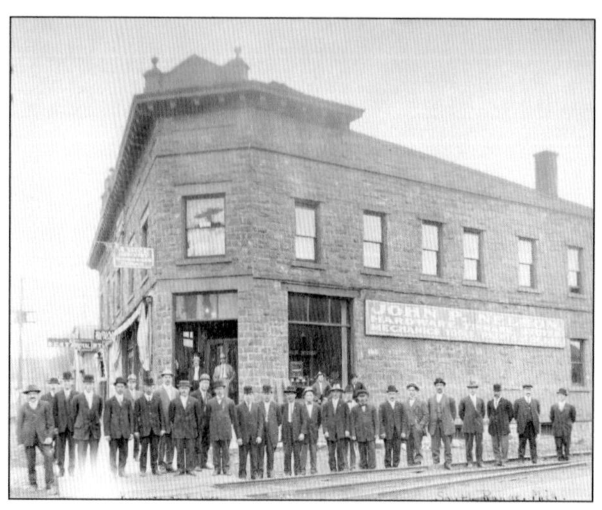

The Knights of Kaleva, which had a chapter in South Range and in many UP communities, was founded by Johannes Oxelstein (John Stone) for the purpose of assisting Finnish immigrants contending with the economic and social pressures of their day and affirming their Finnish heritage. The organization stresses loyalty, benevolence, and respect for one's heritage, and requires full initiation. The roots of the organization will forever be bound to the UP; John Stone is buried in South Range.

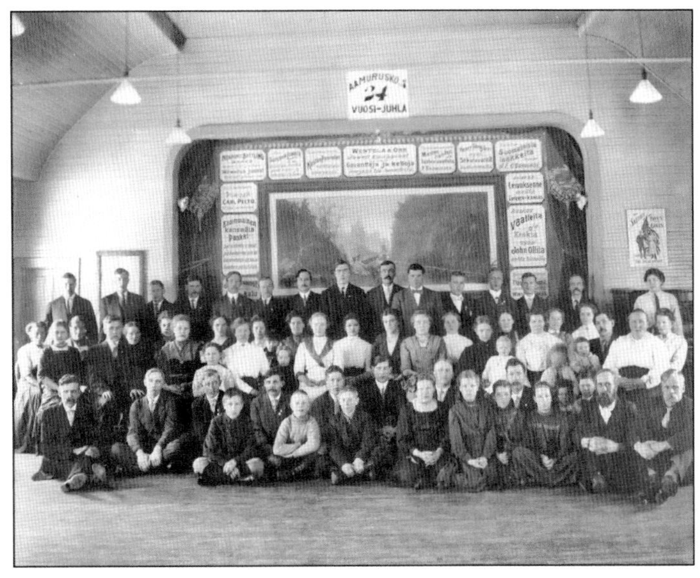

The strongest indication of loyalty to Finnish heritage among UP Finns was perhaps the Knights and Ladies of Kaleva, a society founded in the late 1800s. Many UP towns had a *tupa* (women's lodge) or *maja* (men's lodge), including Negaunee, where the Ahtolainen Tupa was founded in 1909. Eleven years later, the lodge hosted the annual convention of the national Knights and Ladies of Kaleva.

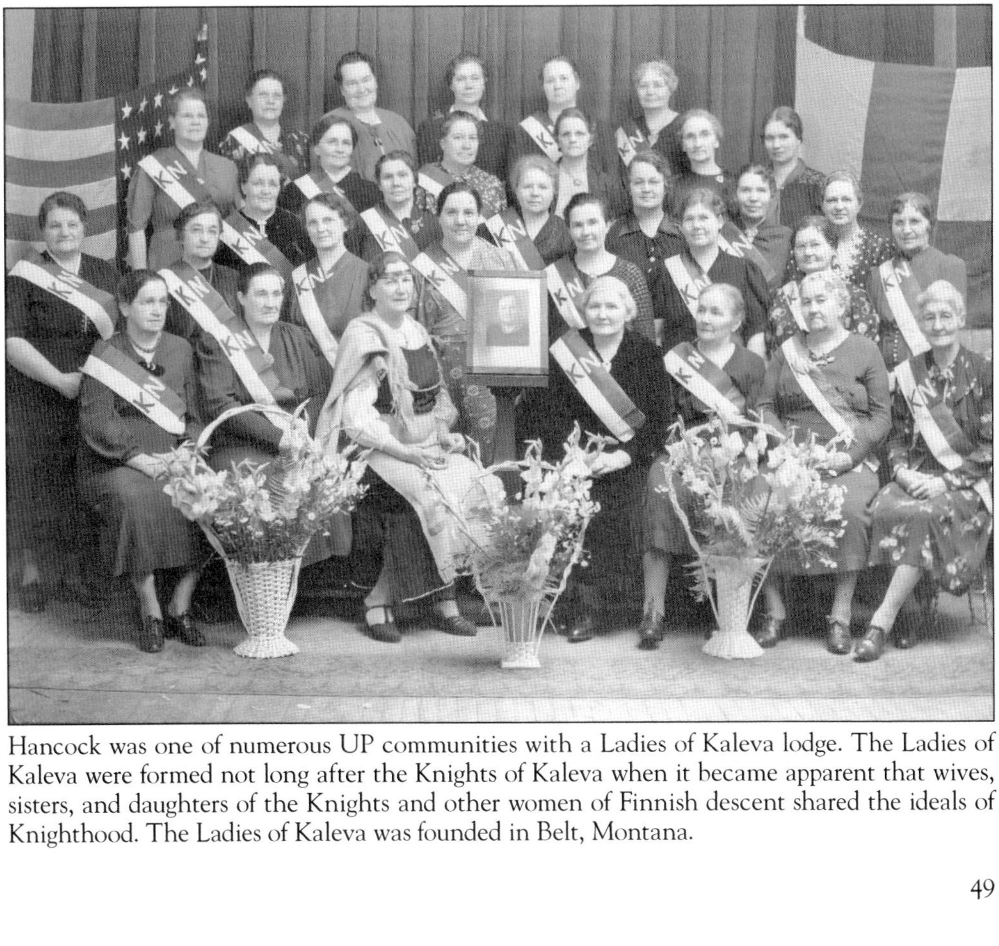

Hancock was one of numerous UP communities with a Ladies of Kaleva lodge. The Ladies of Kaleva were formed not long after the Knights of Kaleva when it became apparent that wives, sisters, and daughters of the Knights and other women of Finnish descent shared the ideals of Knighthood. The Ladies of Kaleva was founded in Belt, Montana.

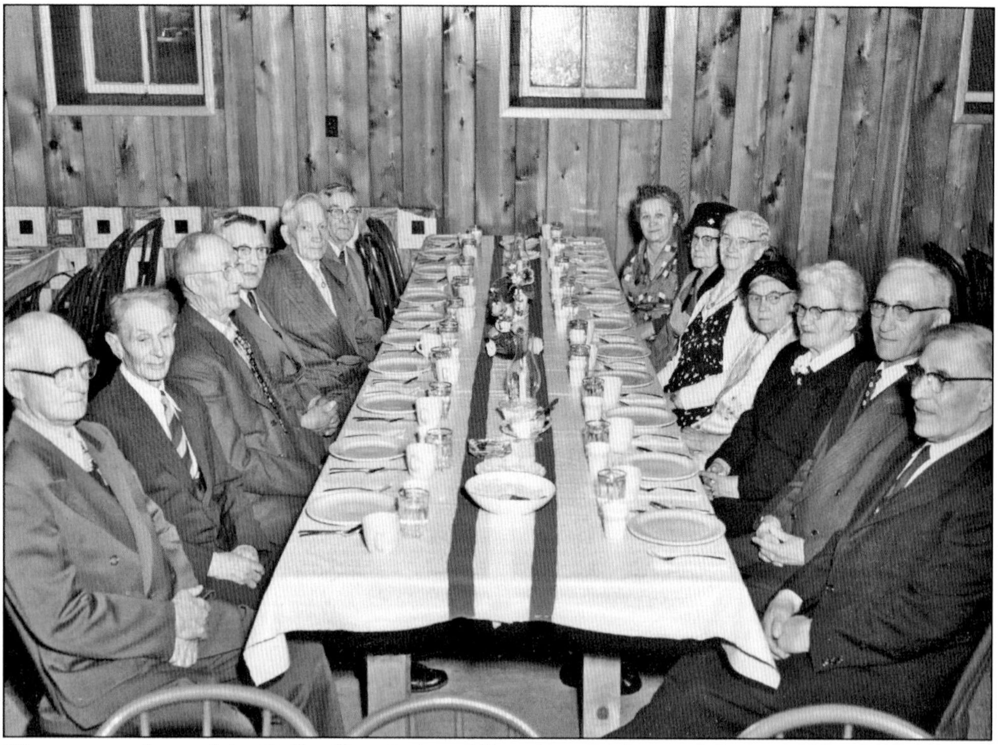

Charter members of the Dollar Bay Order of Runeberg Lodge were honored at a banquet and dance on April 18, 1959. The Dollar Bay order formed in 1903, and the members spent the better part of that summer constructing the hall, which remains active today operating under the name Runeberg Lodge, but serving more as a social club. (John Backman.)

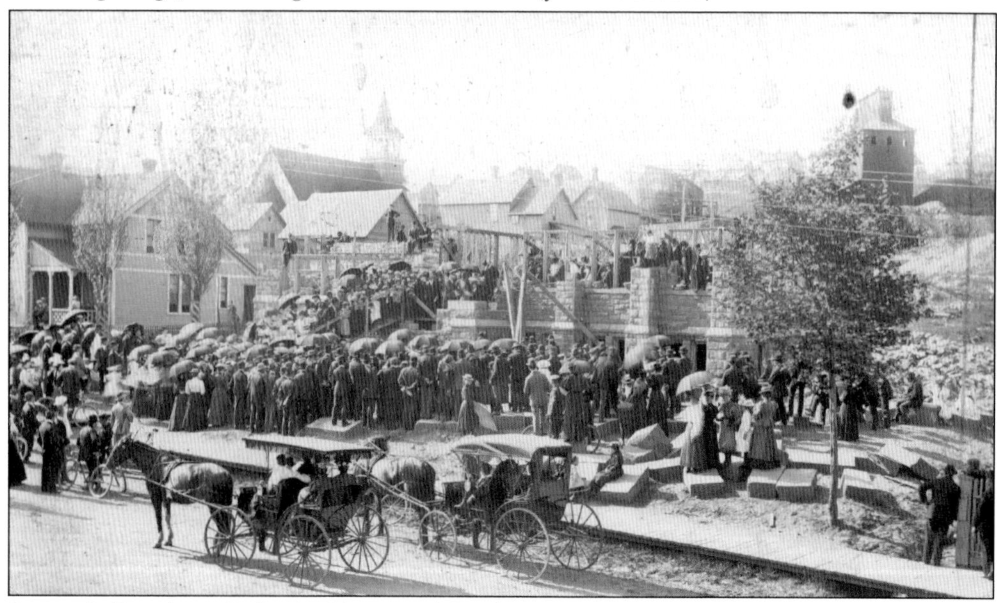

Suomi College (now Finlandia University) has been an influential part of the greater Hancock community for its entire existence, as evidenced by the crowd of onlookers gathered in 1899 to witness history as construction crews build the Old Main building, the first structure on campus.

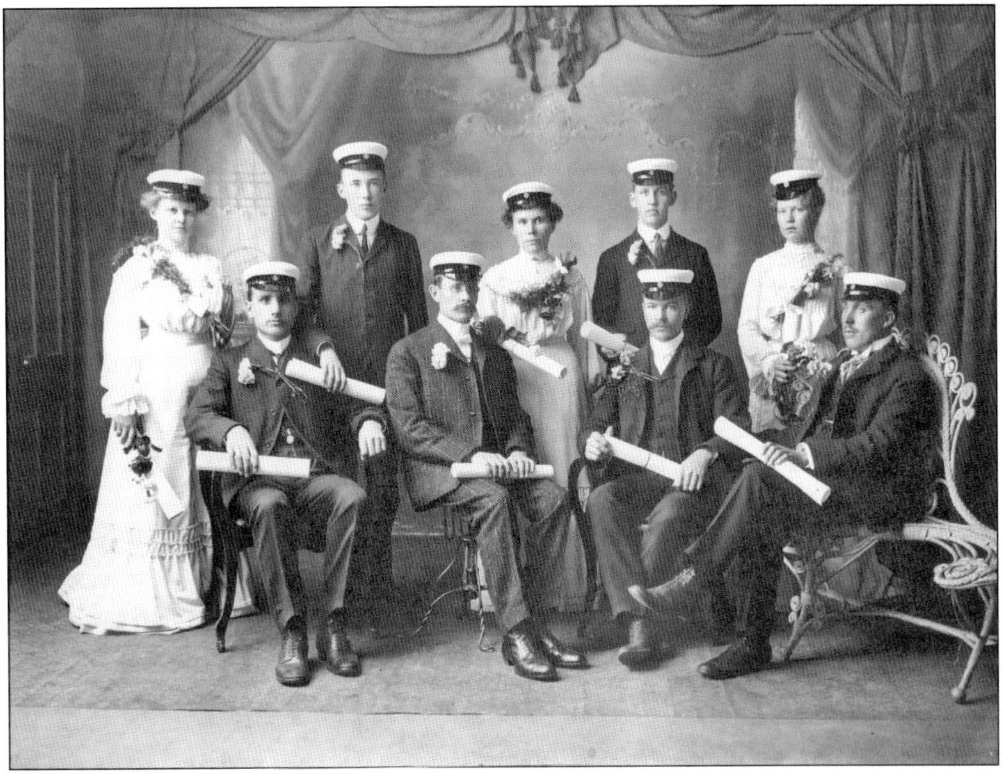

Diplomas in hand, the first graduating class from Suomi College poses for a photograph in 1904 before embarking on their careers. The class included, from left to right, (first row) Alfred Haapanen, Matti Luttinen, Heikki Haapanen, and Solomon Ilmonen; (second row) Lydia Kangas, Victor Koivumäki, Miina "Minnie" Perttula, John Wargelin, and Liisa Paavola.

For more than a century, Old Main, the signature building of Finlandia University (formerly Suomi College), has stood proudly along Quincy Street in Hancock. Having served a variety of needs throughout its existence, ranging from student housing to faculty offices, it currently houses the university's business office and some athletic department employees' workspaces.

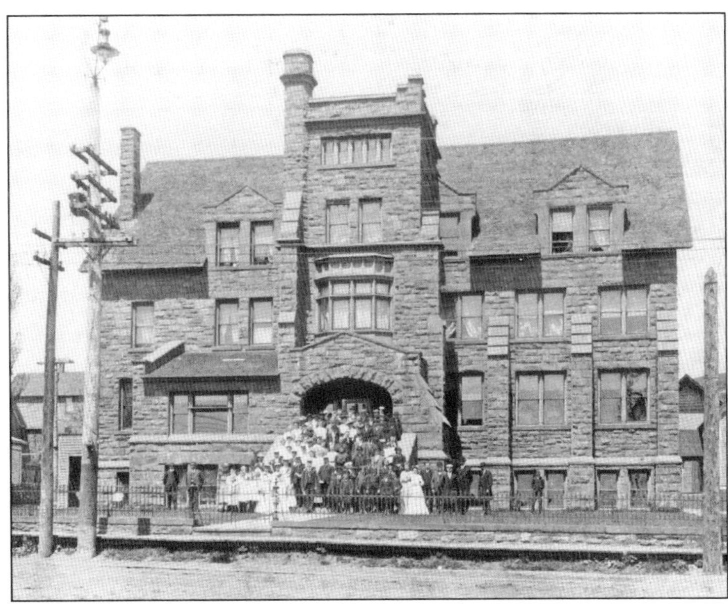

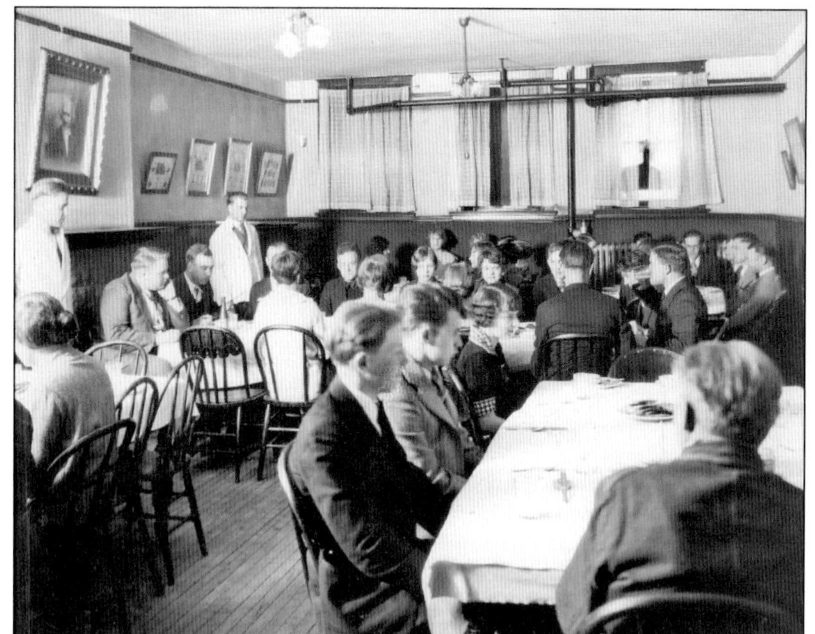

A far cry from the assembly line cafeterias on college campuses today, dinner time for resident students at Suomi College was a more formal affair, with home-cooked meals on properly set tables served to the young men and women who dressed for the occasion.

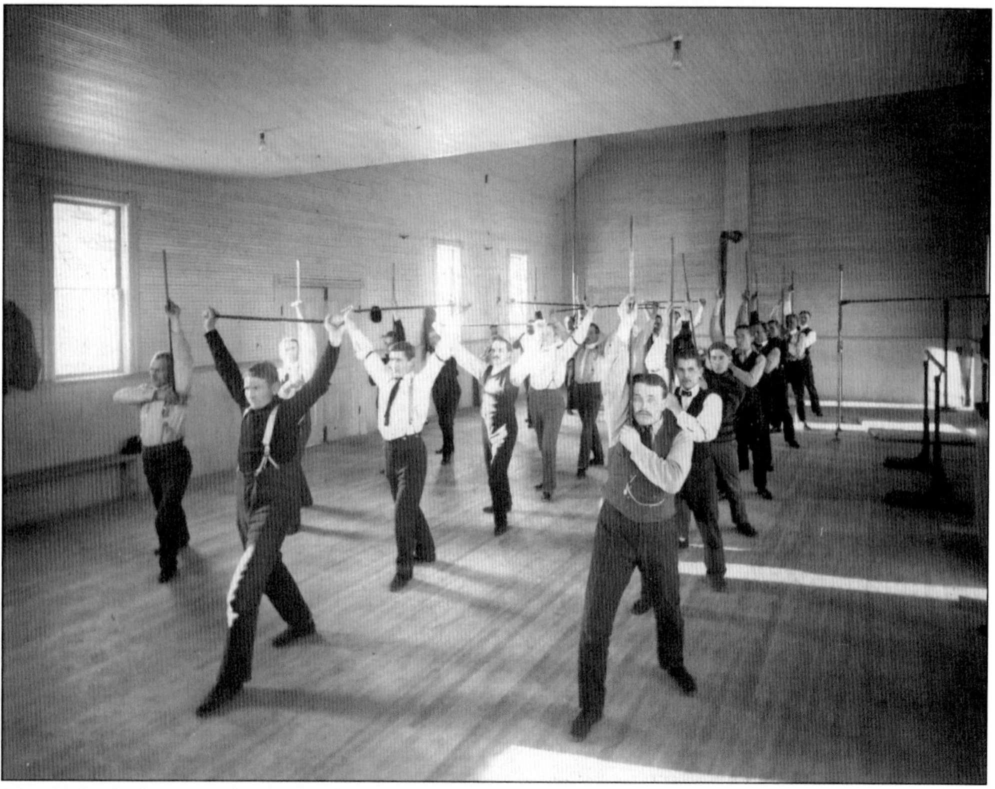

Mindful of educating both the body and the brain, Suomi College course offerings included plenty of opportunities for students to incorporate physical education into their pursuit of their degrees. Calisthenics was a popular choice, much as it was among organizations, such as Finnish Halls, across the spectrum of Finnish America.

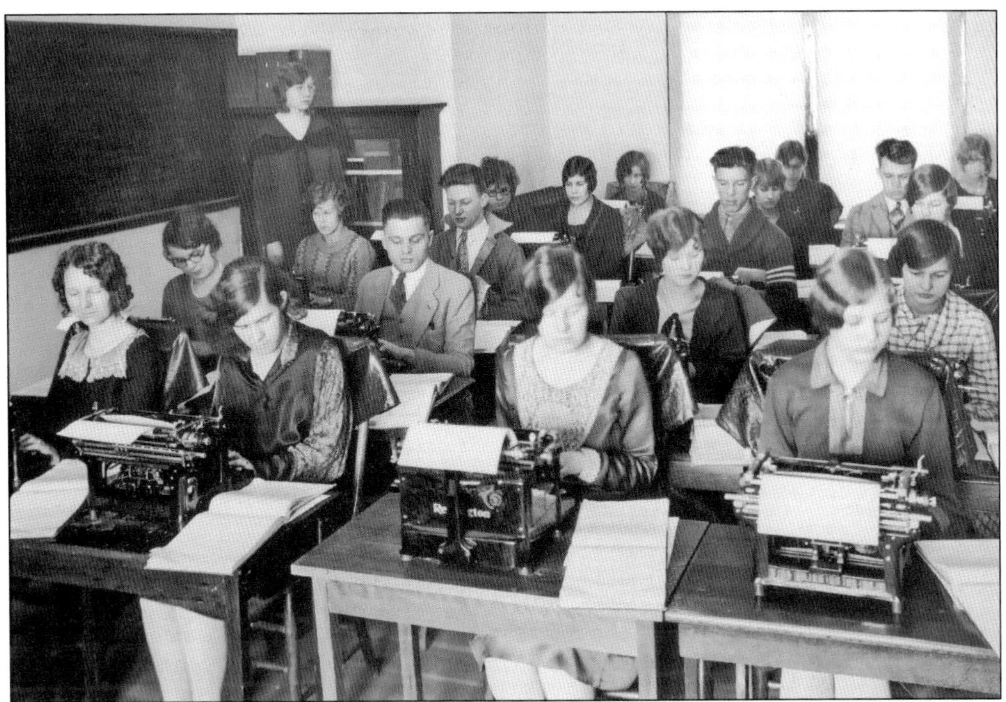

Under the watchful eye of teacher Elizabeth Mitchell, Suomi College students use proper posture and keep their eyes off the keys as they click and clack their way to mastery of the manual typewriter; at the time, it was a valuable tool for those seeking a future in office occupations. This instruction took place in the commercial building on the college's campus.

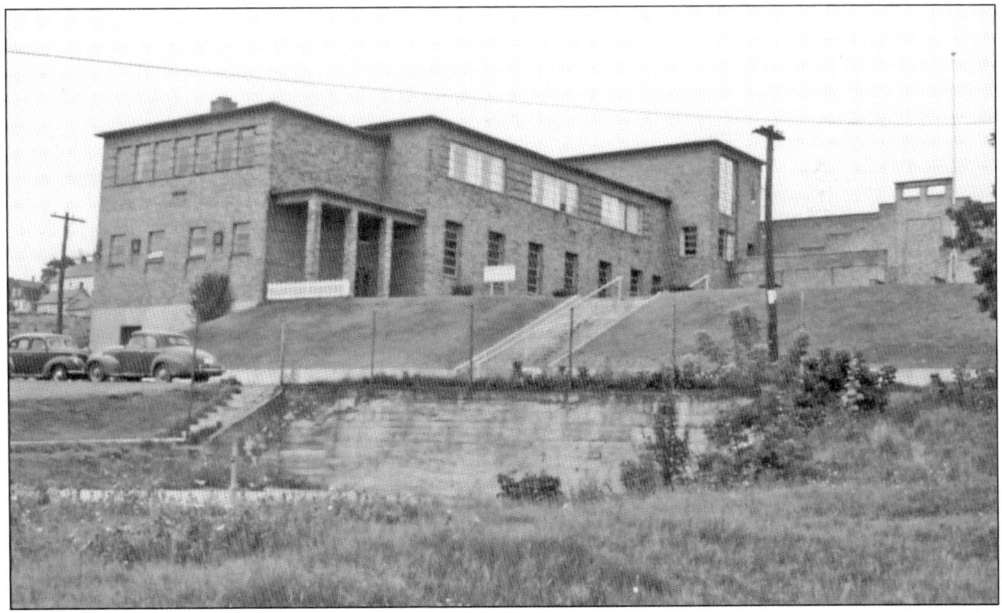

Designed by world-renowned architect Eliel Saarinen and his son-in-law J.R. Swanson, Nikander Hall was the second new building on Suomi College's campus, erected in 1939. Ultra-modern for the time, it housed a gym, library, and classrooms. This building and the brick staircase to the street level above set the stage for future campus development.

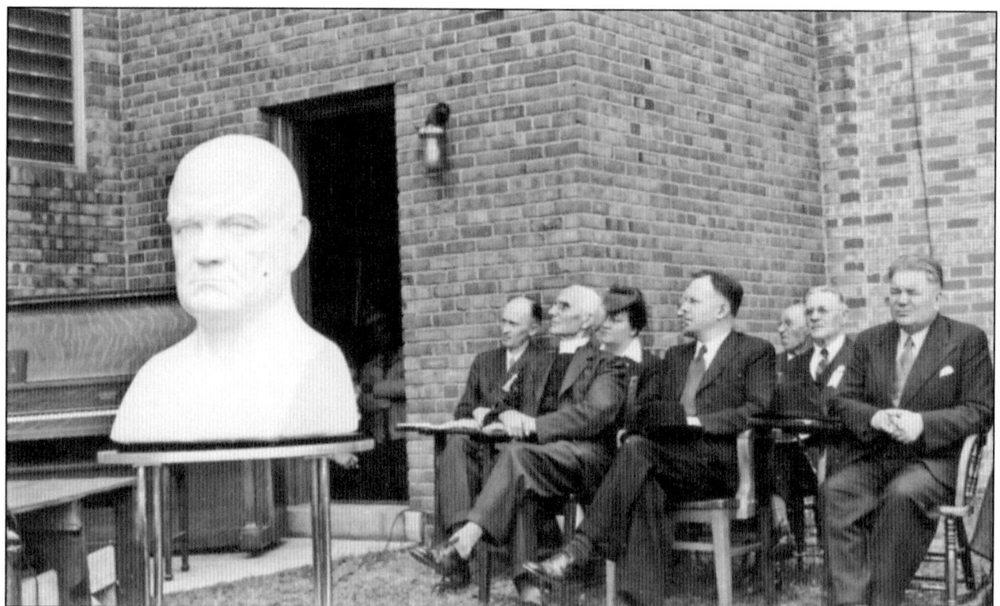

Famed Finnish composer Jean Sibelius was a part of the 50th anniversary celebration at Suomi College—in bust form, at least. Designed, crafted, and donated by Prof. A. Werner of the University of Washington, the bust was delivered to the Hancock campus in 1946, with the giant head a backseat passenger for the entire trek across the United States.

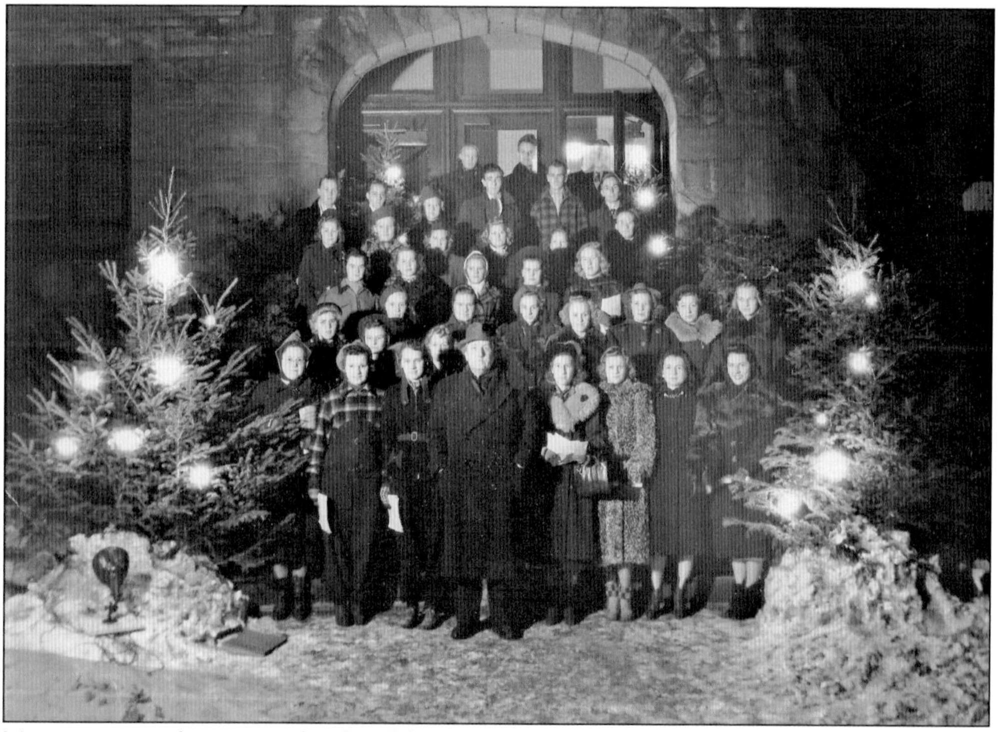

Music was a significant part of student life at Suomi College. Led from 1922 to 1946 by the beloved teacher Martti Nisonen, the choir toured both across the United States and in Finland. Here, they pose for a photograph in front of Old Main while Christmas caroling in 1939.

Three

KEEPING IT CLEAN, YOOPER STYLE

Even today, it is not uncommon to see and smell the enticing plumes of wood smoke emanating from a small outbuilding at a Finnish American home, especially on a Wednesday or Saturday evening.

Old Country tradition dictates that the first structure built is the sauna. The house and barns come later, providing a roof over the settlers' heads as they establish a place in American life. Folkloric beliefs insisted that the sauna had a spirit, and one should never behave badly or speak coarsely nor loudly in the sauna. "The church is the most holy of places, and the sauna is second," according to traditional belief.

For a Finn, the sauna is much more than a place to bathe. Early saunas were *savusauna* (smoke sauna) in which there was no stove, but only large field stones, which were slowly heated by an open fire. In the course of heating, smoke leaked out of every crevice, giving the appearance that the bathhouse was on fire. Once well-heated, the smoke was quickly let out from an opening near the ceiling and more or less everyone together took a cleansing steam (*löyly*) before the sauna cooled down.

The cleanliness and restfulness of the sauna made it conducive to other essential practices. Women gave birth in the sauna, and the dead were prepared for burial there as well. At times, it was the farm's laundry, as well as a place to cure meat and fish.

Public saunas sprang up in Finn towns, sometimes with mens' and ladies' nights or perhaps with private saunas for families and a "bull pen" for the single men.

Modifications developed in both Finland and Finnish America, which led to the advent of fabricated iron sauna stoves designed by Bruce Crossing resident Leo Nippa. Nippa Sauna stoves have been distributed across the country.

The Saturday night sauna remains an integral part of UP, where folks, whether Finnish or not, keep it clean, Yooper style.

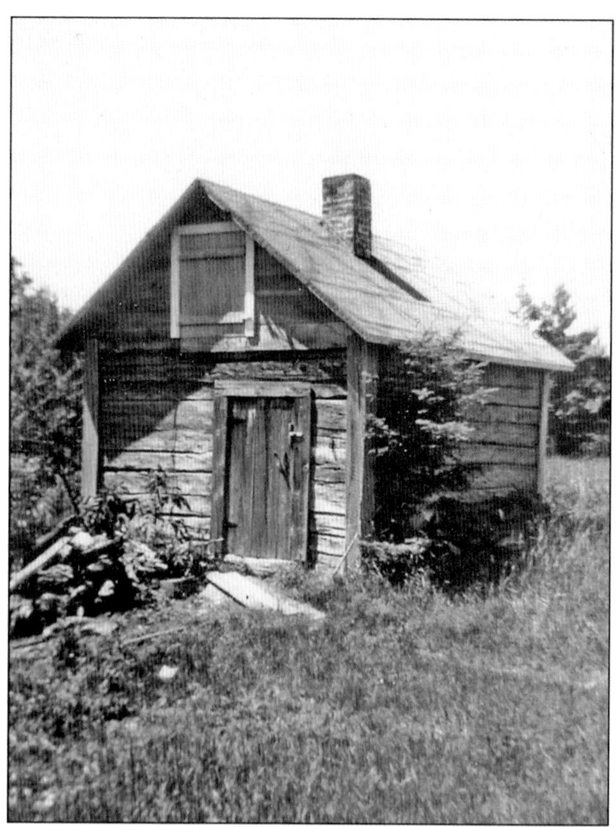

The serenity of the natural setting, the beauty of the clean lines of the hand-hewn construction, and the inviting aroma of wood smoke emanating from the chimney is the recipe that has attracted Upper Michigan's Finns like Antti Kallunki and many of their friends and neighbors to enjoy the sauna tradition that crossed the ocean with immigrants nearly two centuries ago. (James Kurtti.)

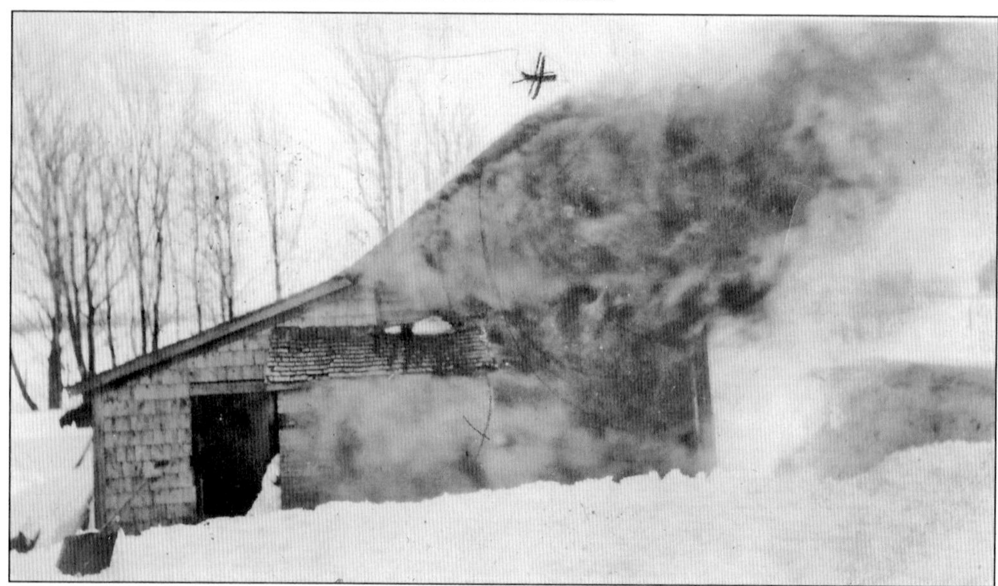

When a *savusauna* (smoke sauna) is heating, smoke spews from the structure, so it was often hard for passersby to know whether the sauna was simply being used or was endangered. This scene at the Komula sauna in Tapiola ended in tragedy; the sauna burned to the ground, confirmed by the photographer marking a cross above the structure in keeping with the Finnish tradition of labeling deceased people in photographs.

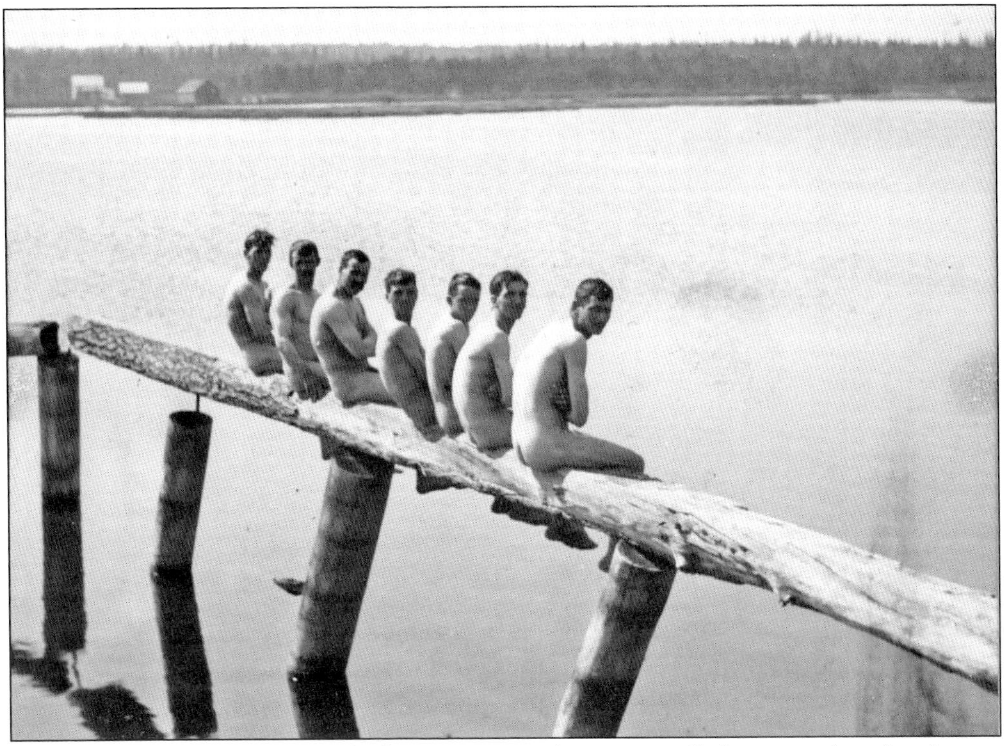

After a deep-cleansing sauna, standard operating procedure—especially for saunas along shorelines—is to dive into the lake, or the snow, to thoroughly refresh the body and spirit and curtail the excessive perspiration. Clothing is not recommended, either in the sauna or afterward.

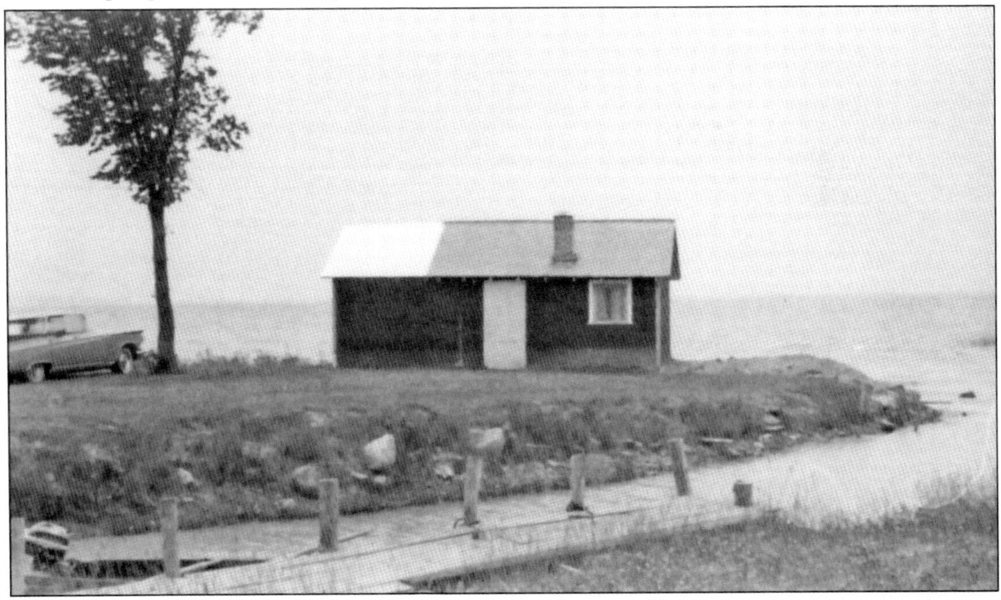

The sauna at the Niemelä Tourist Center at St. George Bay on Sugar Island (Sokerisaari) was a popular destination for locals and visitors to this eastern Upper Michigan island, which Finns first settled in 1916 under the leadership of Frank Adolf Aaltonen, who left his work as an organizer for the Western Federation of Miners.

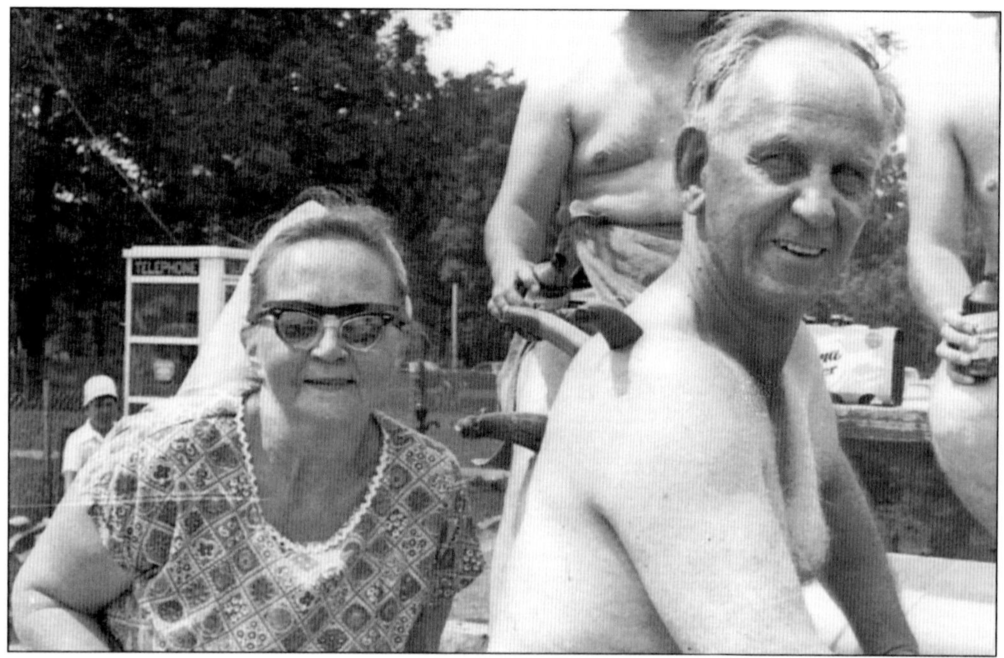

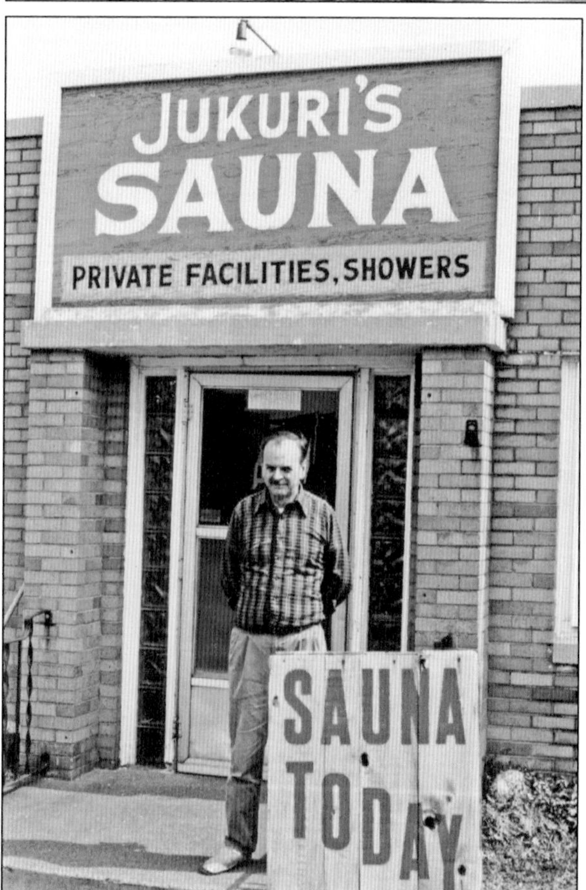

The Finns knew the sauna was an effective way to relieve the day's aches and pains, but for ailments that needed more treatment, cupping was often the answer. Through this process, demonstrated by Kathrine Liimatainen during a Fourth of July parade, "bad" blood is drawn out of the body's problem areas through superficial wounds and suction, typically after the person is warmed and relaxed by using the sauna.

Lawrence "Laury" Jukuri knew a thing or two about water. He is remembered by his friends and neighbors in Laurium for his knack for finding well sites using "water witching," and is best known for owning and operating Jukuri's Sauna, a public sauna in his hometown, where fresh cedar boughs were provided to sauna-goers as part of their user fee. (Immigration History Research Center Archive.)

Four

Religion, Politics, and Other Things to Fight About

The political and religious spectrum of Finnish America is vast, and most would agree, rather ardent in the early days. The region's earliest immigrants came from the Finnish-speaking provinces of Norway and Sweden's far north, as well as the northernmost areas of Finland—a region that had experienced a great religious awakening during the second half of the 19th century known as the Laestadian Movement (commonly called Apostolic Lutheranism in the United States). Although the movement's adherents remained members of the Evangelical Lutheran Churches in their respective countries, the movement was heavily influenced by earlier pietistic confessions from mainland Europe, stressing the absolution of sin through confession and the rejection of worldly pursuits, such as personal adornment, dancing, and the consumption of alcohol.

Later immigration included Finns from other parts of Finland, including many formerly landless farm laborers, as well as working class urbanites. Radicalism and leftist thought, which caught the attention of Finland's reformists and radicals, appealed to the disadvantaged, who were often forced to leave home due to overpopulation and the lack of opportunity. Of these immigrants, who constituted the lion's share of those who left Finland, it was a mixed bag of religiosity and radicalism.

The Swedish-speaking Finns were diverse as well, including leftists, but more often Evangelical Lutherans and, in some cases, Baptists and Free-Church affiliates.

Evangelicals, Socialists, Laestadians (Apostolic Lutherans), Wobblies (Industrial Workers of the World), National Lutherans, Republicans, Democrats, Temperance Movement followers, Methodists, Baptists, and Pentecostals built their churches and halls, each vying for loyal members. Parents warned their children not to cross the threshold of "those others" lest they be led astray.

Should a church allow an organ to play? Can the women cut their hair? Should the hall allow dancing? Can they wear a red ribbon at Christmas? A difference of opinion could easily provoke a parting of ways.

Splits upon painful, long-lasting splits occurred within communities, deeply cutting through families and friendships and, more often than not, have never been healed. If a town has more than one Finnish Lutheran church or co-op store, perhaps it is because the earlier residents disagreed about religion, politics, or other things to fight about.

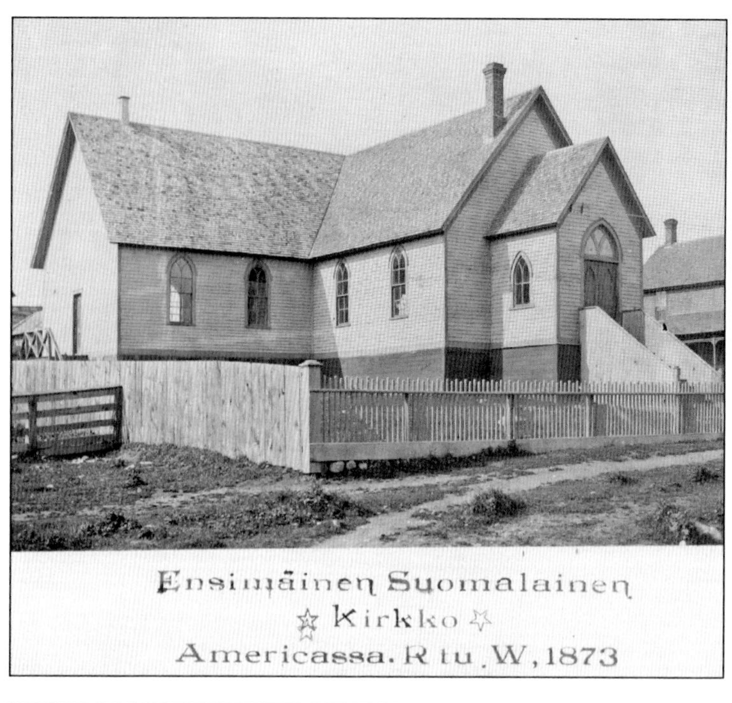

Though Finns in the Copper Country built a joint congregation with the Norwegians and Swedes atop Quincy Hill as early as 1867, a faction of them later came into conflict with the Norwegian Pastor Roernaes and left the congregation. They built the first solely Finnish church on Pine Street in Calumet in 1873, which became the home of Laestadianism in America.

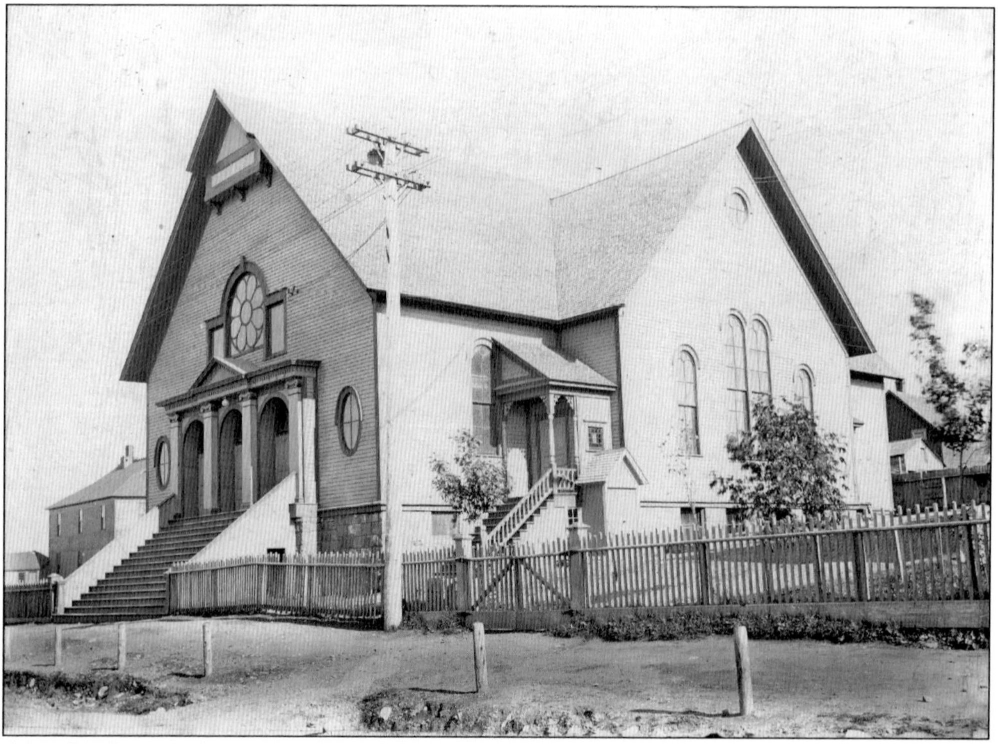

After the election of a new pastor divided the Pine Street congregation in 1888, the dissenting group broke away and built their own church across the street. Known as the Old Apostolic Lutheran Church, the denomination is lay oriented and has a layman approach to the ministry, meaning the preachers are not paid by the church and do not have a theological education or ordination.

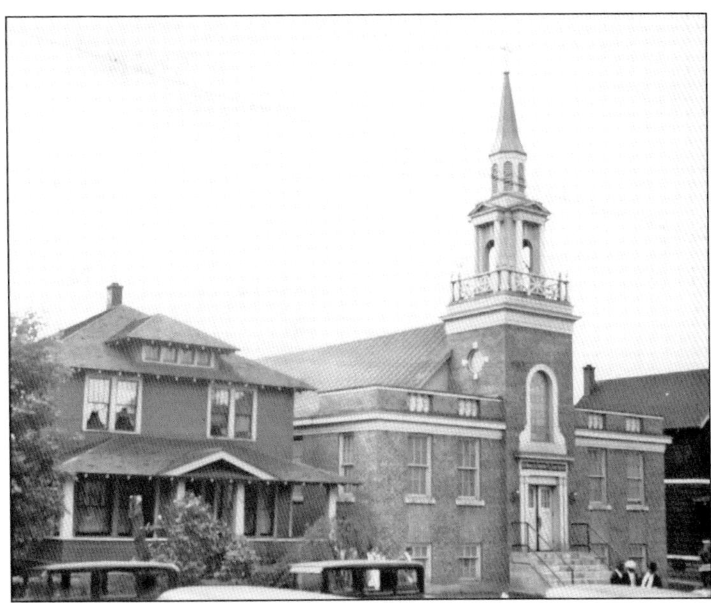

Ironwood was home to a Finnish Evangelical Lutheran congregation, established in 1888. The first pastor was J.W. Eloheimo, who defied the Suomi Synod and formed his own Fenno American Church. Through a contract stipulation, he retained control of the church building. The Suomi Synod eventually bought the building from Eloheimo's wife; the building is now St. Paul's Lutheran Church.

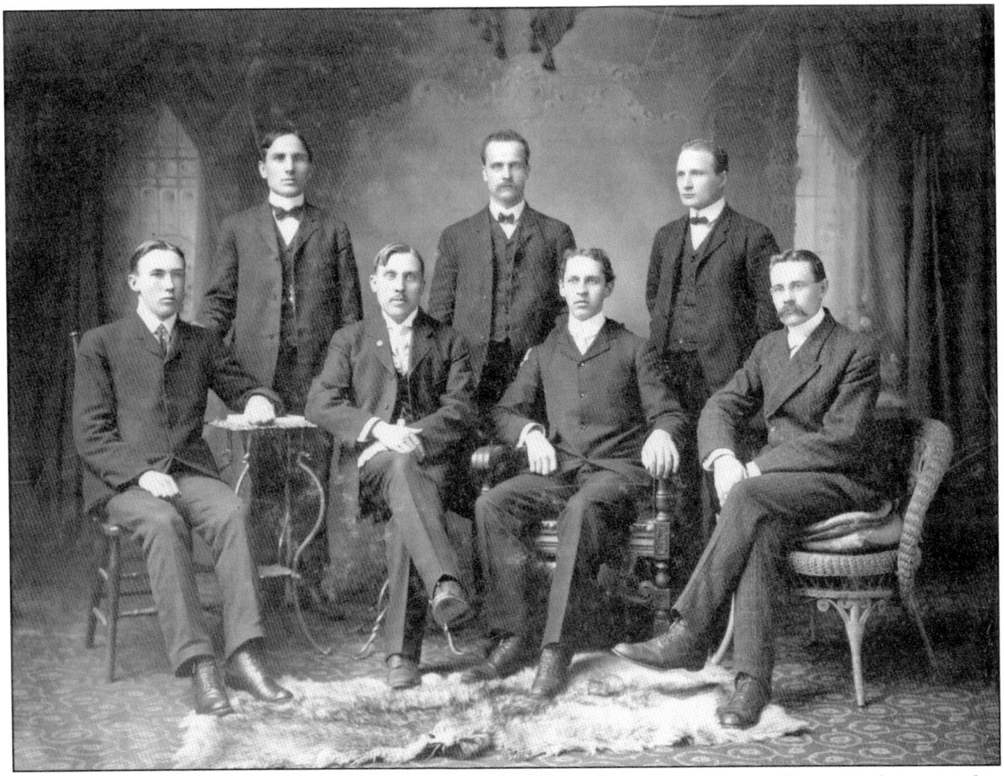

Suomi College not only prepared young Finns for life and employment in America, but was also home to the Suomi Synod Seminary to provide clergy for the growing immigrant communities. These men often had to serve large, multi-location parishes, and needed Finnish language fluency. Shown here are, from left to right, (first row) Victor Koivumaki, Solomon Ilmnonen, John Wargelin, and Matti Luttinen; (second row) Alfred Haapanen, Pekka Keranen, and Jacob Mantta.

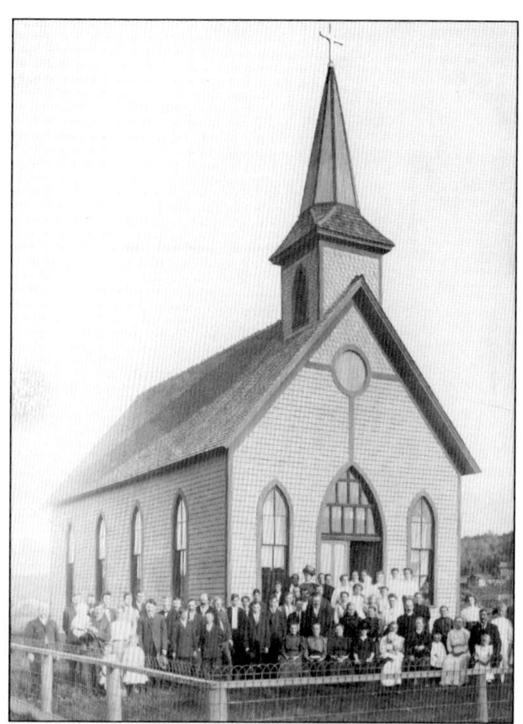

Small communities like Palmer often shared a pastor with neighboring churches. This was far from the only hardship faced by this Suomi Synod congregation. While church construction began in 1890, they had financial difficulties due to the Panic of 1893, a thunderstorm that jarred the church off its foundation in 1900, and a foreclosure on the mortgage. After a series of property exchanges, they regained their original church building in 1907.

The Suomi Synod, established in 1890, had member congregations in almost every community that had Finns. To grow and maintain this membership, the Synod, like other Lutheran denominations, held an annual church convention where delegates discussed church business. These gatherings also provided young people with a means to meet and socialize. In 1914, the convention was held at St. John's Evangelical Lutheran Church in Sault Ste. Marie.

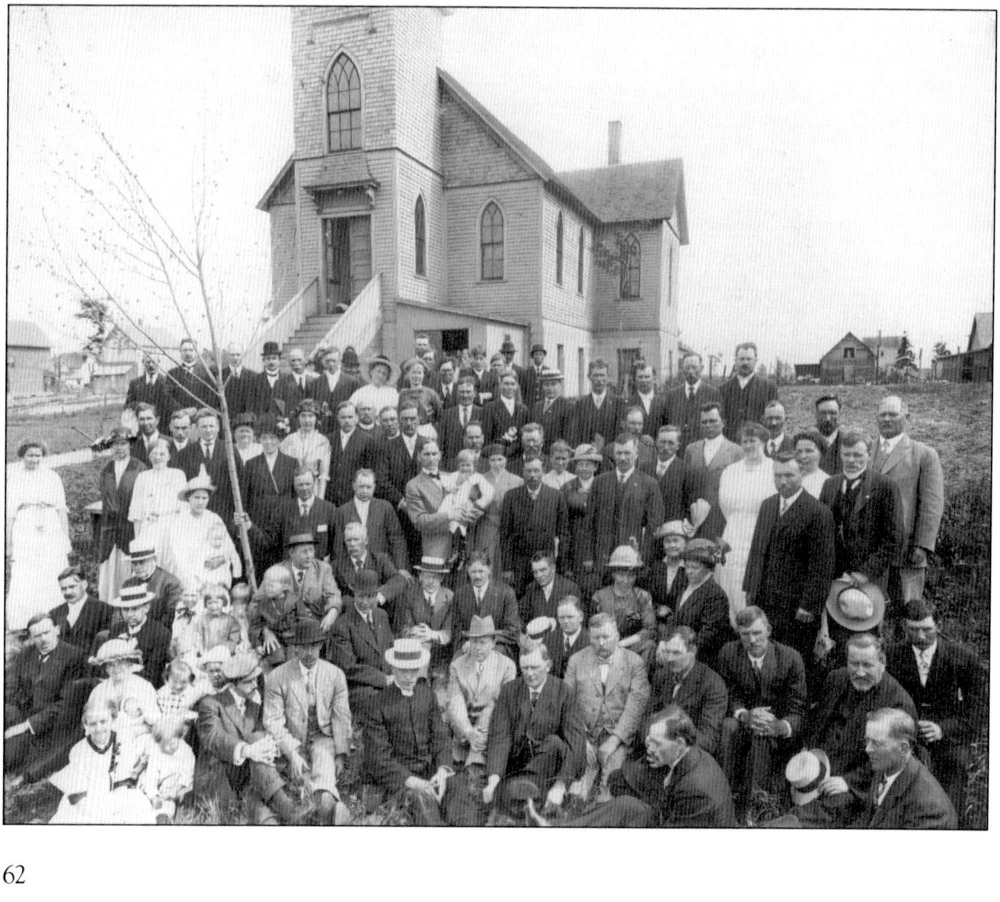

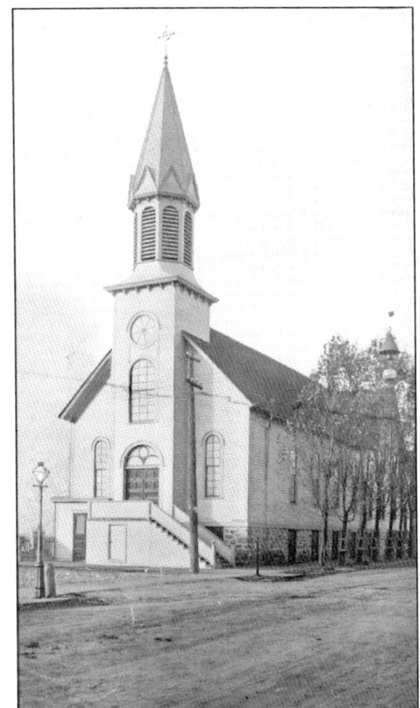

About a decade after the first Finnish settlers arrived in Ishpeming to work in the iron mines, a Finnish Lutheran congregation formed under the leadership of Finnish immigrant Jakob Hoikka. Their first, modest church was built in 1887; it has undergone several renovations during its life and is still in use today. It is pictured here between 1903 and 1932.

This is a 1900 confirmation class of Pastor John Back at Our Saviour's Lutheran Church in Atlantic Mine. Young people in this denomination were often confirmed around the age of 15 and would attend classes for several weeks in the summer prior to confirmation in order for the pastor to be sure they were prepared.

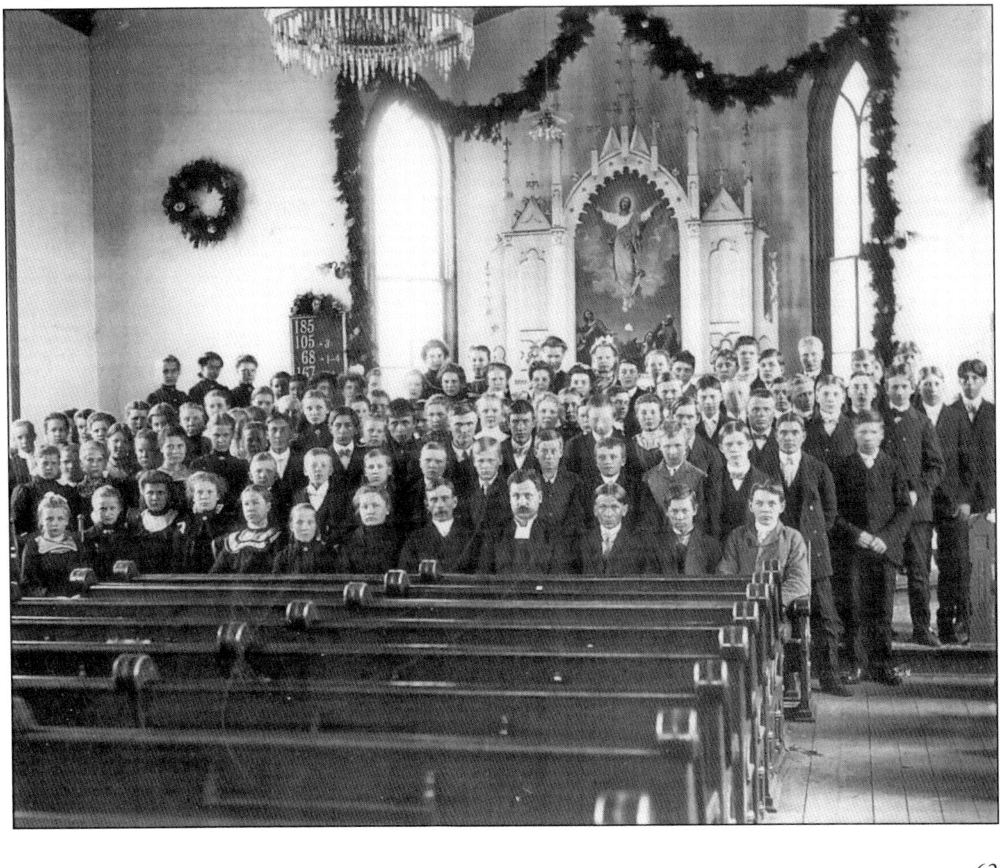

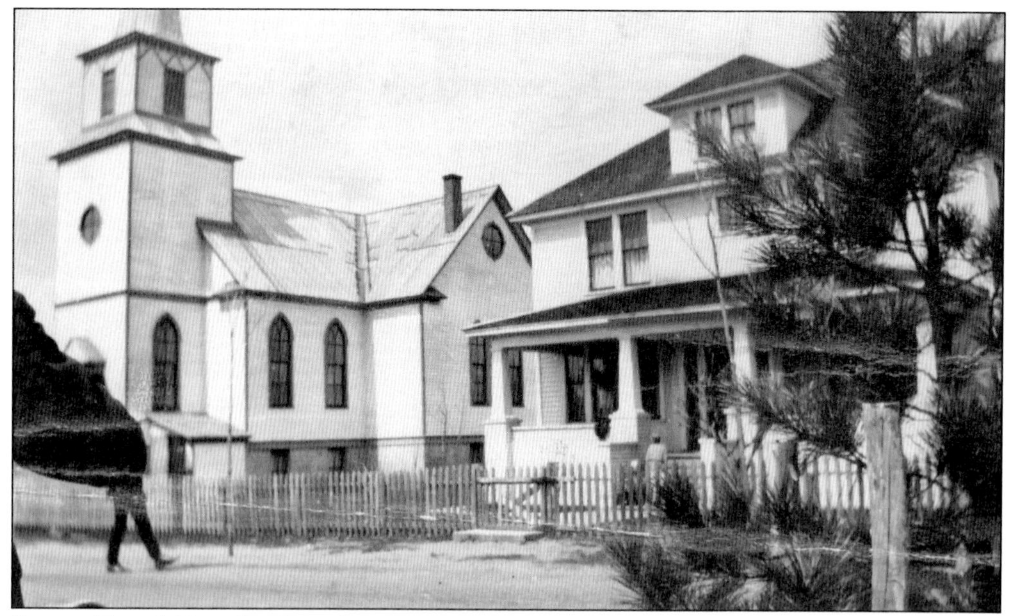

Finns in Forsyth Township formed a temperance society in 1900, and two years later, the temperance hall was hosting religious services. It was common then for practical-minded Finns to share spaces, regardless of differences. The Princeton Finnish Evangelical Church (later Grace Lutheran) built a church and joined the Suomi Synod in 1909; it burned in 1942 and was rebuilt, but the congregation, still active today, moved to Gwinn in 1973.

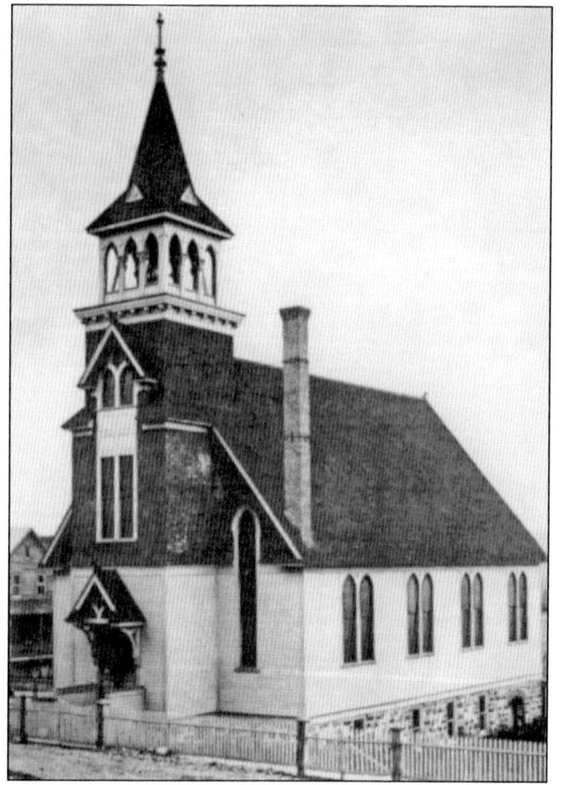

In 1908, the mainstream of American Laestadianism began to divide into two branches, often referred to by the names of their respective pastors, Arthur Heideman and Andrew Mickelsen. The home of the Mickelsen group was the church on Franklin Street in Hancock. In 1929, they organized as the Finnish Apostolic Lutheran Church of America. Also known as the Federation, member congregations were autonomous but met annually to discuss ecumenical matters.

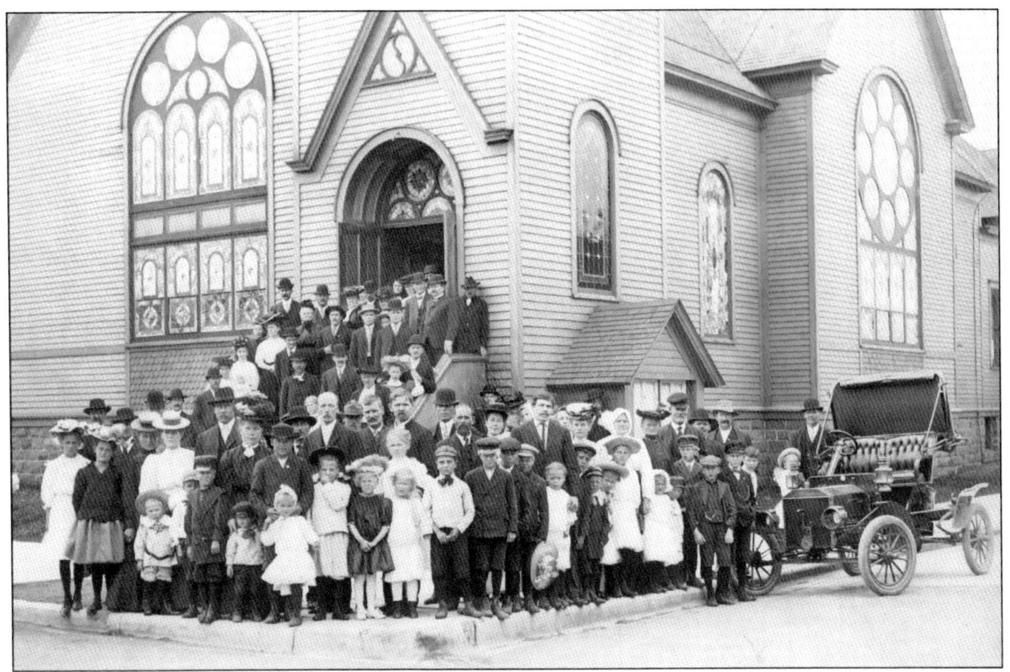

When the Suomi Synod was established in 1890, many Calumet Finnish congregants did not approve the synod's constitution, believing it gave too much authority to clergy. Because of this, the pastor, J.W. Eloheimo, excommunicated about 500 members. They organized their own independent congregation, which they called *Kansallisseurakunta* (National Church). This group shared a building with the Suomi Synod for a while until they built the church seen here in 1900.

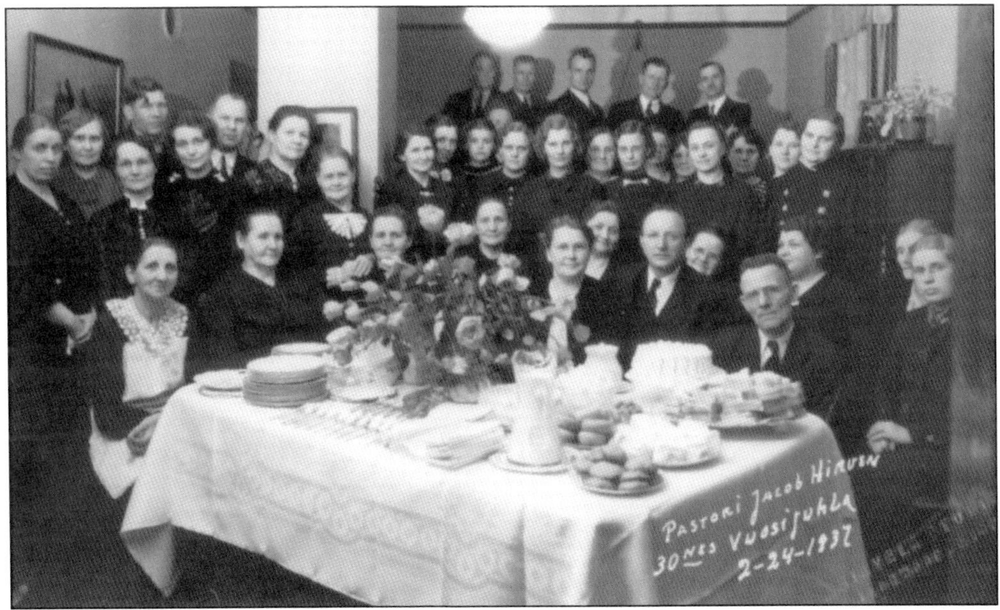

Milestones and anniversaries are significant occasions to Finns, which the good people of Zion National Lutheran Church of Ironwood proved as they acknowledged the 30th anniversary of the ordination of their pastor, Jacob Hirvi. A Finland native, Hirvi emigrated as a young man and served Zion, which was formed in 1897, for 17 years. He died in 1950 of a heart attack.

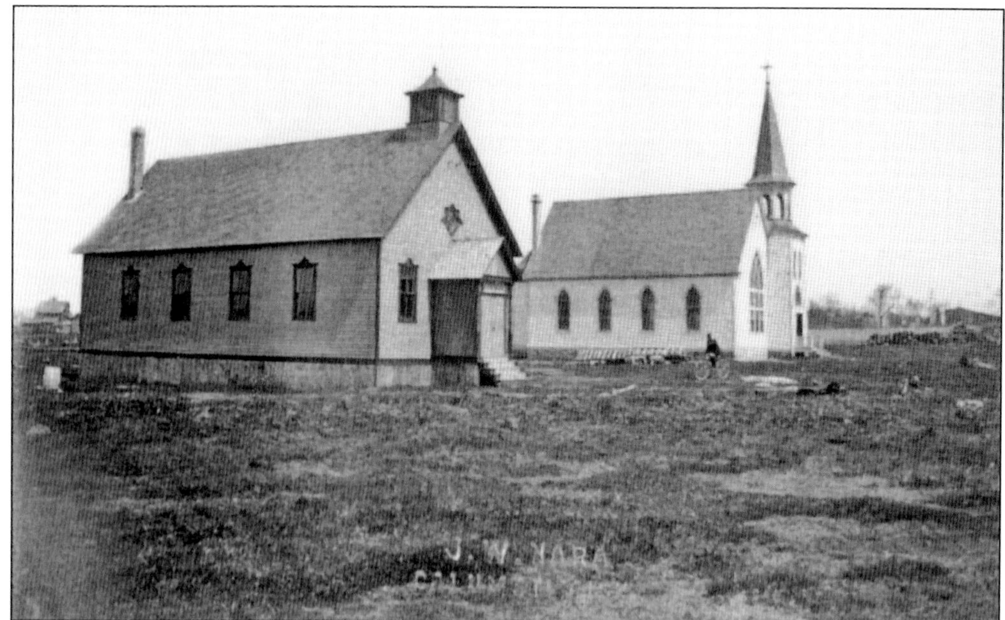

Representative of the diversity within Finnish Lutheran life in the late 19th century, the Finns in Atlantic Mine in 1899 had three Finnish Lutheran churches, two of which were built side-by-side. The Apostolic Lutheran Church, on the left, had ties to the Laestadian Movement of northern Finland and Sweden. Our Savior's Lutheran Church, at right, was affiliated with the State Church of Finland.

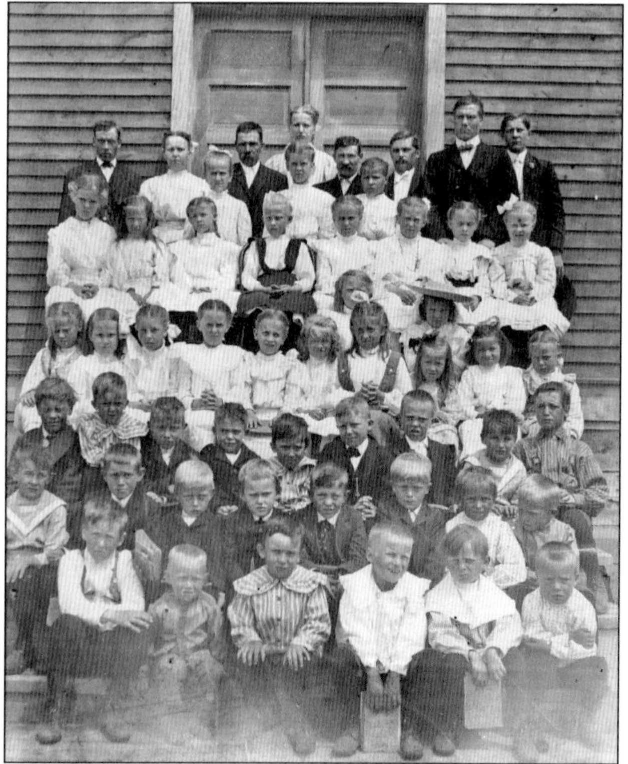

Children in all the Finnish churches often attended Sunday school—like this group from Mass City—from a very young age, through to when they were confirmed in their mid-teens. Very often, they practiced needed skills like reading and writing along with their spiritual education while benefitting from the social interaction.

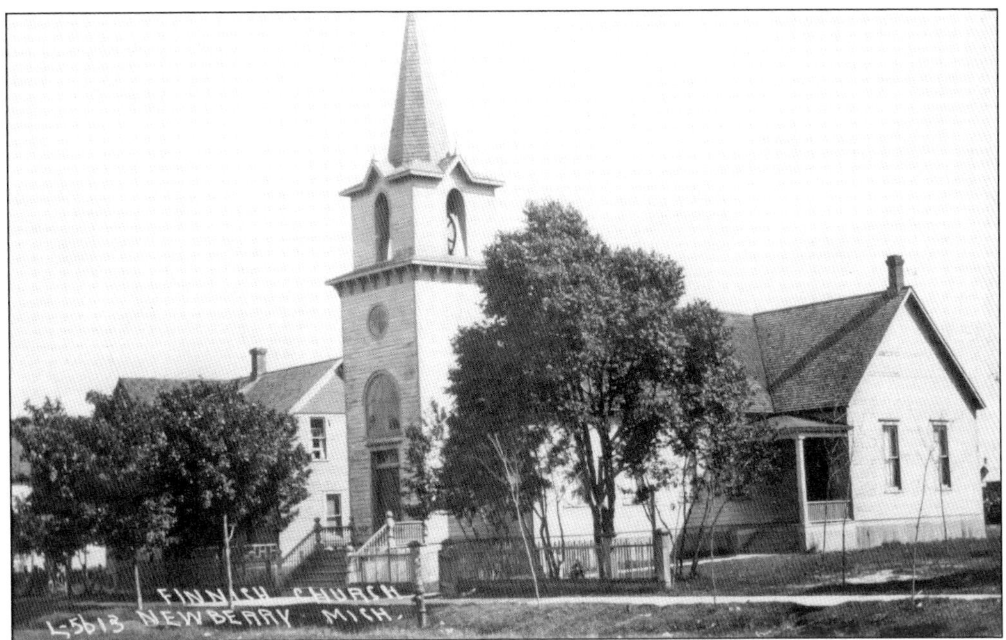

Finns were first drawn to Newberry by the lumber camps. Finnish-owned businesses and organizations like a cooperative store, a socialist hall, boardinghouses, and public saunas soon followed. The founding meeting for what would become Bethlehem Lutheran Church, one of the nine charter congregations of the Suomi Synod, was held May 29, 1888. Construction was completed by the end of 1889.

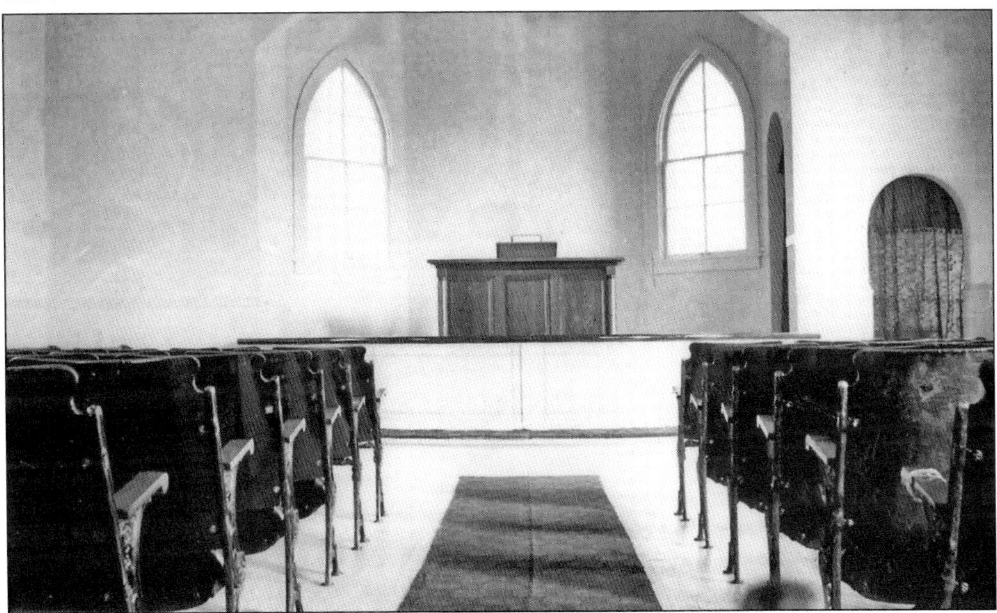

In its heyday, the tiny community of Toivola, like other villages that size, had both an Evangelical Lutheran and an Apostolic Lutheran church. The Toivola Apostolics bought the unused Congregational church from the nearby community of Freda and moved it to its present site in 1938. This photograph shows a traditional Laestadian (Finnish Apostolic Lutheran) edifice, unadorned and with a speaker's table, rather than a pulpit, as the focal point.

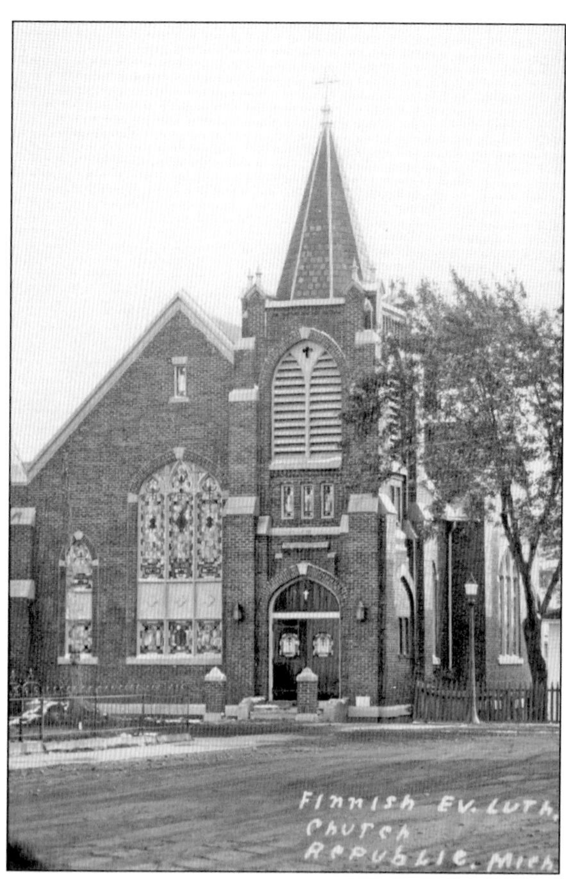

The lure of iron mining and the corresponding wages brought droves of Finnish immigrants to the Marquette County village of Republic, enough to support both an Apostolic Lutheran and an Evangelical Lutheran church, as well as other Finnish businesses and organizations. As the mine continued to encroach on the town, many buildings, including the Evangelical Lutheran church, were moved to new sites in South Republic during the early 1970s.

With roots in Finland, and with the Evangelical Lutheran Church, it is fitting that for decades Suomi College had a Martha and Mary Society, shown here on its 25th anniversary in 1938. The name of the society, which provided services such as fundraising, spiritual growth, and education, comes from Bible references to Mary and Martha.

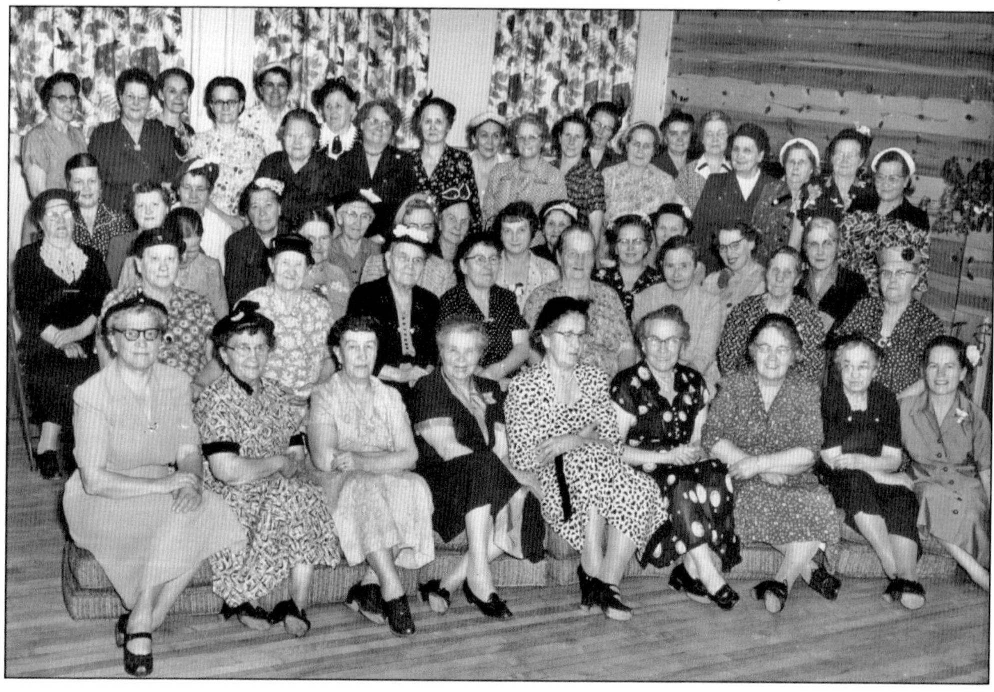

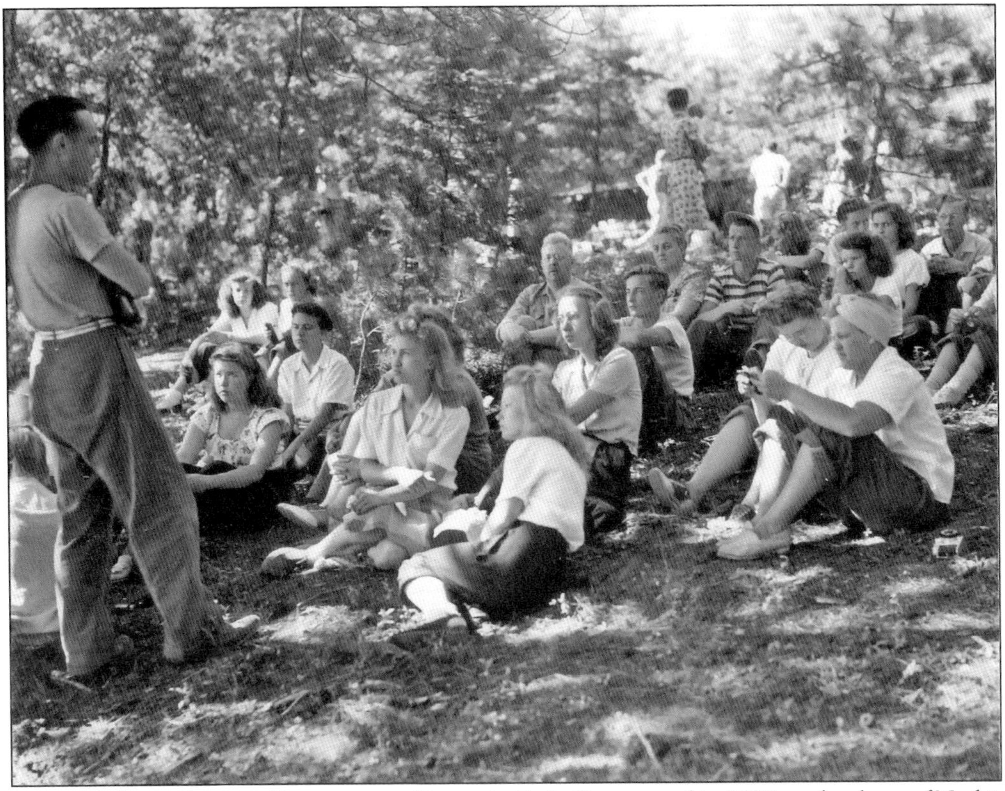

Camp Nesbit, a Civilian Conservation Corps–built facility erected in 1938 on the shore of Nesbit Lake in northwest Iron County, was the site of a Luther League Bible Camp for several summers. For over 90 years, youth ministry in Lutheran congregations was united under one name: Luther League. Its primary function was gatherings that incorporated fun activities, service projects, and planning for future events.

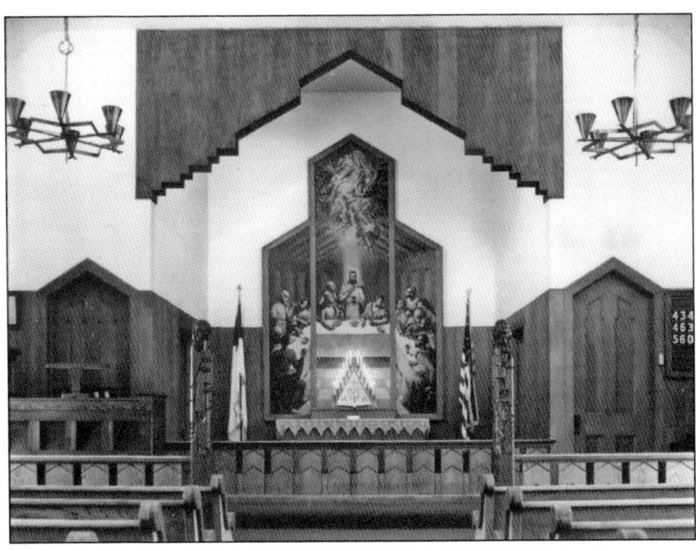

Sixteen families from a local temperance society came together in 1900 to form Bethany Lutheran Church in Covington. A group of Chicago artists, led by School of the Art Institute professor and Finnish consul Elmer Forsberg, remodeled the church in the 1930s, transforming it to a warm, wondrous chapel with rural Finnish-style Art Deco effects. The artists, helped by men from the congregation, did it gratis.

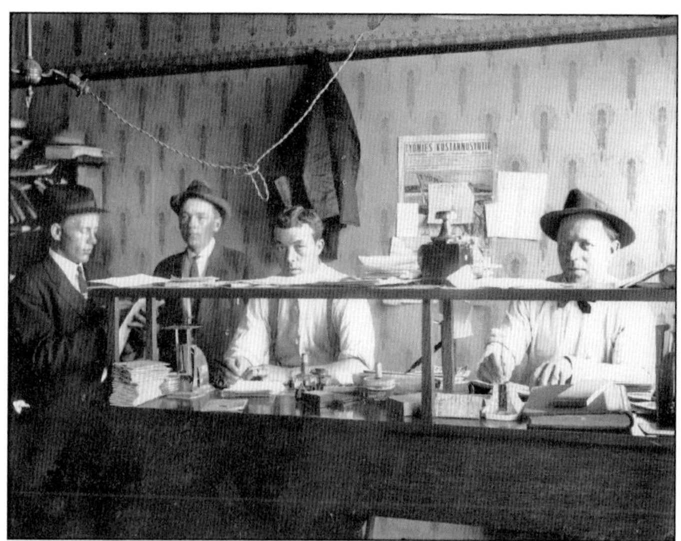

The Western Federation of Miners office in Hancock is seen here sometime after 1903 and before the strikes of 1913. On the wall is a poster of the *Työmies* (Worker) newspaper, one of the most widely distributed Finnish American working-class newspapers in the United States. Other working class Finnish newspapers included *Raivaaja* (Pioneer), published in Worchester, Massachusetts, and *Toveri* (Comrade) published in Astoria, Oregon.

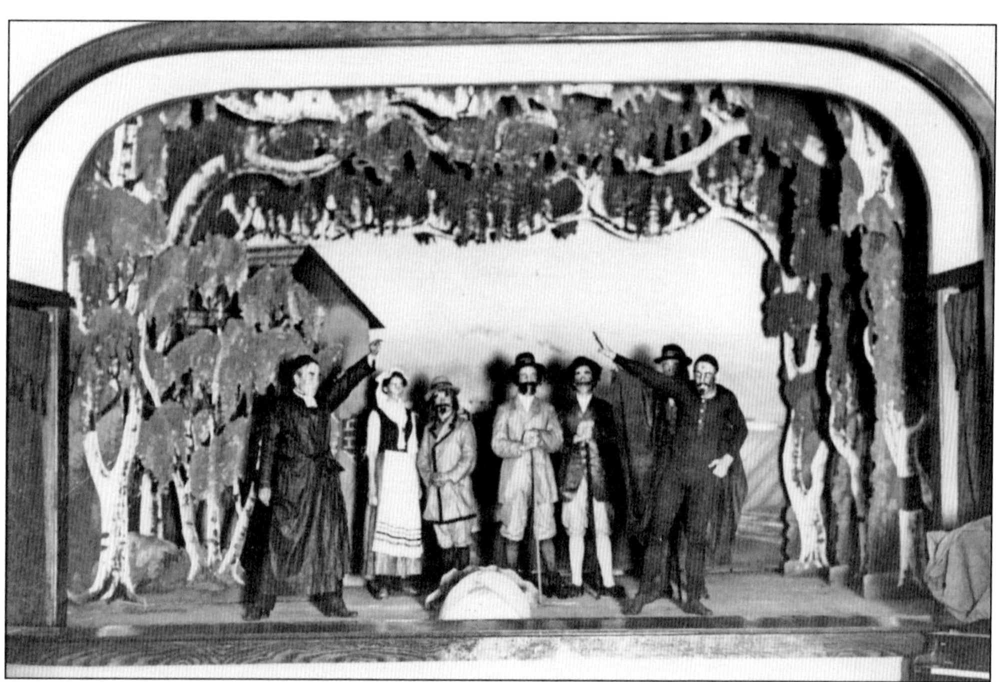

Finnish halls across the UP were constructed with a stage in their primary gathering space because theatrical performances were popular among "Hall Finns." At the opening ceremony for Liberty Hall in Marquette, a troupe performed the well-known theatrical performance *Pirunkirkko* (Devil's Church). The socialist organization in Marquette formed in 1906, and after three decades of a rather difficult existence, ceased operations in 1938.

Representatives from the Finnish Socialist Federation gathered in Hancock in 1909. The federation was well known for its network of federation-owned halls located in the major centers of the Finnish American community. These halls provided facilities for meetings, speeches, and social events such as dances. The group also produced several publications, including a biweekly comic called *Lappatossu* and a women's newspaper named *Toveritar.*

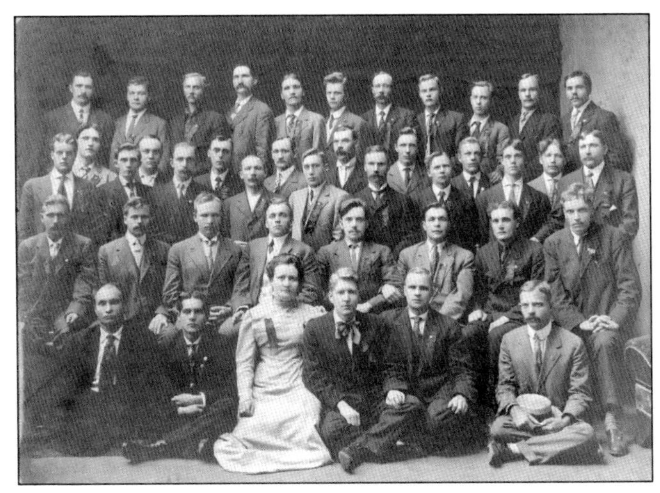

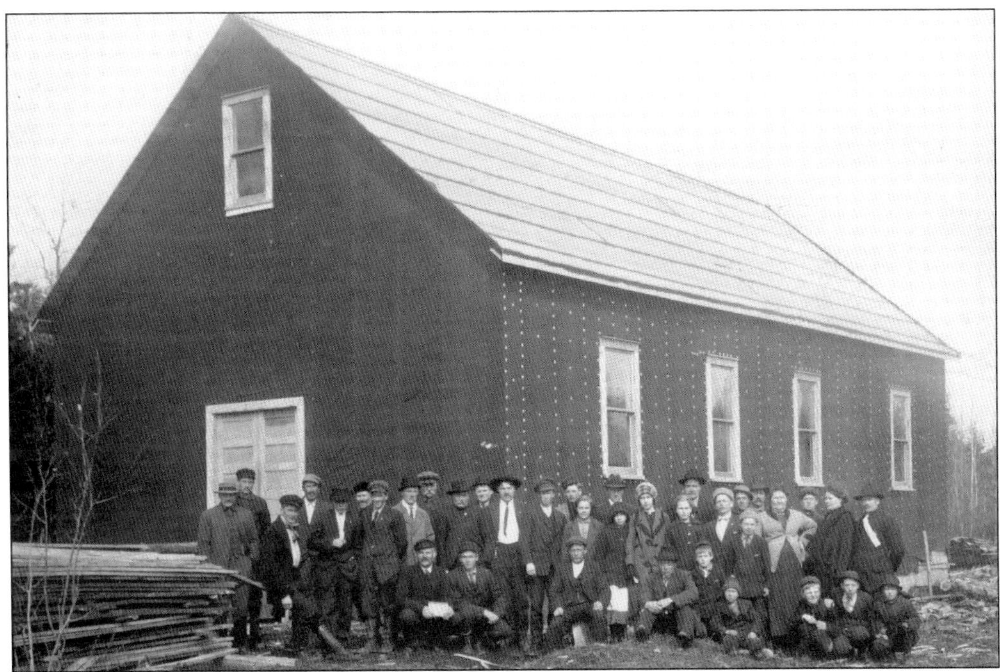

Built in 1913, the Finn Hall on Drummond Island hosted plays, parties, dramatic readings, and athletic events like boxing and gymnastics, and contained a stage, restaurant, and library. Youth groups, women's meetings, theater troupes, and athletic teams all met there as well. Before long, more "worldly" activities were taking place there, including dancing and alcohol use, contrary to the Christian utopian vision set out by Maggie Walz.

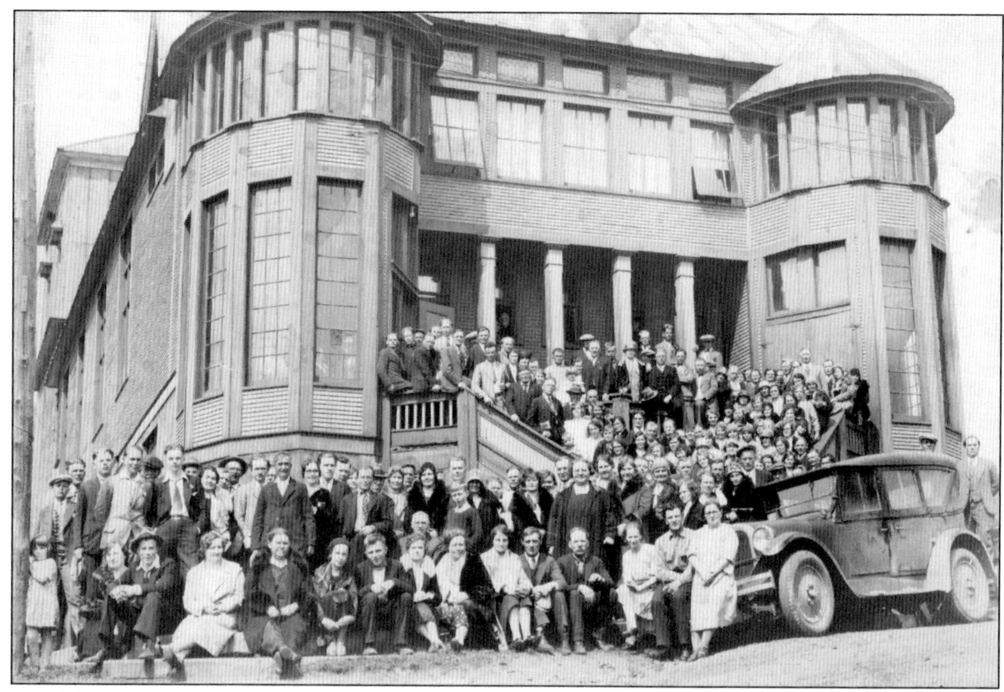

A celebration at the Labor Temple in Negaunee drew dozens of people. The Labor Temple opened on July 31, 1910, and was demolished in May 1946. It was an impressive Victorian-style structure and boasted plush seats and a large stage. The temple was an important meeting place for the Finnish community. It was better known for its dancing and live music than for its political education programs.

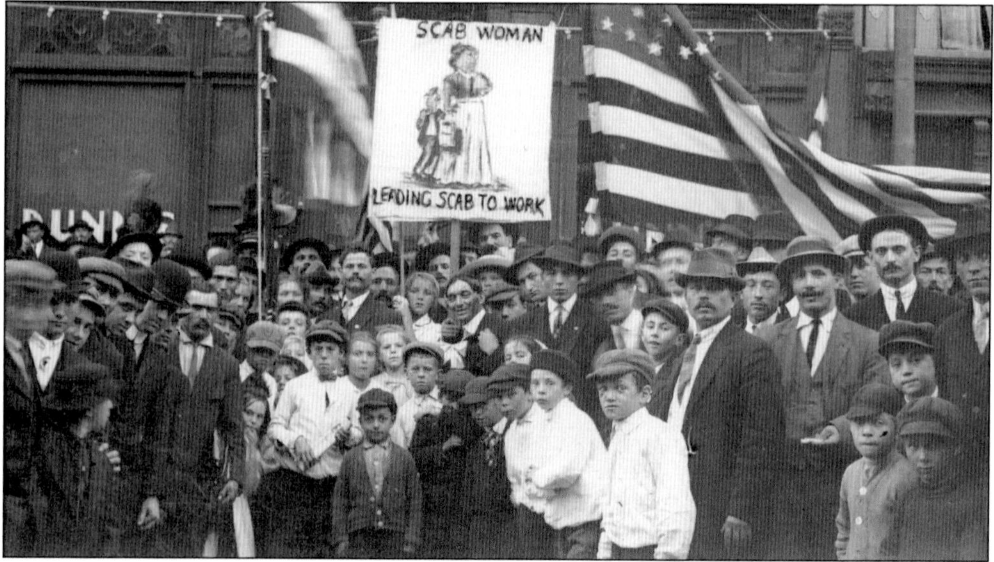

Beginning July 23, 1913, a strike was waged between an inter-ethnic group of thousands of mineworkers and massive mining companies like Calumet & Hecla. The strike was fought primarily over such bread-and-butter issues as wage increases, the eight-hour day, and the elimination of the one-man drill, a labor-saving device that workers believed would cost them jobs. The strike lasted until April 1914.

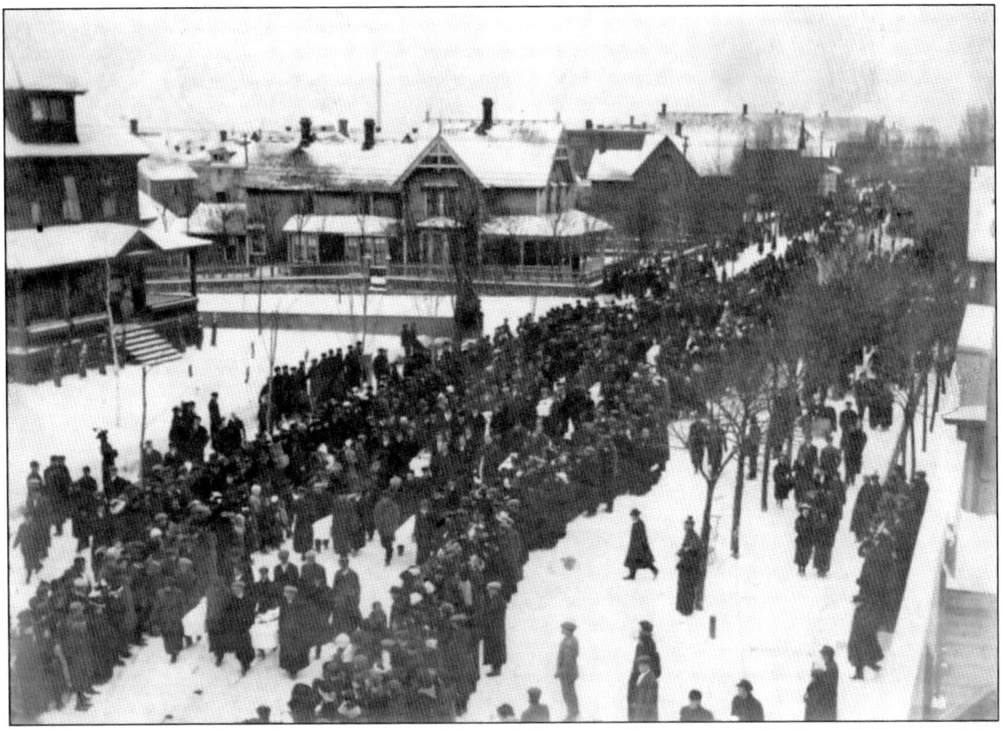

Undoubtedly the most infamous event in Upper Michigan history is the Italian Hall tragedy in Calumet, where several dozen people, mostly children, were killed evacuating a Christmas party for striking copper miners after a false cry of "fire." The funeral processions for the victims took place shortly after Christmas and traveled along two miles of road lined with mourners.

Even a mining town that dealt with its share of deaths was not prepared for a mass casualty as significant as the Italian Hall tragedy. Coffins were express shipped to Calumet. The days following the tragedy saw a flurry of cooperation between funeral homes and churches as caskets were filled—small white ones with flowers atop for the children—and horse-drawn hearses were arranged.

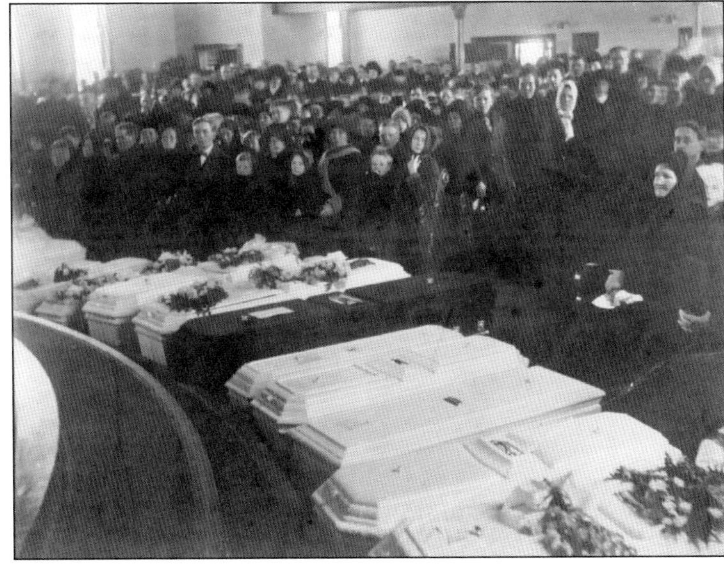

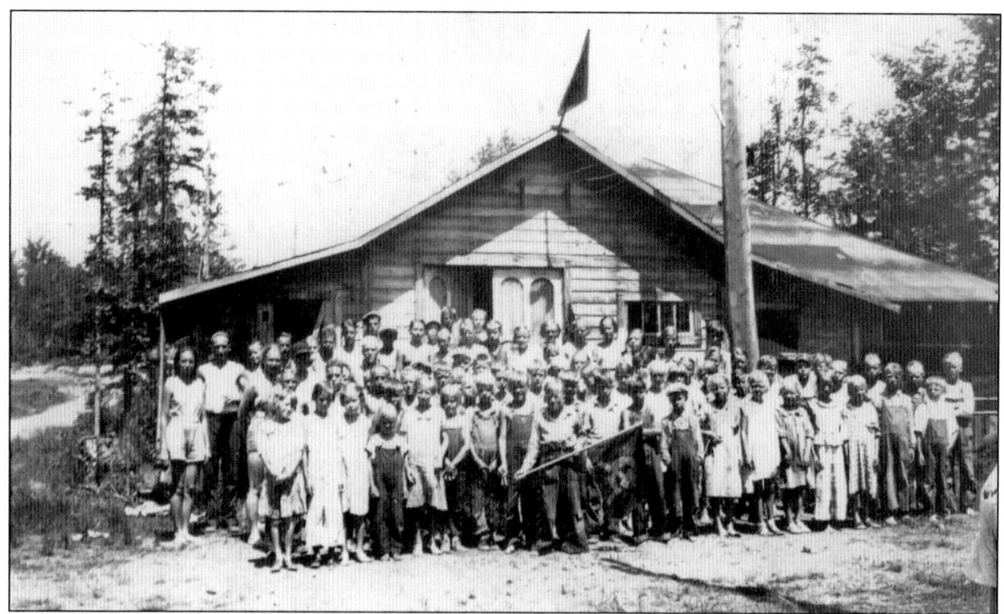

The summer school of the Ironwood Socialist Organization gathered in the western Ontonagon County village of Bergland at Wirtanen Hall. The concept of socialism, often misunderstood as being synonymous with communism, was stigmatized by many Upper Michigan residents, but despite this, interest and membership in socialist organizations was notably strong in the early 20th century.

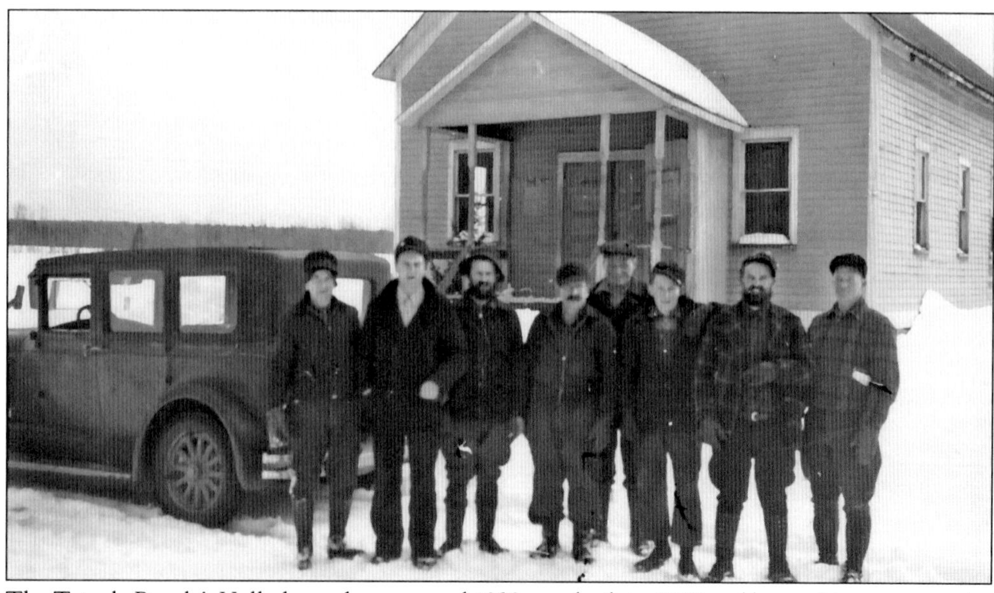

The Toivola People's Hall, shown here around 1939, was built in 1919 and burned (some say under suspicious circumstances) on July 20, 1952. Even small rural communities often had enough diversity of opinion to support many different social and political groups. Since dancing was forbidden in the community's temperance hall (Toivola Soihtu), the area's young people banded together and erected a building where they could conduct their preferred social functions.

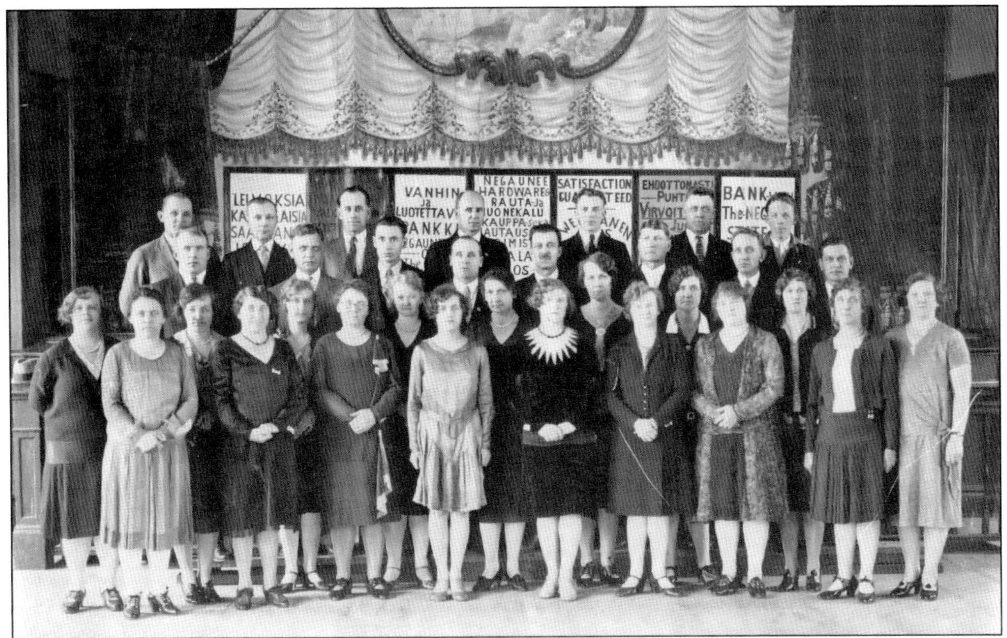

The Negaunee and Ishpeming Joint Songwriting Workers' Association had a strong membership in the early 1900s. The advertising banners, which were surely thoughtfully positioned behind the group when they posed for this photograph, reveal the support they received from various businesses in the area, known as Upper Michigan's Iron Range.

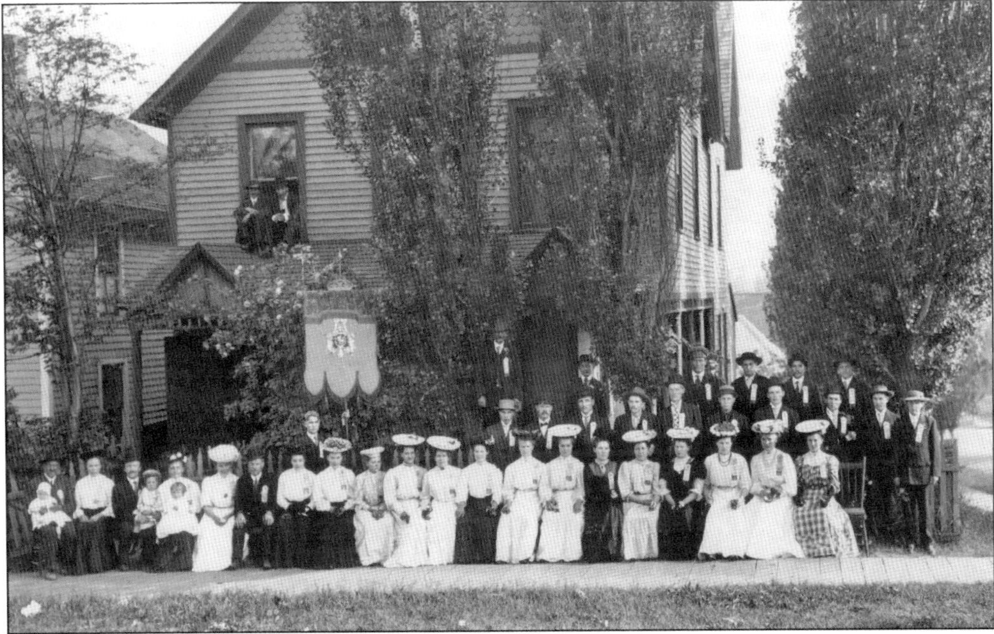

The Aalto Temperance Society, located on Bluff Street in the city of Marquette, was one of many societies of its kind formed in Upper Michigan. Temperance societies were formed in many communities where there were Finnish immigrant workers. They were organized to provide a wholesome alternative to the saloons, gambling, and prostitution that many young immigrants without families or community responsibilities often found attractive.

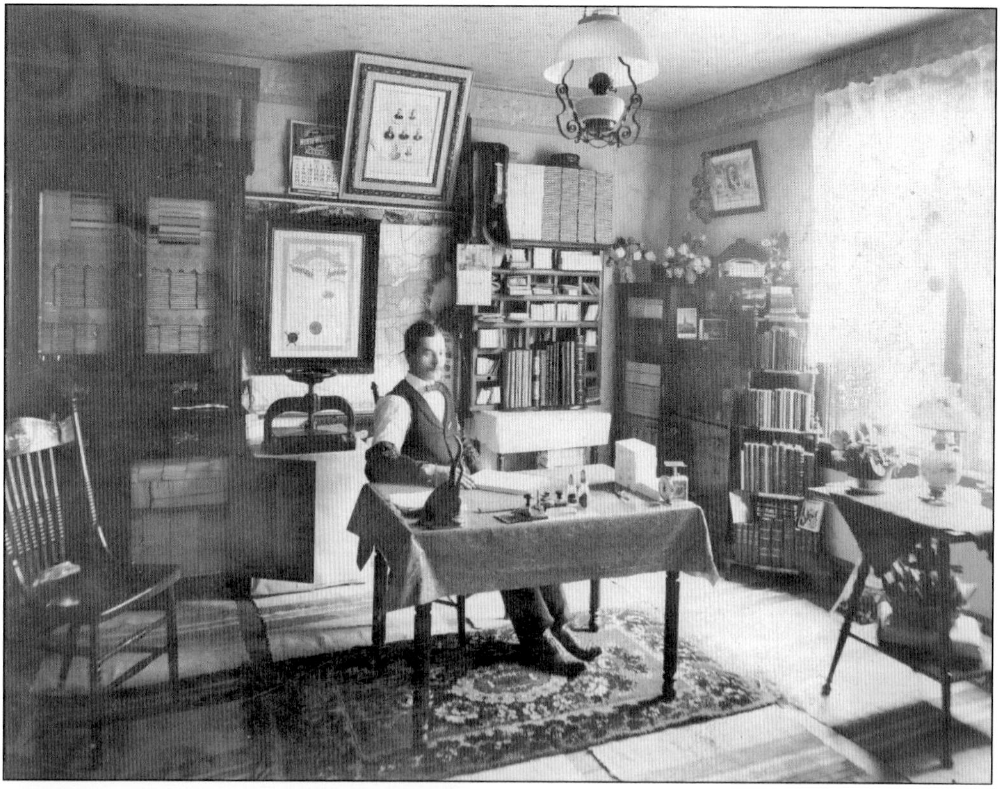

The Finnish National Temperance Brotherhood (Suomalainen Kansallis Raittius Weljeys Seura) office in Negaunee, seen here in 1898, was the headquarters for an organization that formed to coordinate the many societies that had formed during the temperance movement. Between 1888 and 1902, a total of 161 temperance societies joined the larger association.

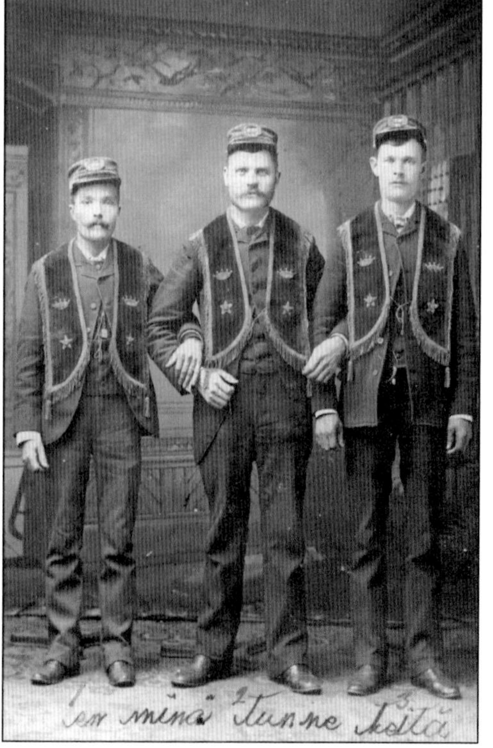

Temperance organizations typically issued medals or badges to their members to mark a given number of years of good standing with the organization. While these men, who had spent years striving to reduce their countrymen's use of alcohol, were proud to display the honors they had earned in this photograph, the regalia was not typically worn in public.

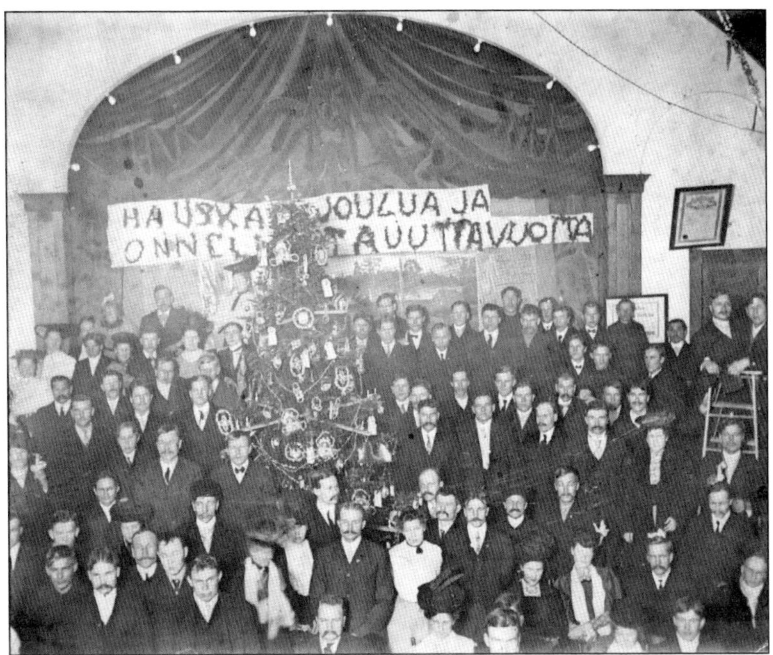

With banner-sized Finnish-language wishes of "Merry Christmas and Happy New Year" adorning the stage area and a traditional Finnish-style Christmas tree (direct from nature with hand-made ornaments), the folks gathered at the Finnish Hall in South Range were ready to celebrate "the most wonderful time of the year."

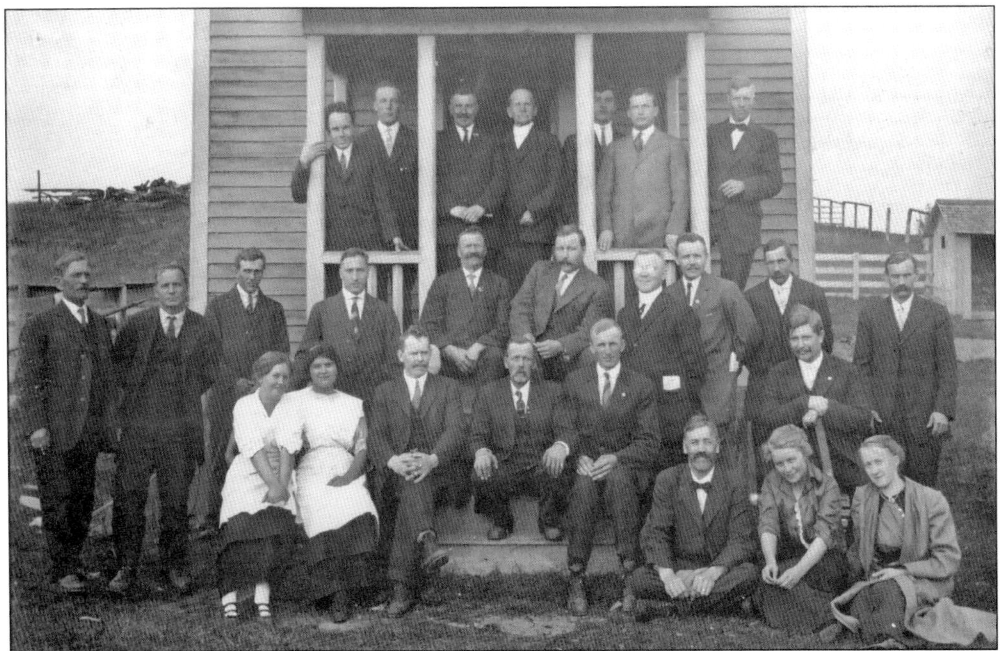

Members of the Ranna Ruusu Temperance Society gathered in 1913 in Oskar, along the shores of the Portage Lake Shipping Canal in Houghton County. In an area populated by many single, immigrant miners, lumberjacks, and other laborers, the temperance societies of Upper Michigan tasked themselves with providing alternatives to the "evils" these new immigrants might find by using alcohol.

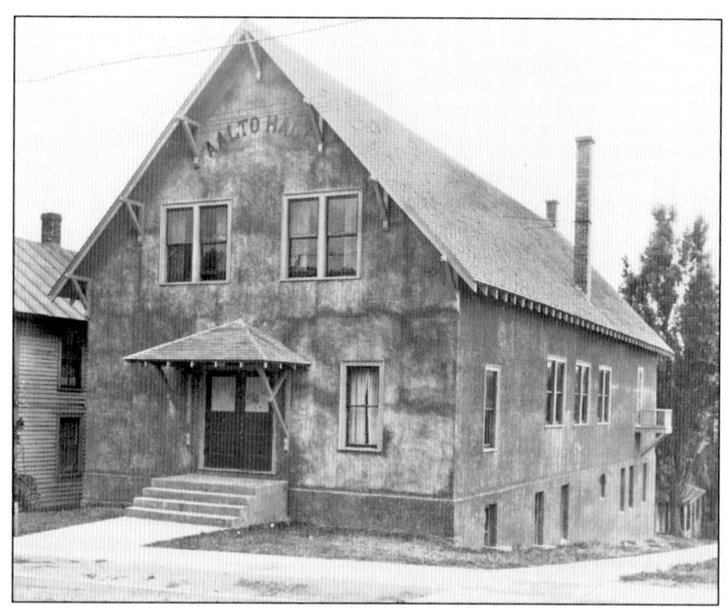

Aalto Hall in Marquette was built by the temperance society of the same name in 1922. It was sold 25 years later, but the society remained active, conducting meetings in member's homes as late as the 1960s. By 1906, the Finnish temperance movement on the Marquette Iron Range actively joined the national effort for Prohibition. In 1908, all the groups met and formed the Marquette County Temperance League.

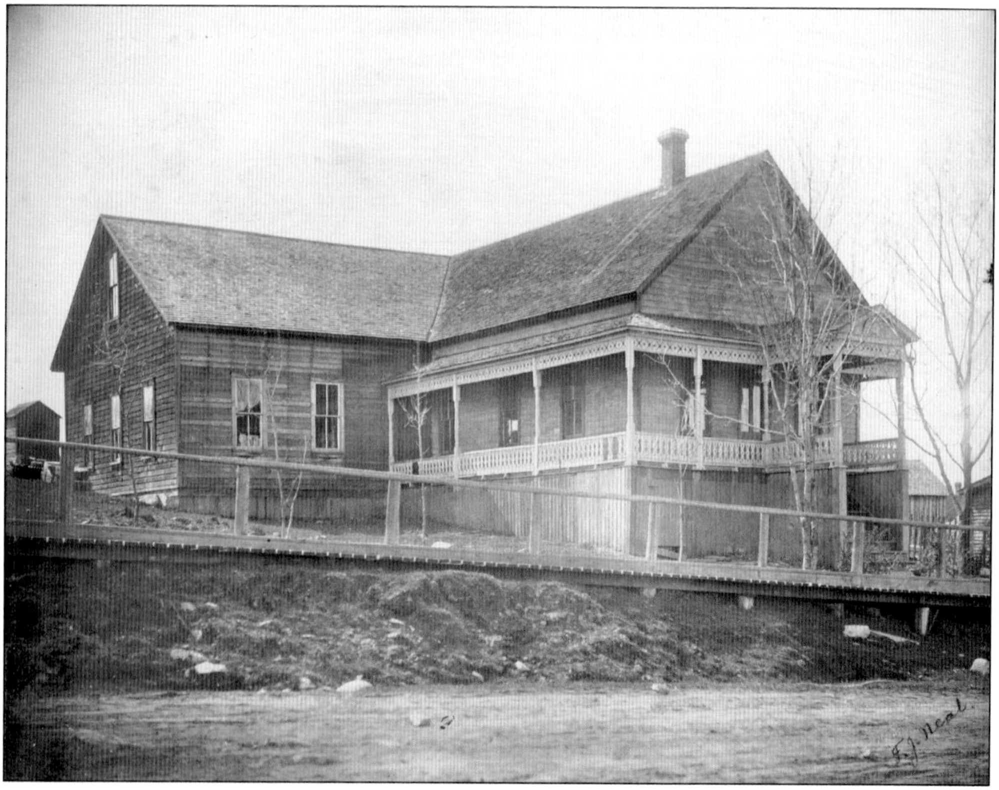

Temperance societies gave themselves names imbued with meaning. The temperance group in Crystal Falls called themselves *Toivola*, or "Place of Hope." Like other such organizations, they believed they were a civilizing force in towns where saloons often outnumbered churches, and temperance halls offered an alternative place to spend free time.

Five

Sooner or Later, You'll Be a Co-Operator

Finnish Americans, much like their Finnish counterparts, embraced the ideals of the cooperative movement coming out of Rochdale, England, including the idea that all members, regardless of gender, race, or class, had one vote, despite the number of shares held. Furthermore, co-operatives strived to keep prices affordable for members rather than making huge profits. Getting fair prices for the farm products and buying in bulk provided the immigrant Finns a chance to keep their small-parcel stump farms going in the early years.

The success of cooperative stores gave way to expanded cooperative efforts, including service stations, fuel oil and propane gas services, fisheries, gristmills, dairies, credit unions, and even a funeral home. "If the co-op doesn't have it, you don't need it," was a commonly expressed axiom among the membership.

Furthermore, the co-ops provided the non–English speaking grandmothers and grandfathers a safe haven when doing business. Well into the 1960s, and perhaps beyond, a good co-op manager made sure there were bilingual employees to provide full service.

In the years 1921–1931, Communists within the Central Co-operative Exchange membership tried to develop ties with the American Communist Party. Their attempts were thwarted at the annual convention by a vote of 129 to 16. The Communists were expelled from the exchange and formed their own network, the Workers and Farmers Unity Alliance, which at its peak had 20 stores across the Midwest, mostly in the UP.

Over time, the red sickle and hammer symbol on co-op products was replaced by simply the name "co-op." The cooperative stores were not prepared to respond to the advent of supermarkets in the mid-20th century. They did not realize quality and lower prices could not compete with glitzy advertisements and wide aisles.

Today, there remain three Finnish-founded cooperative stores in the UP, in Rudyard, Trenary, and Bruce Crossing. Although the cooperative movement has waned in the past few decades, there still remain those who believe in the marketing phrase, "Sooner or later, you'll be a co-operator."

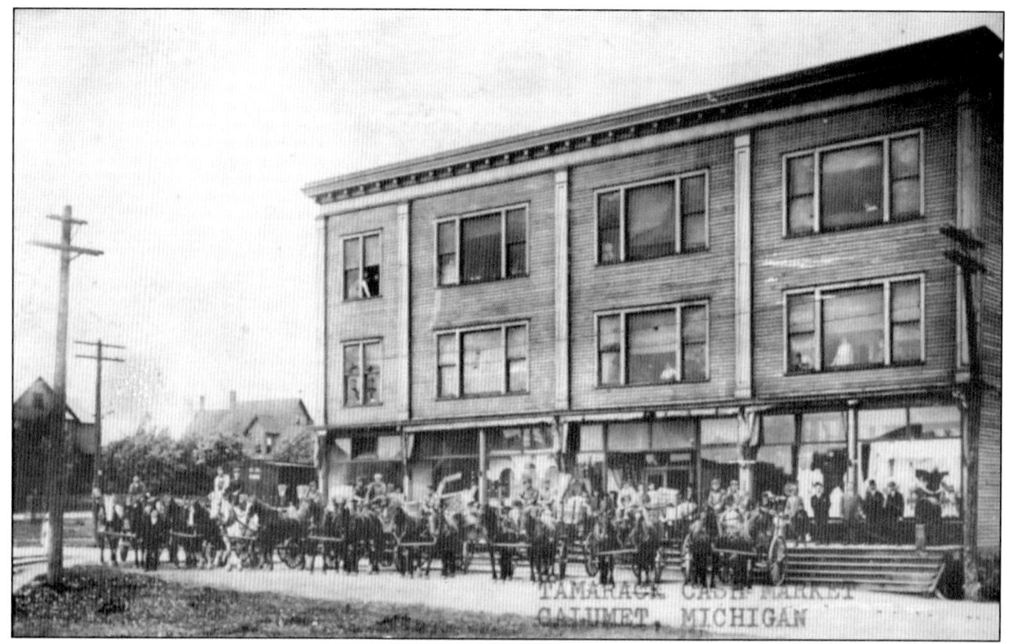

The Tamarack Cash Market in Calumet was one of numerous cooperatives sparked by the influence of Finnish immigrants who brought with them the principles of cooperation. In its peak years, the cooperative movement had stores in virtually every UP community; some villages had more than one, dependent on the political leanings of the area.

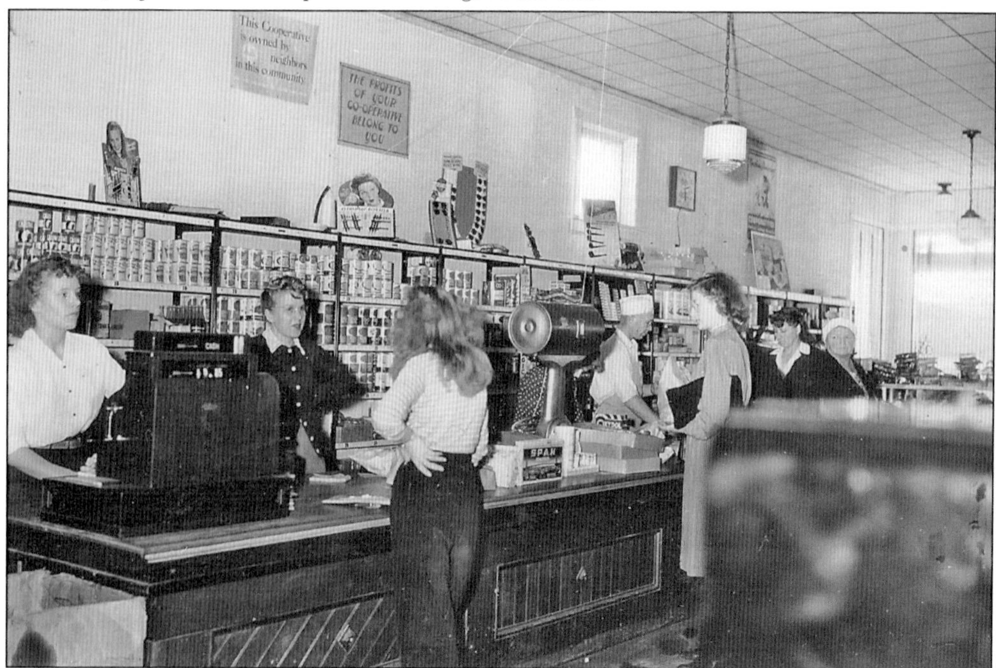

In co-operative stores across the UP like Settlers Co-op in Bruce Crossing, it was more likely customers would hear Finnish spoken than English, especially in the early years when the markets were full-service, and sales clerks and other employees who dealt with customers had to speak both languages.

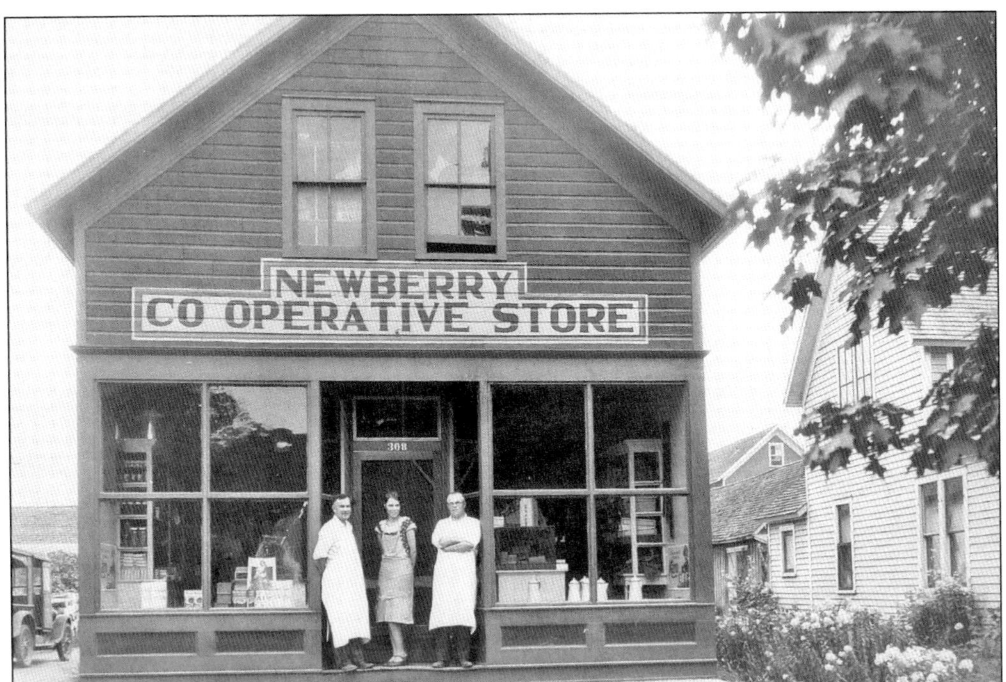

The Luce County community of Newberry was first settled by French Canadians, followed soon after by the Finns. When logging camp officials showed their preference for the Finns and their greater physical strength, there began a struggle between the ethnic groups. Like most physical conflicts, this soon resolved itself, and the Finns began establishing businesses in the town, such as the Newberry Co-operative Store.

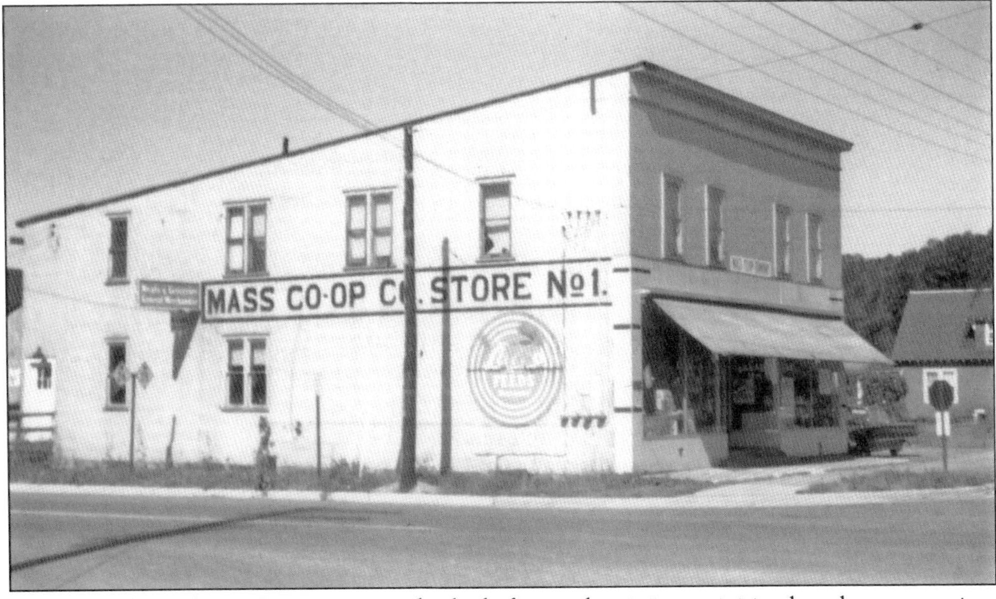

The tiny village of Mass City was once a hotbed of not only mining activities, but also cooperatives and radical politics. The Mass Co-op Company Store No. 1 was affiliated with the Cooperative Unity Alliance and was also known as the "Red" co-op, started by the leftist-leaning folks in town who sought an alternative to the "White" co-op less than a block to the north.

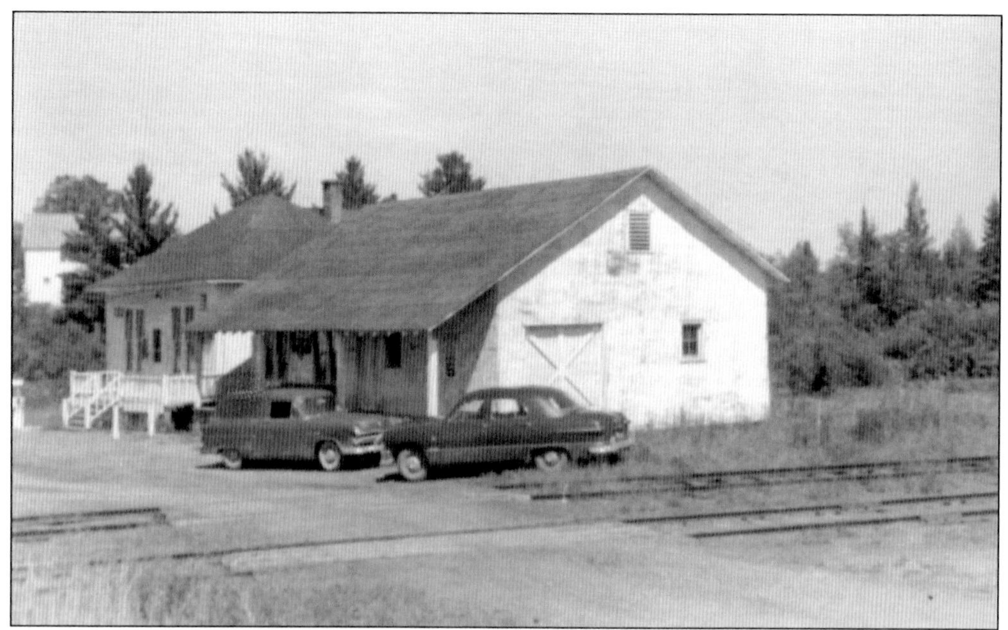

Cooperatives were common wherever Finnish farming communities were established. Such was the case in the Baraga County enclave of Herman, which was founded by Herman Keränen, an immigrant from Finland who, with the money he earned from lumbering, established the largest and most productive farm in the area. The cooperative store in this community was opened in 1919.

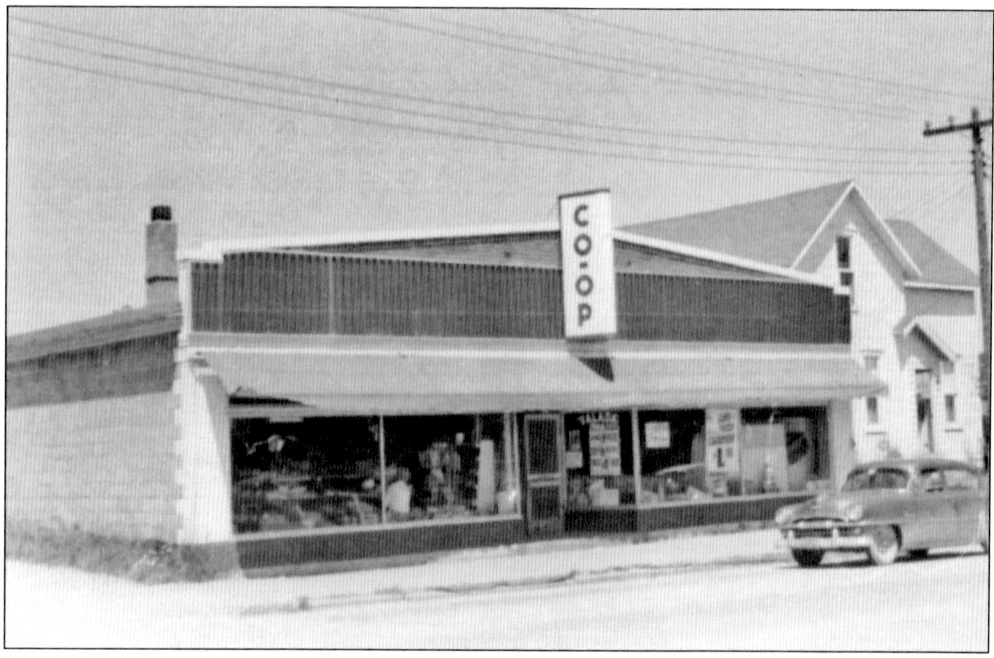

The Finnish cooperative in Rudyard is one of the few co-ops across the peninsula founded by Finnish immigrants that remains in full operation today. Many longtime residents of the area likely remember storekeeper Hans Lankinen, who managed the co-op, which was the largest business in the community, for many years until his death in the 1960s.

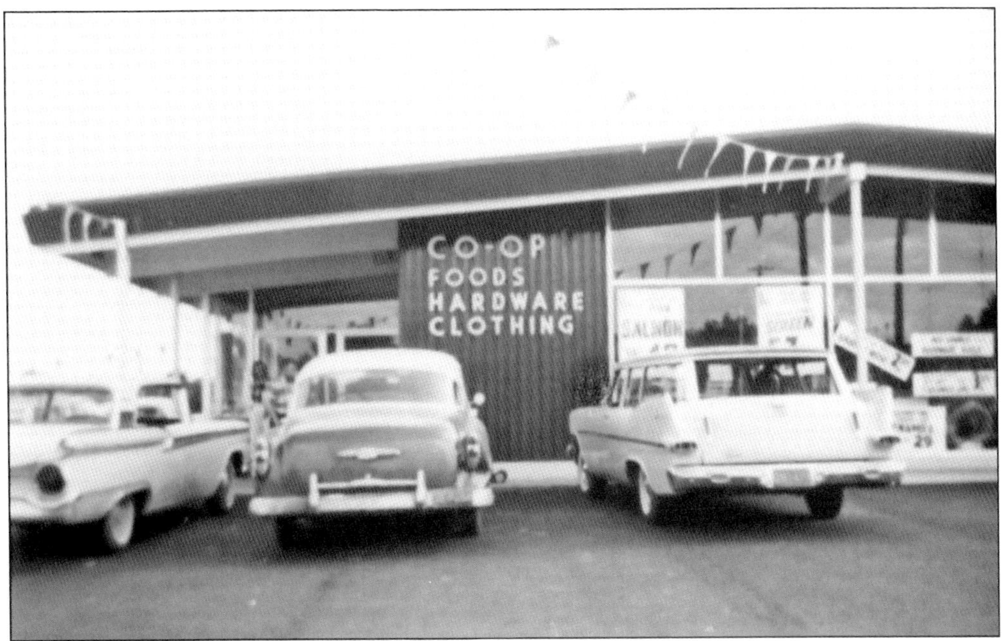

There have been Finns in Wakefield since 1886, with the earliest settlers coming from Lapua and Kuusamo. Like their counterparts in other UP communities, they organized and established numerous organizations, such as temperance societies and church congregations. The Wakefield Cooperative Association, seen here in July 1959, was one of the many entities founded by the Wakefield Finns.

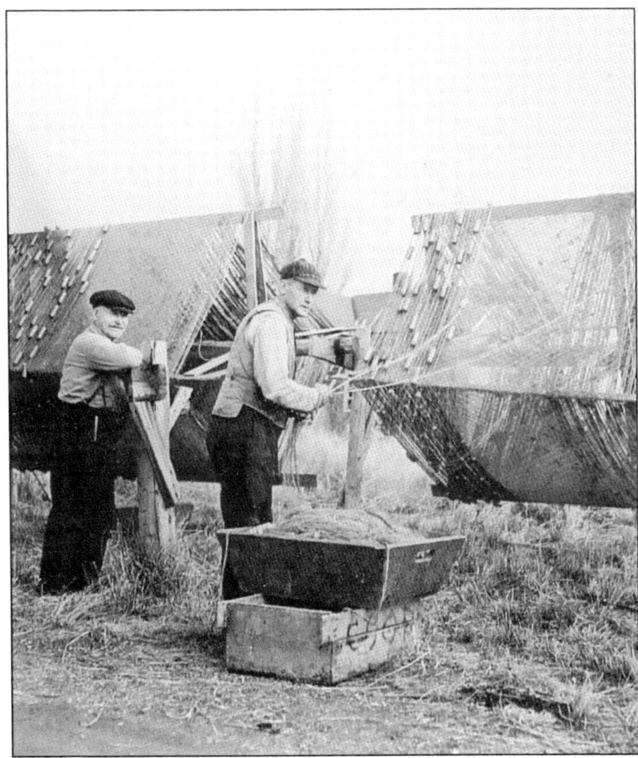

Cooperative endeavors were not limited to farmers' products. In Chassell, a small village in Houghton County, cooperative fishing activities were a primary source of income for many Finnish American men, such as Fred Rautiola (left) and Arthur Törmälä, seen here repairing their nets. The Portage Shipping Canal, which Chassell borders, provides access to the waters of Lake Superior. (Chassell Historical Organization.)

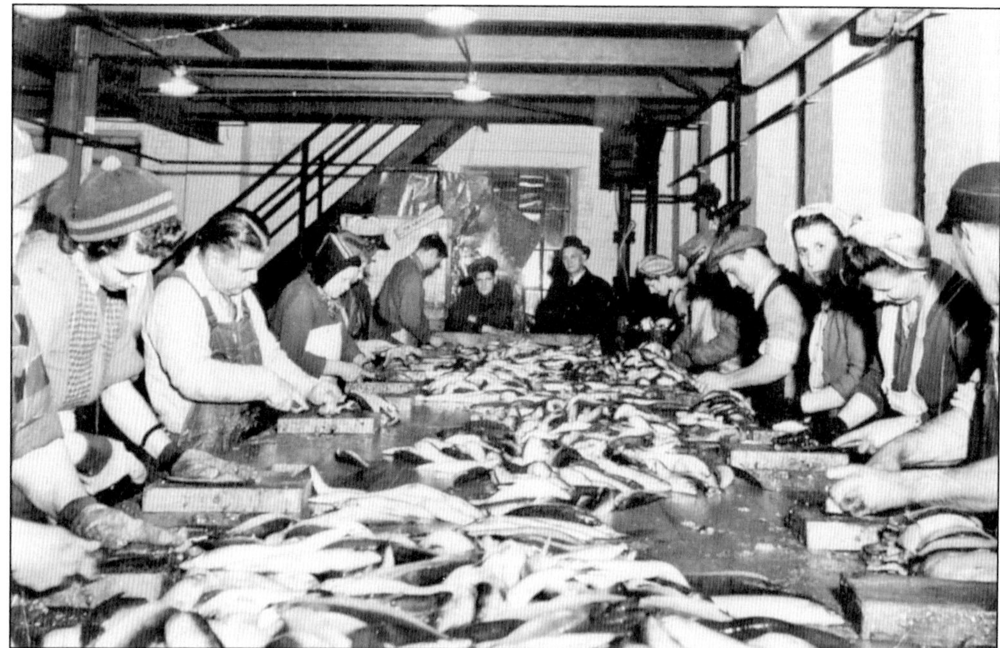

The Lake Superior Fisheries of Hancock was one of several cooperative commercial fishing operations based in Houghton County and served as a source of employment for many local Finnish Americans, both male and female, either on the fishing boats themselves or in the on-land facilities cleaning and preparing fish for both retail consumers and restaurants. (Chassell Historical Organization.)

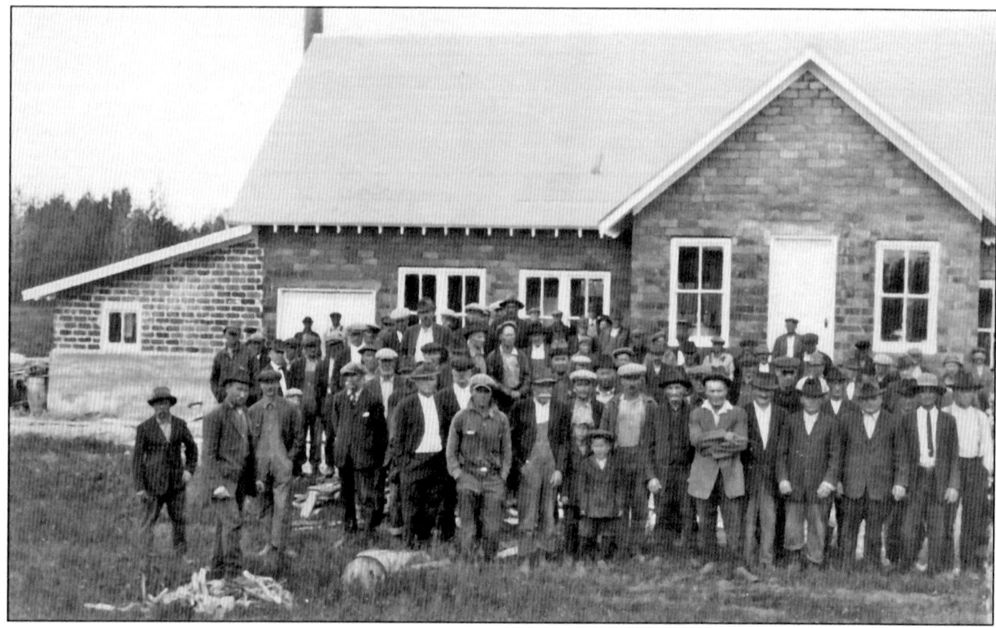

The North Star Creamery, based in Bruce Crossing, employed a significant number of local residents and was yet another example of the broad outreach of the Settlers' Cooperative. The results of their work were sought after from several counties over, because the creamery produced cheese and other products that were frequently awarded for their quality. (James Kurtti.)

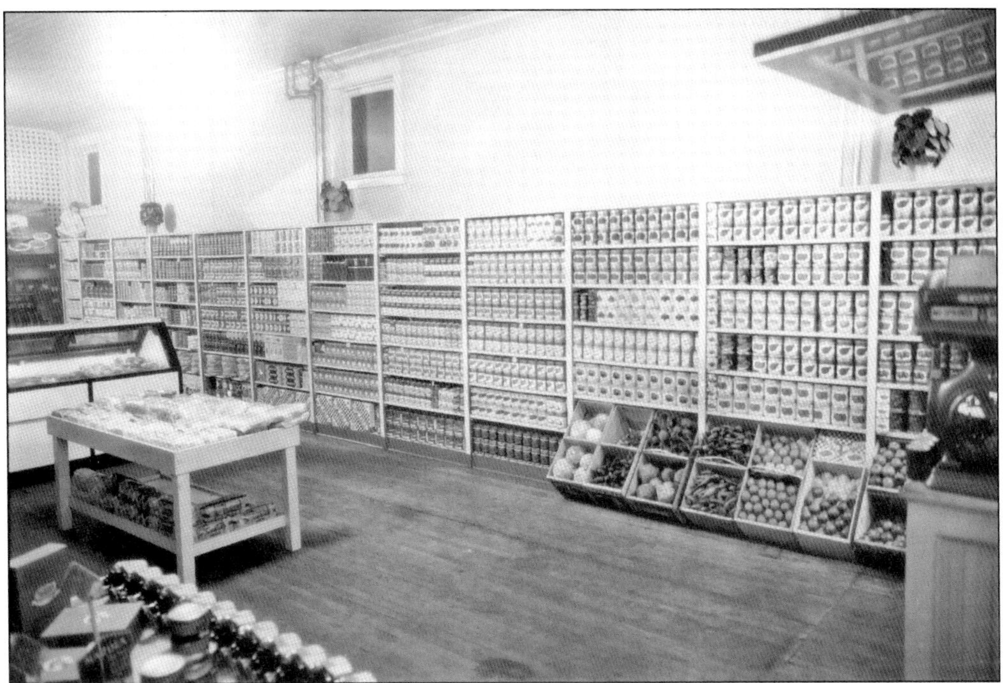

Since it was home to a shipping port and railway center—both providing numerous employment opportunities—as well as being the site of Northern Michigan Normal School, a hub of teacher development, the city of Marquette attracted a number of Finns to settle there. These Finns' influence became apparent in many ways, including the establishment of the Marquette Co-op Dairy in the early to mid-20th century.

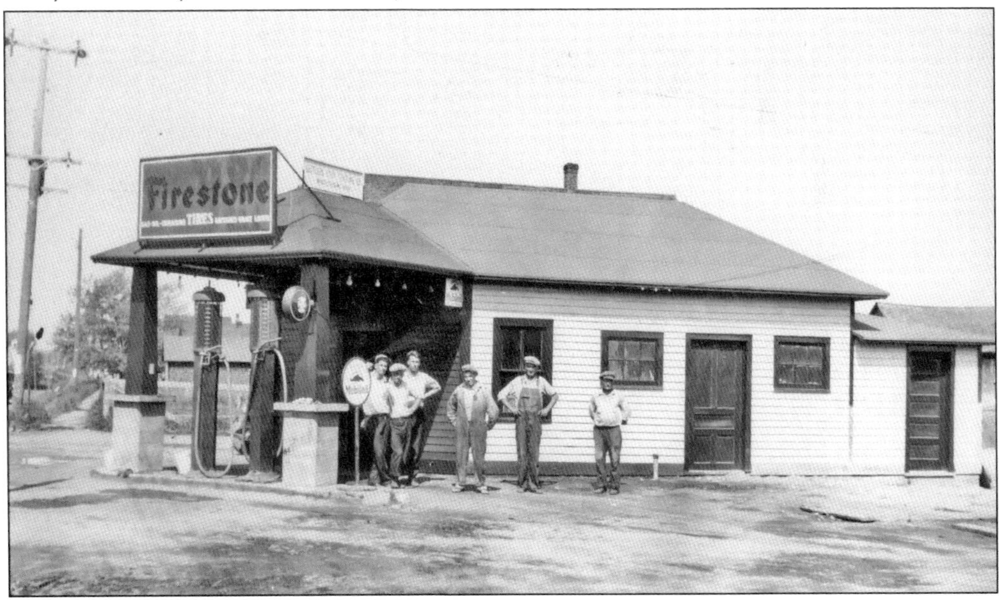

Much like many UP co-ops, the Settlers' Cooperative of Bruce Crossing expanded to include a full-service fuel station. Locals still remember getting their tank filled, windshield washed, and oil checked, all with a dash of Finnish spoken by the attendant. In fact, the station manager preferred to hire employees who could speak Finnish, since many customers could not communicate in English.

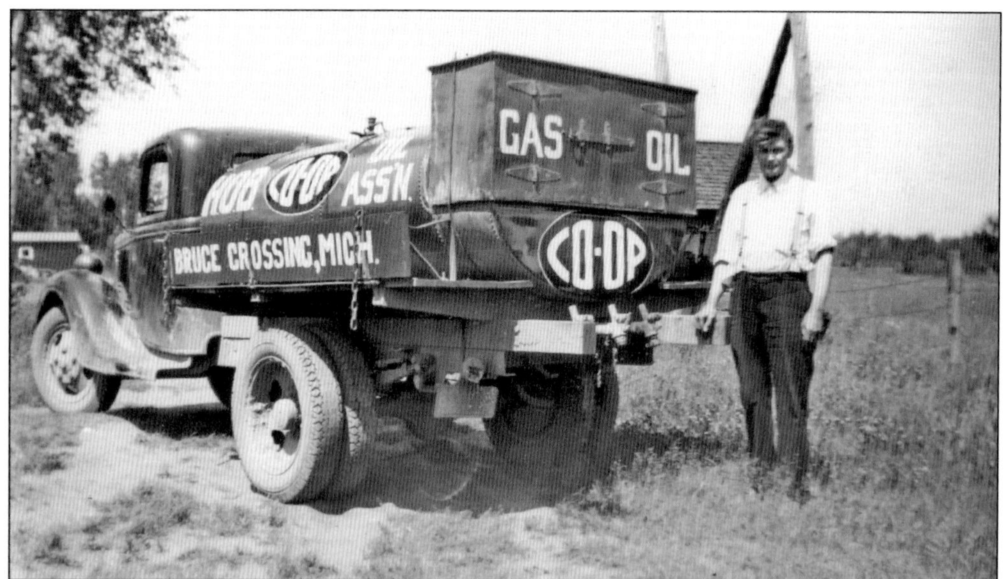

The cooperative philosophy extended well beyond the store and its affiliated businesses. The Settlers' Cooperative branched into many service-driven endeavors, including HVAC repair and maintenance, and home delivery of gasoline and other fuels. The co-op served customers throughout Ontonagon County and, in many cases, even beyond those borders.

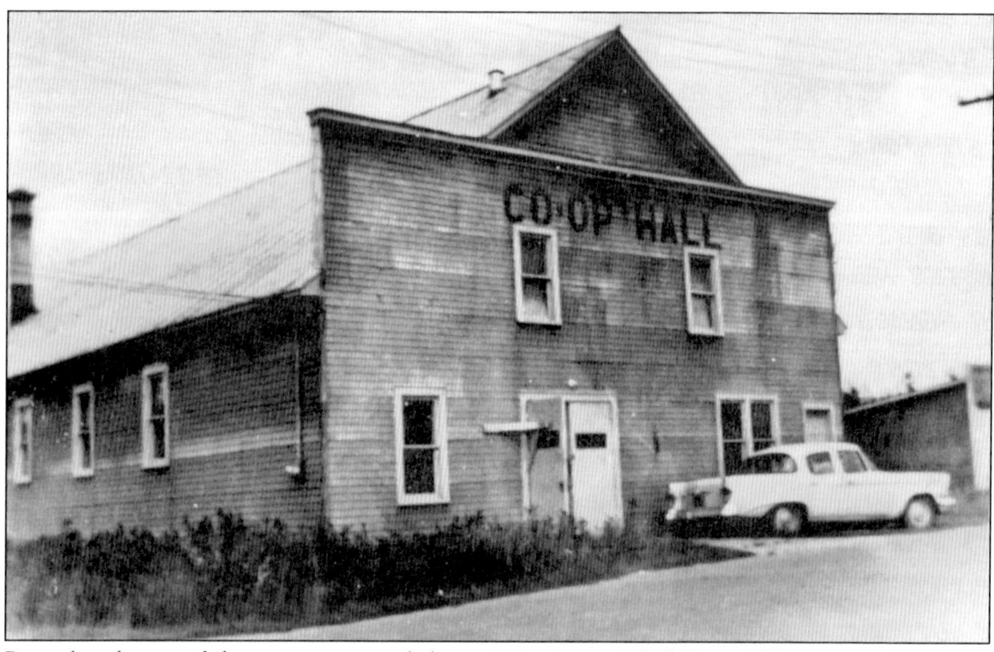

Prevailing biases of the time prevented the cooperative-minded Finns of Bruce Crossing from using the township hall for their annual meeting, so they built their own. It is believed that the Co-op Hall is the only one of its kind anywhere in the United States. The hall evolved into a community center, hosting plays, movies, funerals, and *Suomi Kutsuu* dances.

Everyone was welcome at the co-op, as exemplified by this photograph of store manager Martin Keränen offering a treat to an unlikely patron. This was just one of many incidents that showed why Keränen was beloved by all his customers throughout his tenure managing the Trout Creek store. (James Kurtti.)

Manager John Pölkky shows Sadie Linna (left) and Ida Nordberg the fine china that could one day be in their homes through a shopper loyalty incentive program. Through this concept, shoppers could over the course of weeks or months build a set of china piece-by-piece as a reward of sorts for doing their business at the co-op.

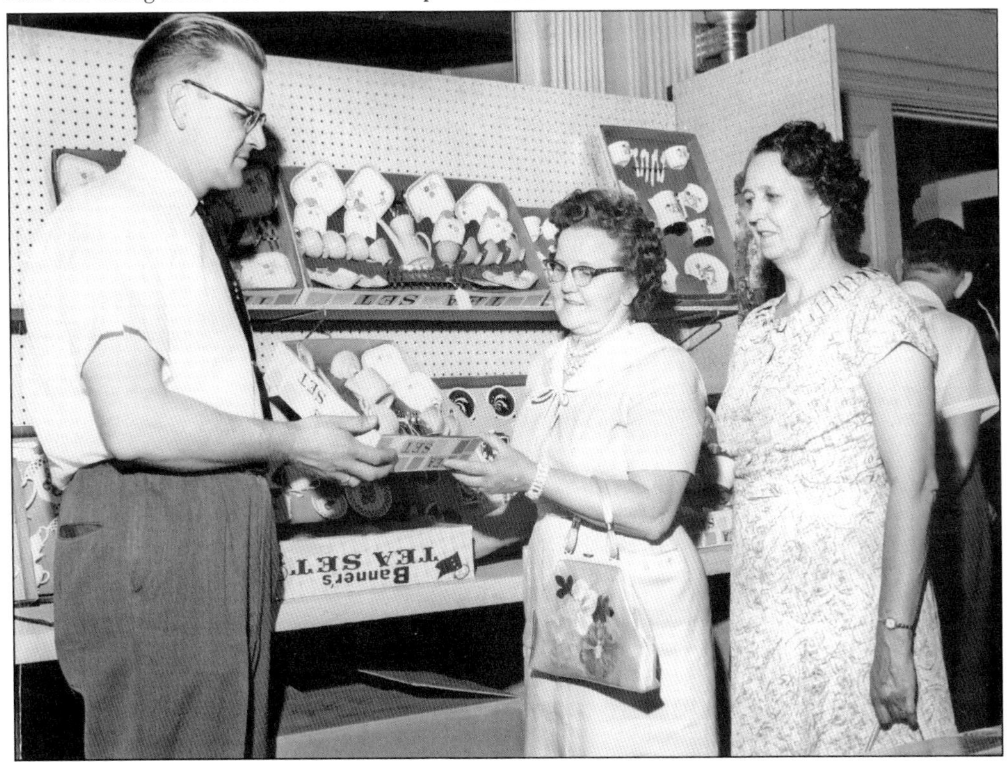

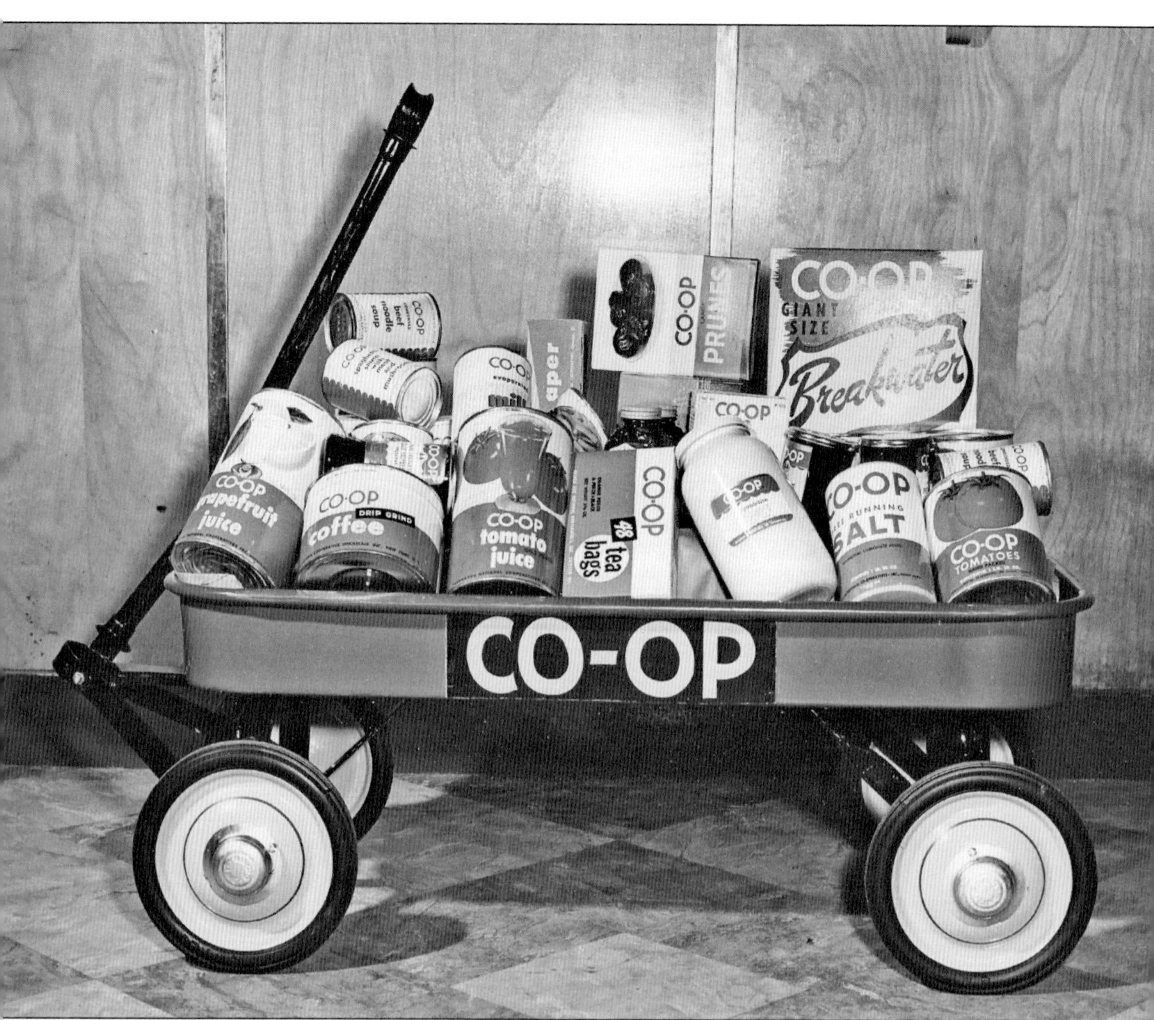

Sooner or later, you'll be a co-operator, especially in towns settled by progressive-minded Finns in Upper Michigan. The co-op label was a frequent sight in the cupboards of homes in these towns, and the distinct lettering of the brand was not exclusive to foodstuffs and grocery items. Virtually everything from fruit juice to furnaces proudly touted the co-op brand.

Six

It's All Fun and Games

Those who work hard need to play hard as well, whether that play is musical, theatrical, or physical. Or perhaps it was the art of working hard to relax. This chapter explores how Finns in the UP had their fun in all its marvelous dimensions.

The vast tracts of public lands and waterways provided ample opportunities for Finns to do what they do best—escape to nature. The woods, lakes, and heavy winter snows reminded them of Finland, inspiring them to make skis, snowshoes, or perhaps a *potkukelkka* (kick sled) for the children. Ice fishing, skating, and rolling in the snow from the sauna were all ways the Finns snubbed their noses at Old Man Winter. If the snows were particularly heavy, people hunkered down indoors with board and card games, playing the accordion and the like.

In summer months, folks had a ball honing their skills at America's pastime (baseball), taking a sauna or dancing on a Saturday night, singing in the church choir on Sunday, enjoying a picnic or a fishing trip, or taking in a play at the Finn Hall. Berry picking of all kinds was essential work for families, and yet many would argue that it was great fun, in particular, if you could avoid shoveling manure or boiling clothes in the summer kitchen on a hot day.

Women dog-tired from running a home filled with children and men exhausted from working long shifts in the mine or pitching hay were still inspired to travel to the church or hall to practice their lines and their music, cook the meals, or repair the edifices—all for the common good and to have a little fun. If they happened to have to walk home in the dark, they stepped gingerly hoping not to trip over a sleeping cow, nor step in what she may have left behind, for that, too, could become a source of fodder for others' fun.

They were the days of making one's own fun. Barrel staves became skis; clothes destined for carpet rags, with a little imagination, transformed into play costumes; and a paper clip could double as a fish hook. If a young woman did not have silk stockings with a fashionable seam up the back, her sister carefully drew one on with an eyebrow pencil. If she laughed, the seam would not be straight, but it was all fun and games.

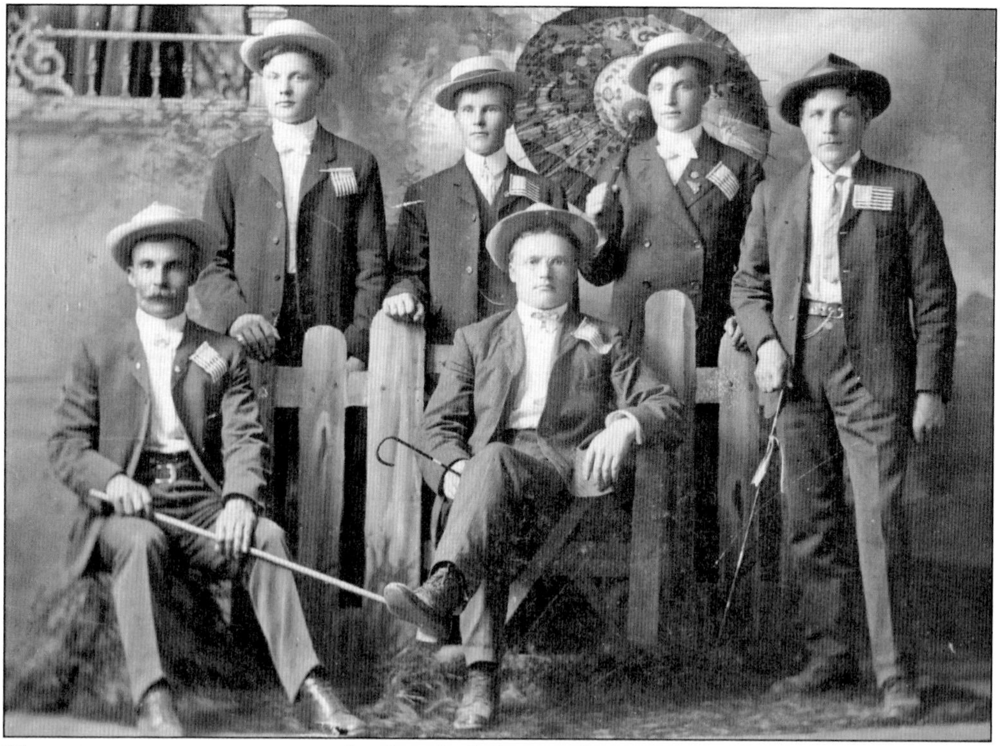

These immigrant copper miner dandies, fresh from a cleansing sauna, donned their finest on "Fortsulai" (American Independence Day) for a photograph in a Calumet studio. From left to right are (first row) Jacob Virranniemi and Charles Palosaari; (second row) Arvid Kallunki, John Kurtti, Charles Virranniemi, and Jaakko Pitkanen. (James Kurtti)

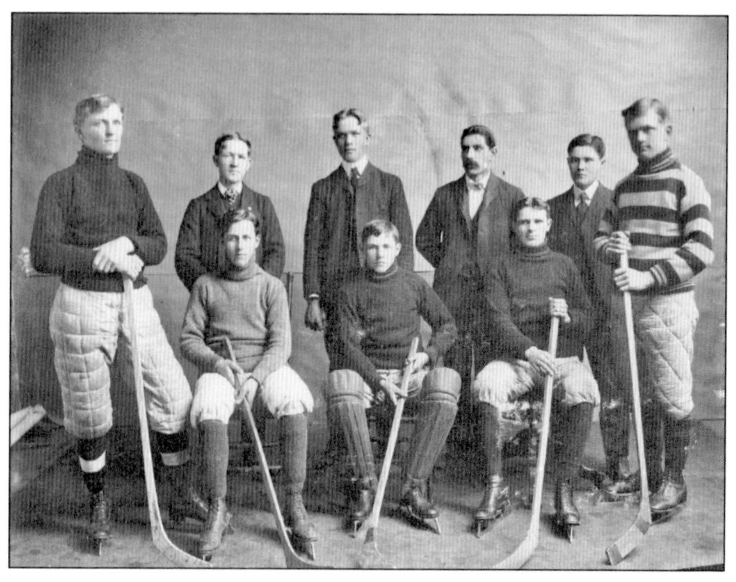

The Copper Country is recognized as the birthplace of professional ice hockey, and along with the pros, it was the home for many community squads as well. This team, the Atlantin Suomalaiset (Atlantic Finns) consisted of players from the Atlantic Mine area, a small community in Houghton County where many Finnish immigrants established farms.

Winters can be long and snowy in Upper Michigan, so skiing was often a means of practical transportation, especially in the pre-automobile era. It is also a frequent choice for winter athletic competition, one in which Finnish Americans often excelled, like Matt Oja (left) and Tomi Partanen of South Range.

Karl Lehto, a Tampere, Finland, native, chose Upper Michigan as the place to buy a farm and one day bring his parents. However, World War I intervened. Despite that setback, Lehto (left) was able to achieve international success as a multi-sport athlete, earning accolades in both the United States and Canada, defeating opponents such as Karl Wirtanen in this 1910 bout.

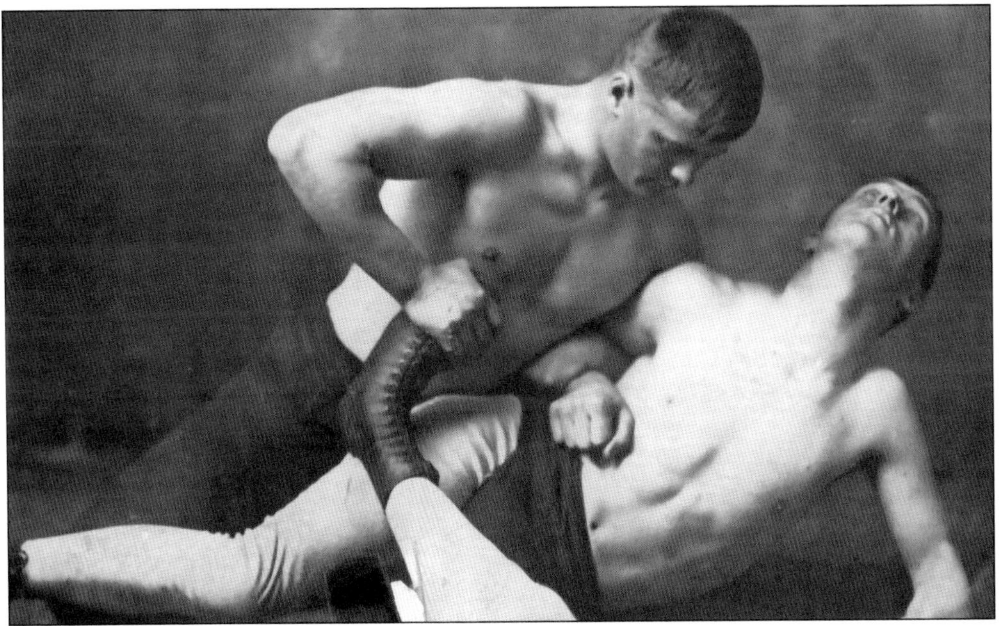

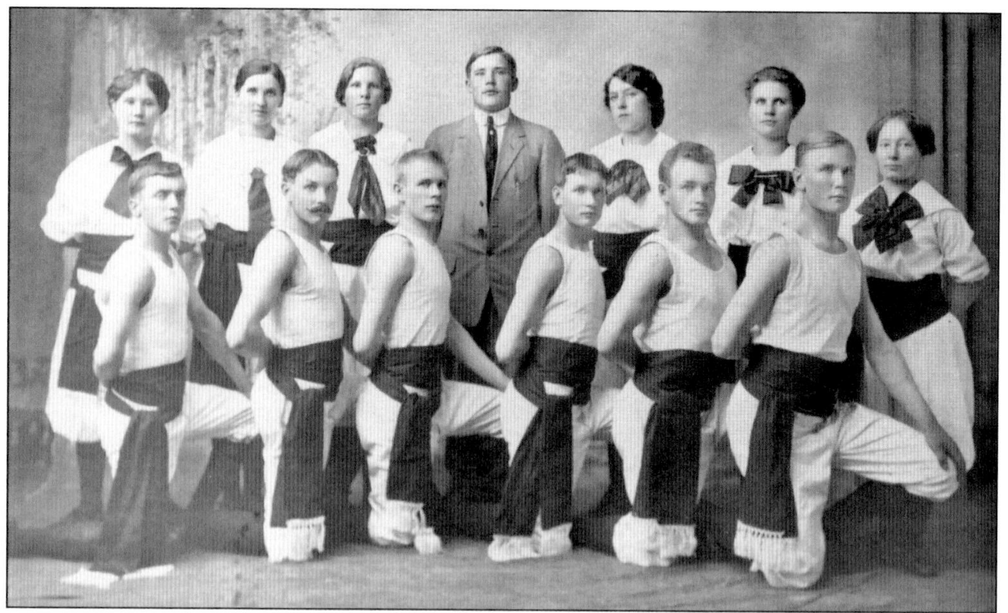

Physical fitness and social activity were a large part of Finnish immigrants' lives in Upper Michigan. This philosophy led to the establishment of many sport-based organizations, including the Marquette-area gymnastics club Köntys. That group's members posed for this photograph in 1913.

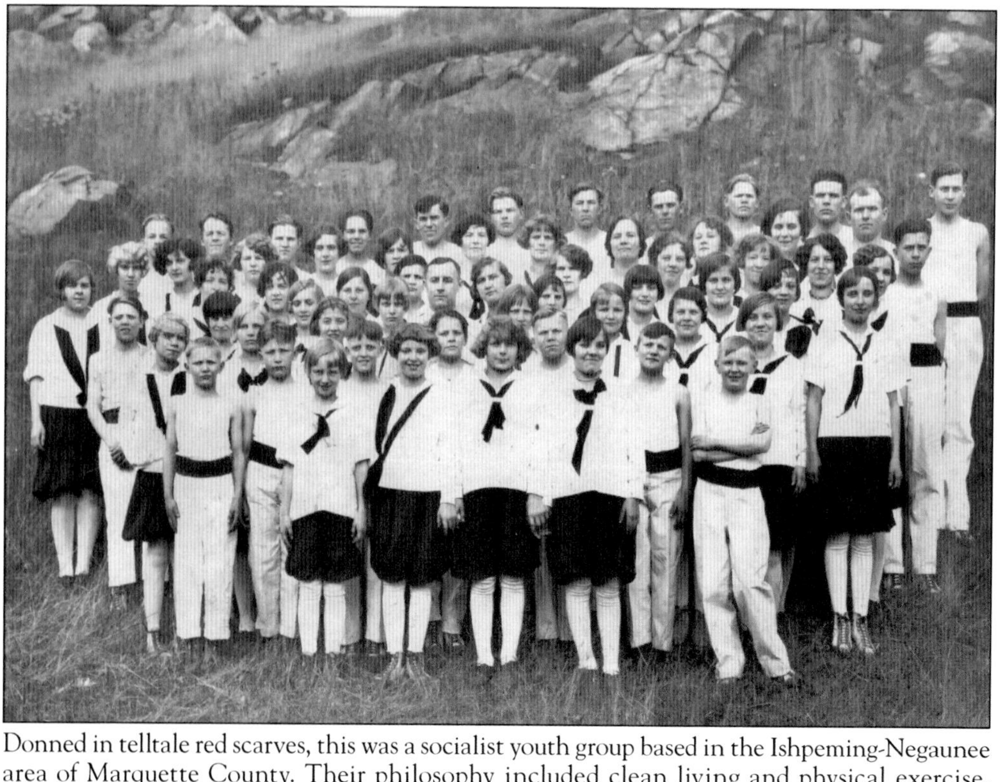

Donned in telltale red scarves, this was a socialist youth group based in the Ishpeming-Negaunee area of Marquette County. Their philosophy included clean living and physical exercise, particularly gymnastics.

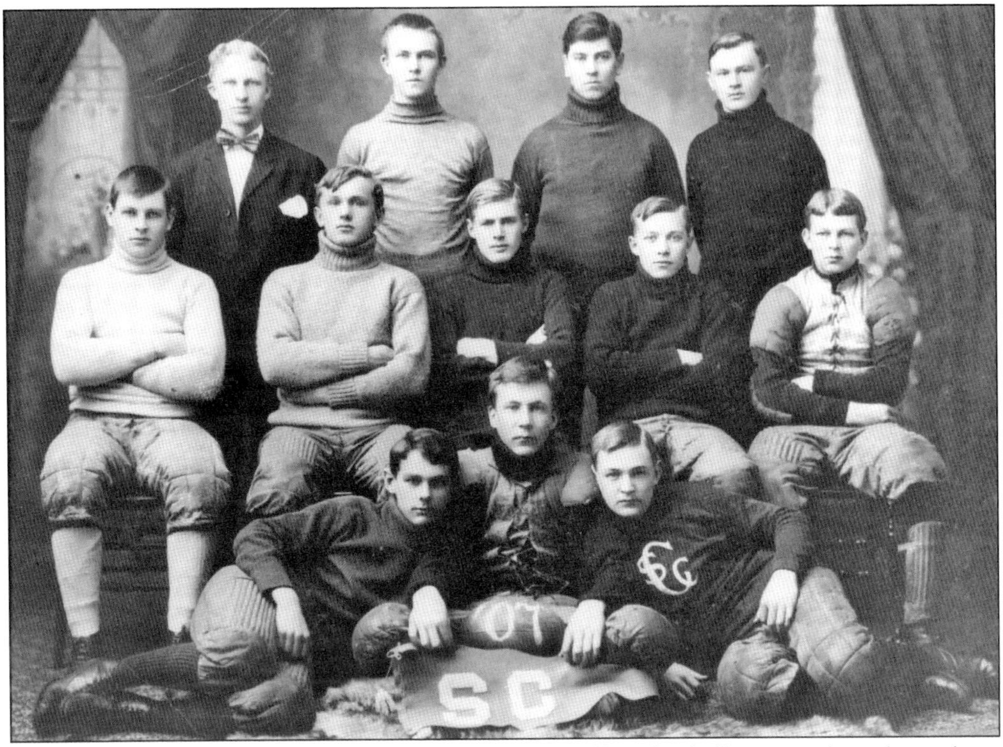

Featuring a roster of Finnish Americans, the Suomi College football team took to the gridiron in 1907. Suomi College provided numerous opportunities for college-level athletes in a variety of sports to continue competing while earning an education. After a brief hiatus, the school's athletic programs have been revived in recent years.

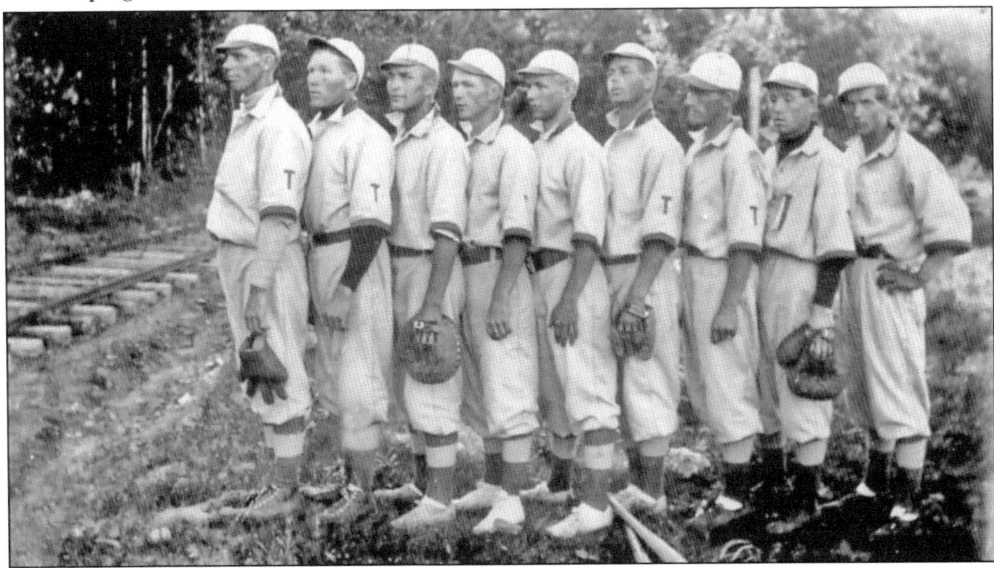

The Finns of Tapiola were people for all seasons when it came to sports and recreation. The tiny community brought together enough men to form a baseball team, complete with uniforms typical of the era. For many years, the Copper Country had a men's hardball league, with commercially sponsored teams that played each other several times each summer. (James Kurtti.)

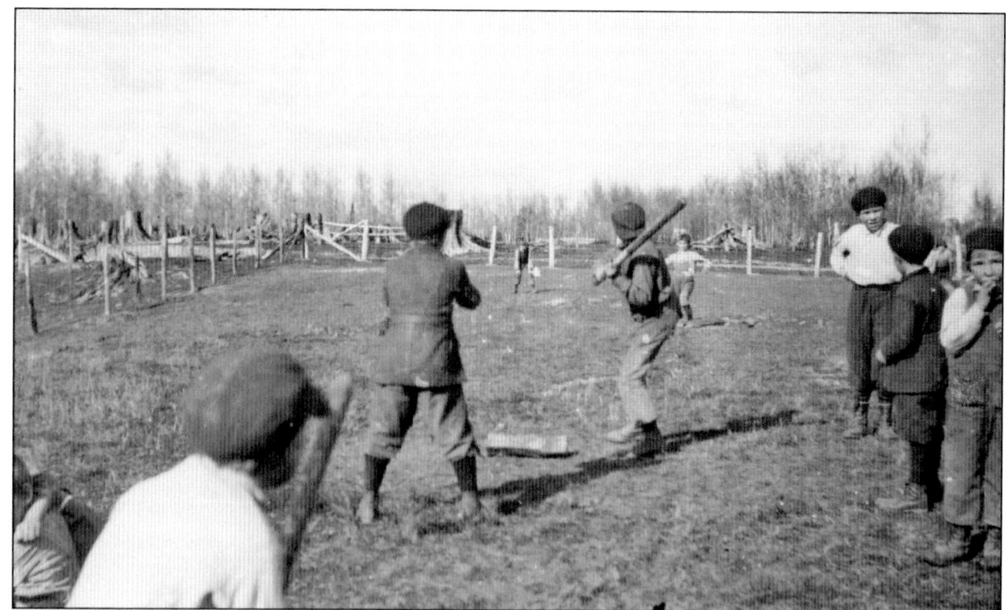

The Finns play it by some notably different rules, but the immigrants to the UP picked up the game of baseball rather quickly. Pickup games and rudimentary fields popped up across the region, in locations such as Askel in Baraga County, where this group of youngsters found time to play between farm chores.

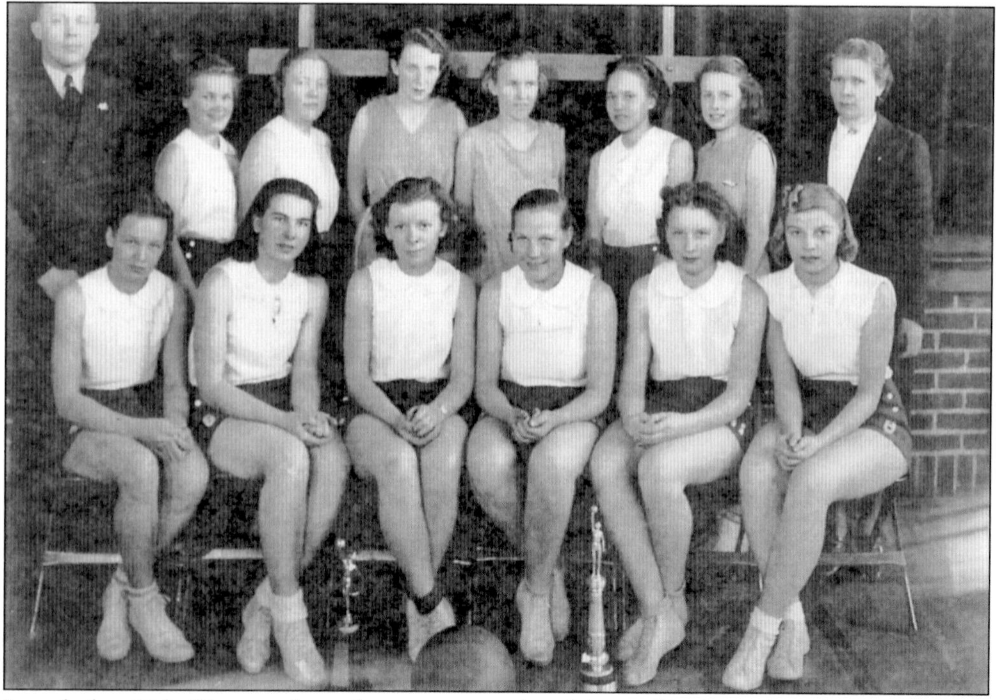

Long before Title IX ensured equal opportunities for athletes of both genders, the UP's Finnish communities offered athletic opportunities for both males and females. Such was the case at the Doelle School, in Houghton County's Tapiola, where Hilda Kangas coached a 12-player girls' basketball team whose roster was entirely Finns in 1939. (James Kurtti.)

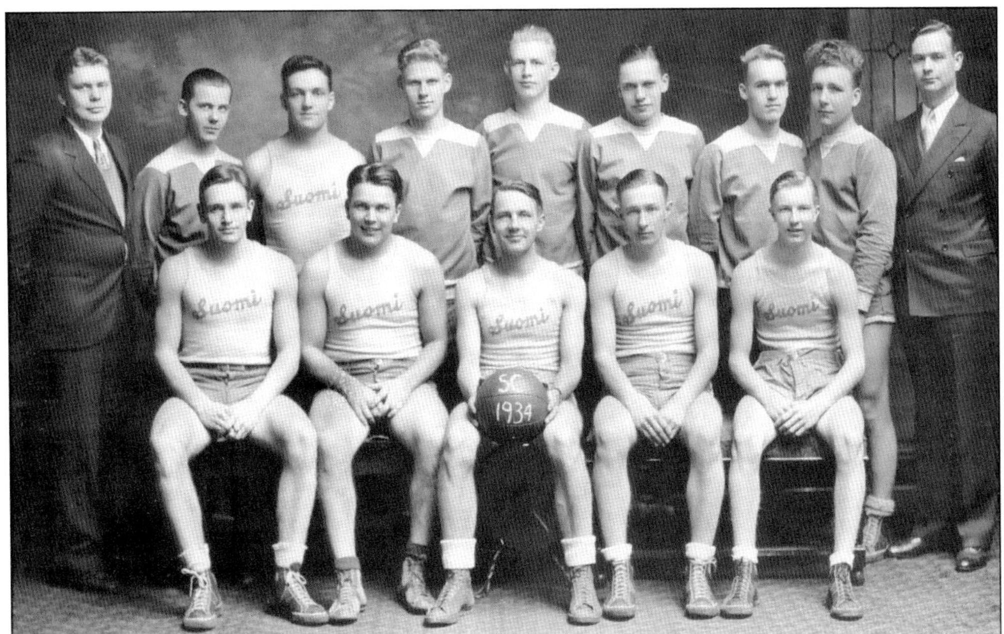

Suomi College's basketball program has a storied history, with many successes on the hardwood over the decades. This 1934 team, like others who took the court in the years before and after, played a schedule against several local opponents, including matches against community-based teams that were established in Finnish-settled towns and villages.

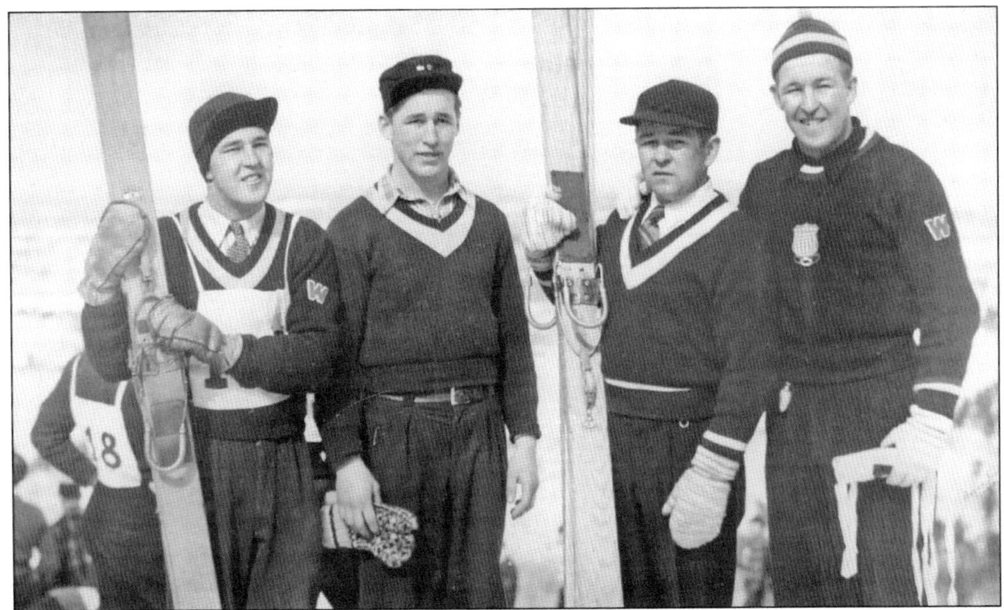

Parents sometimes ask their children, "If your friends jumped off a bridge, would you too?" Substitute "ski hill" for "bridge" and the answer from the Bietila boys would have been "yes." The Bietilas—seen here from left to right, Roy, Ralph, Leonard, and Walter (Anselm and Paul not pictured)—made their name synonymous with ski jumping, especially in the area near Ishpeming known as Cleveland Location. Walter made the US Olympic team in 1936 and 1948, while Ralph was an Olympian in 1948 and 1952. (US Ski and Snowboard Hall of Fame.)

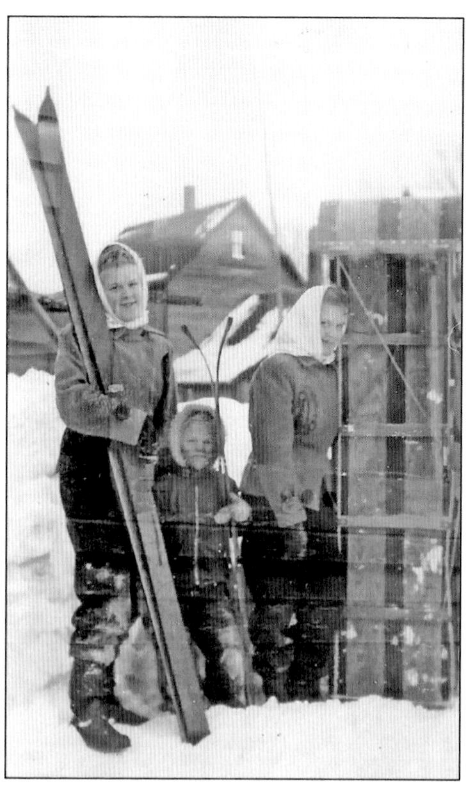

The cold, snow, and occasionally brisk winds of Upper Michigan winters can be enough to keep many folks indoors, but not Ruth, Irma, and Elaine Jurmu of Negaunee, who simply bundled up, grabbed their snow gear—much of which was typically handcrafted—and made the most of what Mother Nature had to offer. (James Kurtti.)

A peek from behind the curtain on the stage at the Doelle School in Tapiola revealed a capacity audience of community members eager to see the performance. Theater was a key part of Finnish American life, with many troupes including Finnish classics such as *Seitsemän Veljestä* (Seven Brothers) in their repertoire.

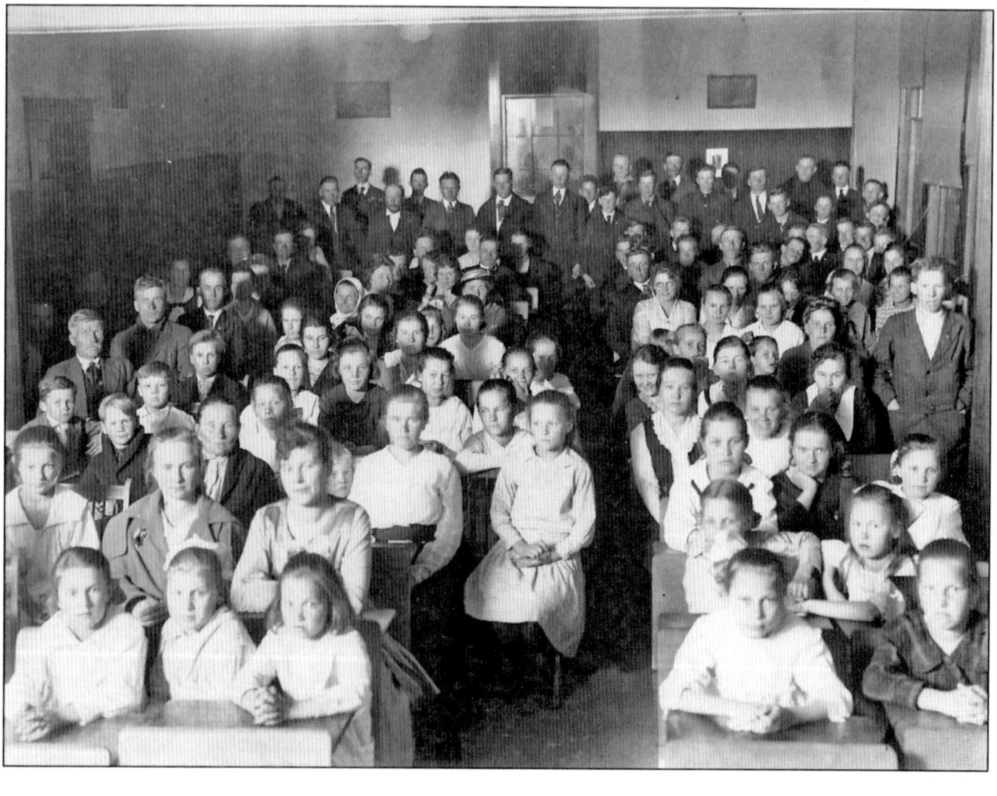

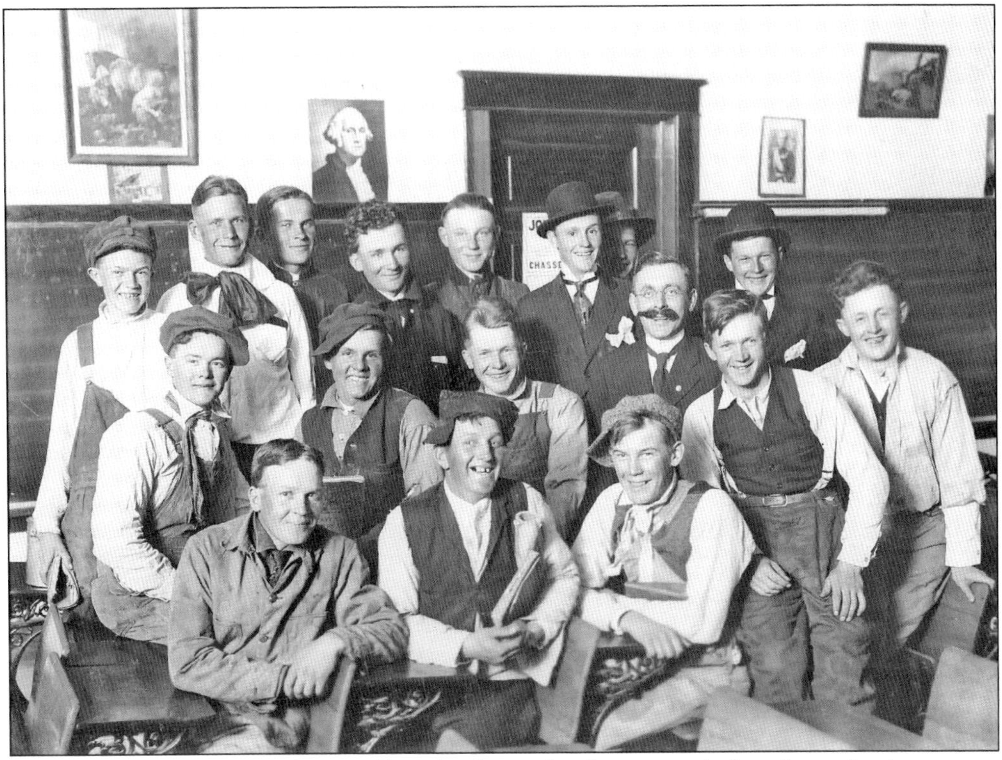

The male students of Tapiola's Doelle School pose for the camera before they take the stage to perform one of numerous plays.

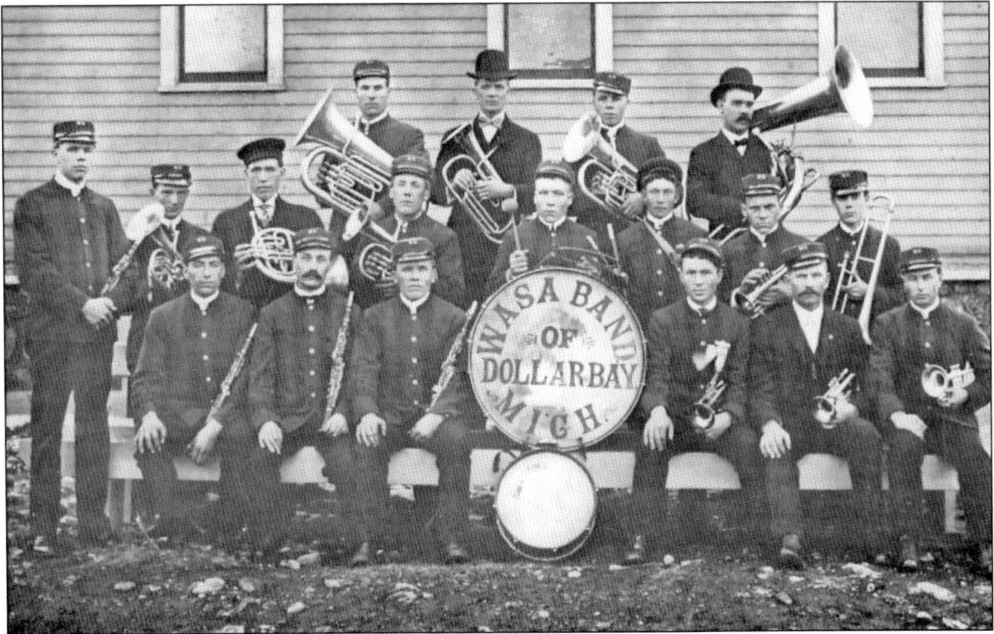

The Wasa Band played for dances and events hosted at the Runeberg Hall of Dollar Bay. The Order of Runeberg was a national Swedish temperance society organized by Swedish-speaking Finns. (John Backman.)

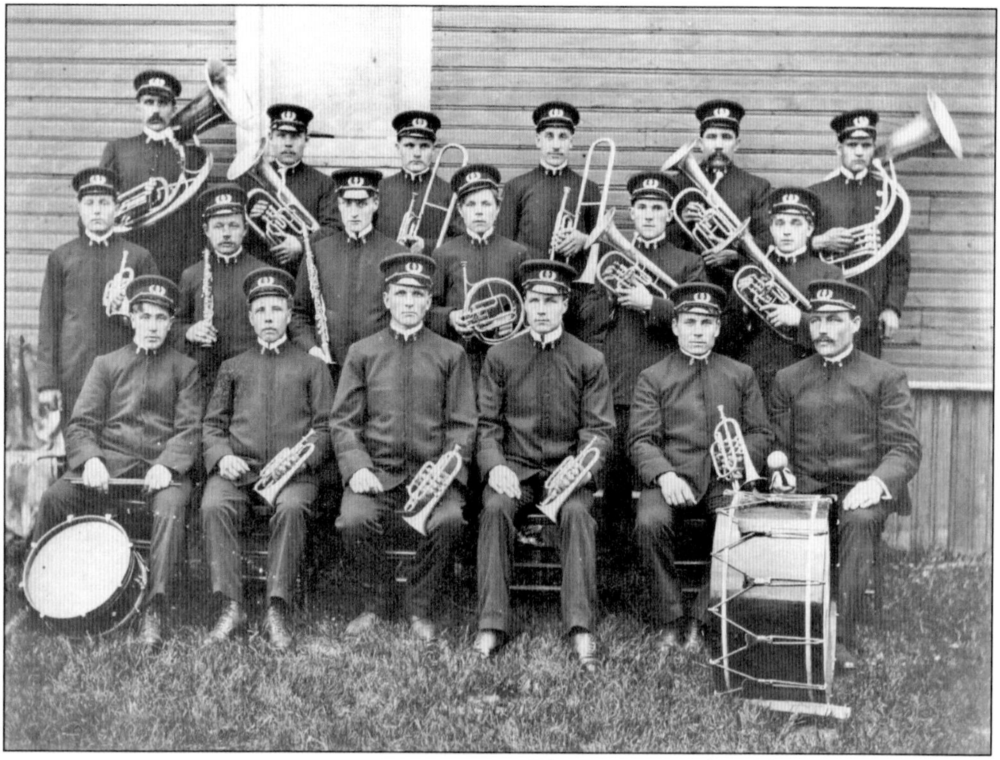

The community band became almost a standard of Finnish-American life in Upper Michigan, with many—if not most—towns and cities forming one. Such was the case in the southern Marquette County village of Princeton, which had an 18-member brass and percussion ensemble as early as 1909, operating under the name Suomalainen Soittokunta Leivo.

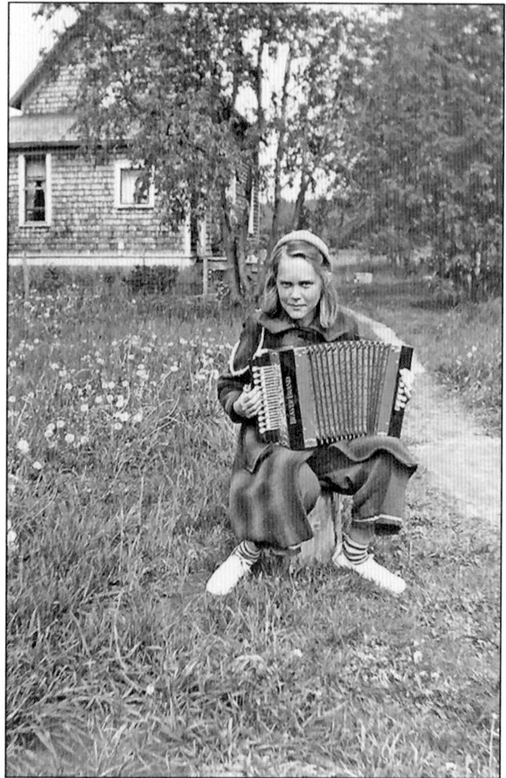

Since the first Finnish immigrants disembarked in Upper Michigan, music has been a part of Finnish American life in the UP, with tunes and playing techniques passed down across the generations. Many a second-generation Finnish American learned to play on an instrument that once belonged to their father, mother, or grandparent.

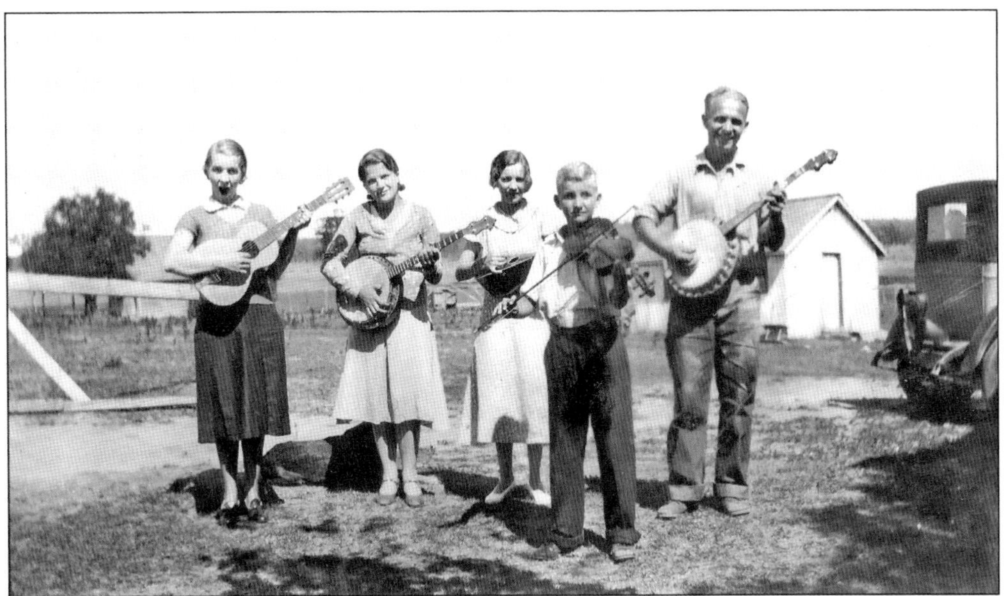

For the Haapala family of Bruce Crossing, joined by neighbor Irene Kurtti for this August 1933 impromptu jam session, music was a part of nearly every day. While today's families wind down at the end of a full day's work by watching television, folks like the Haapalas instead grabbed their instruments and unwound by creating their own entertainment. (James Kurtti.)

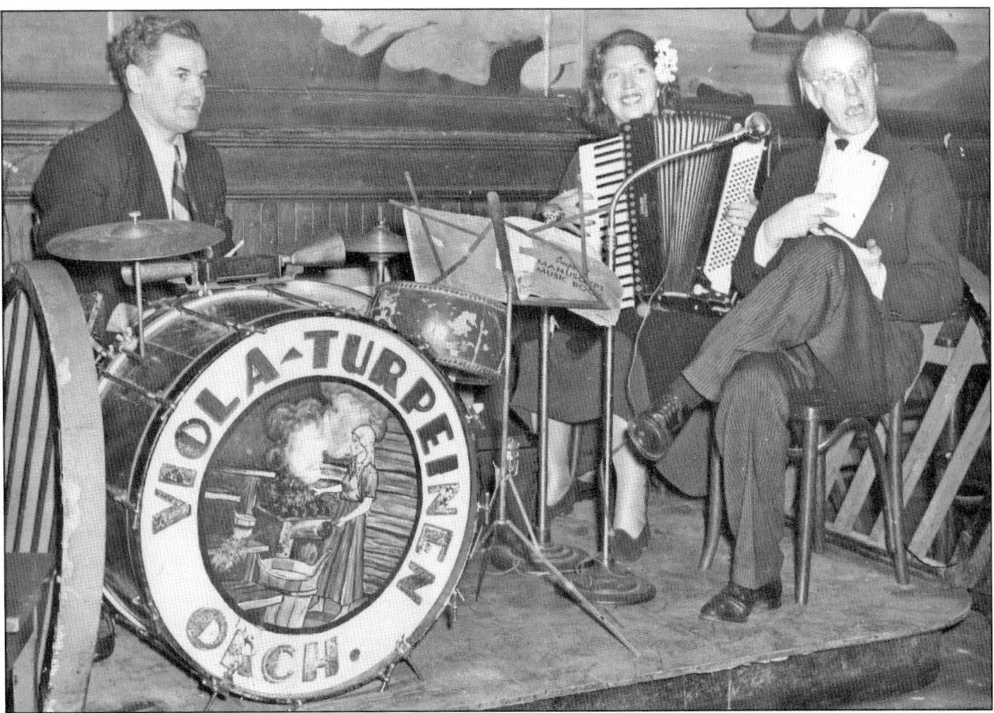

William "Bill" Syrjälä (left) and his wife, Viola Turpeinen, were premiere dance musicians among Finns across the United States. Viola, who hailed from Champion, drew crowds wherever she played. The band's drum heads, as well as other paraphernalia, are part of the Finnish American Heritage Center's artifact collection.

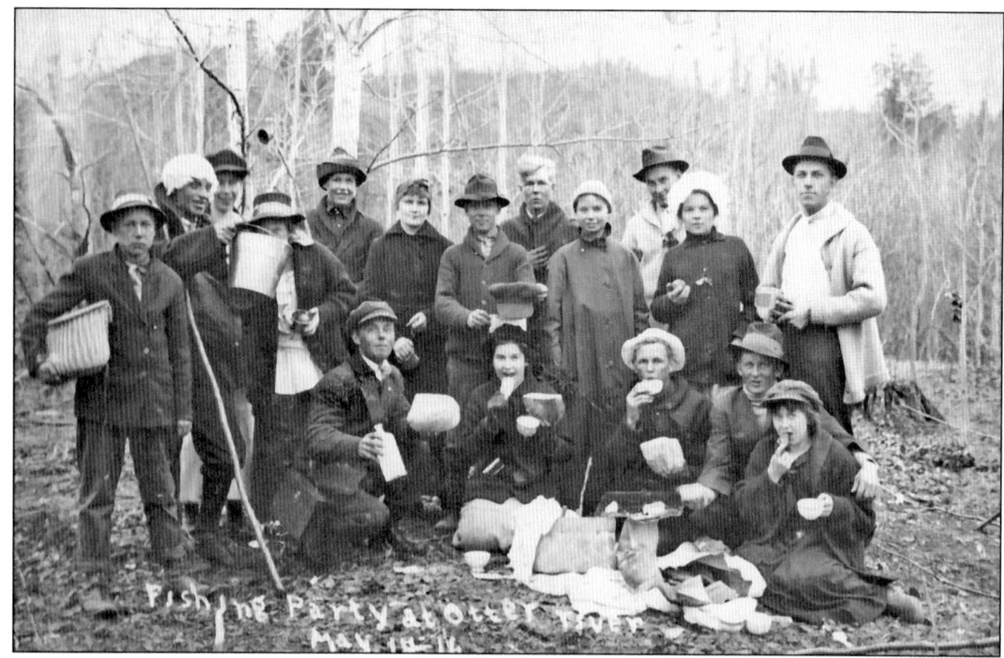

One of the many traditions passed from generation to generation is the idea of the fishing trip. A basket full of food, fire-brewed coffee, a day full of fun (May 19, 1916, in this case), and laughs at locations like the Otter River near Nisula, made it so it did not matter if a single fish was caught.

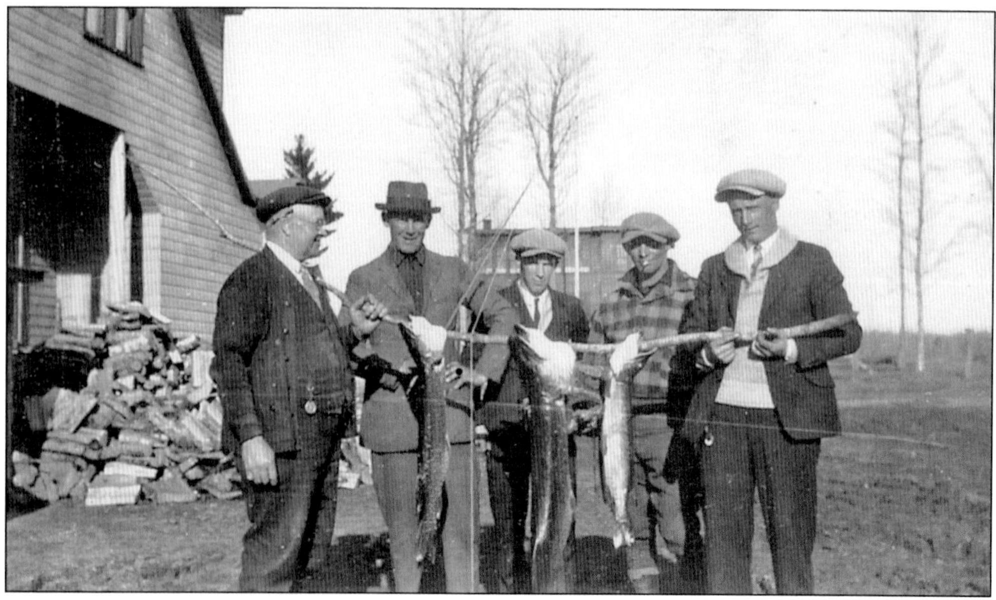

"A bad day fishing is better than a good day doing most anything else," is a saying used regularly by Upper Michigan fishermen. It was on the minds, if not the lips, of this quintet who proudly displayed their day's catch outside the Karvakka-Jarvenpää store in the Houghton County village of Tapiola.

On the farm it was useful when everyone could handle a gun; perhaps one would spot crows in the corn patch or a deer in the carrots. Whether truly hunters or not, these two Finnish lasses pose near Otter Lake (Saukkojärvi) in Baraga County as if it is not just a man's world anymore.

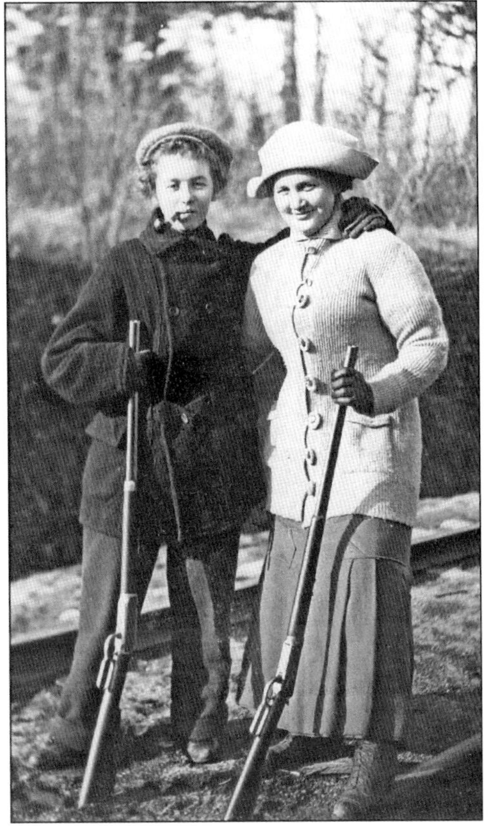

Hunters for generations have told and shared stories of the one that got away, but Albert Kurtti of Paynesville kept his cool and his aim was true, allowing him to harvest this remarkable 23-point buck near his home in Ontonagon County. Since most "big" bucks are between 8 and 10 points, one can imagine the reactions of Kurtti's fellow hunters when he bagged this monster. (James Kurtti.)

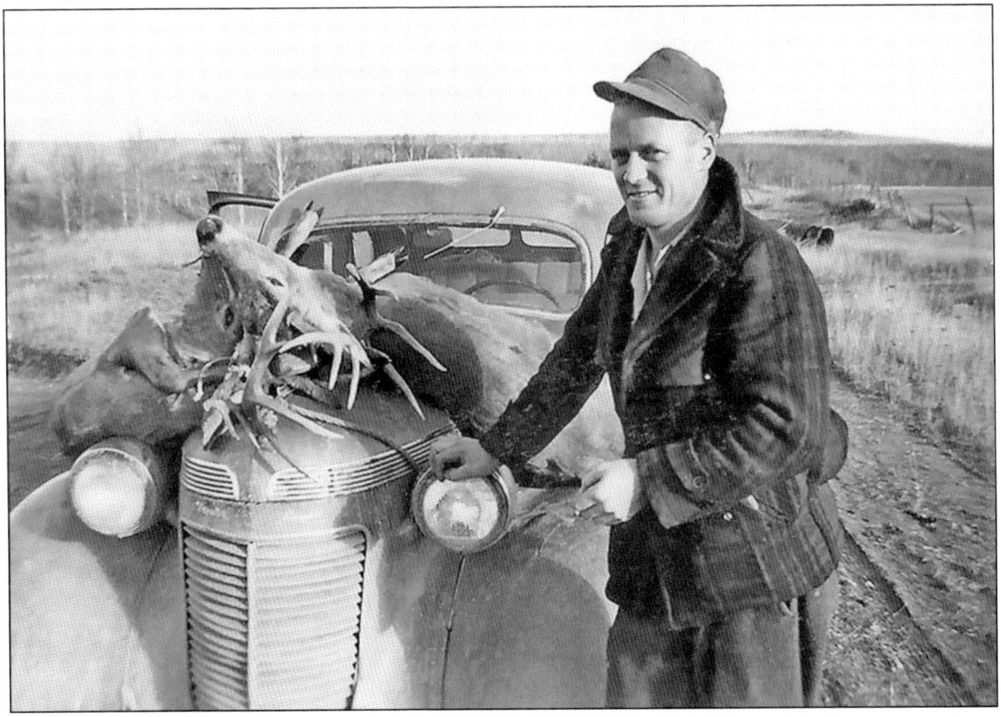

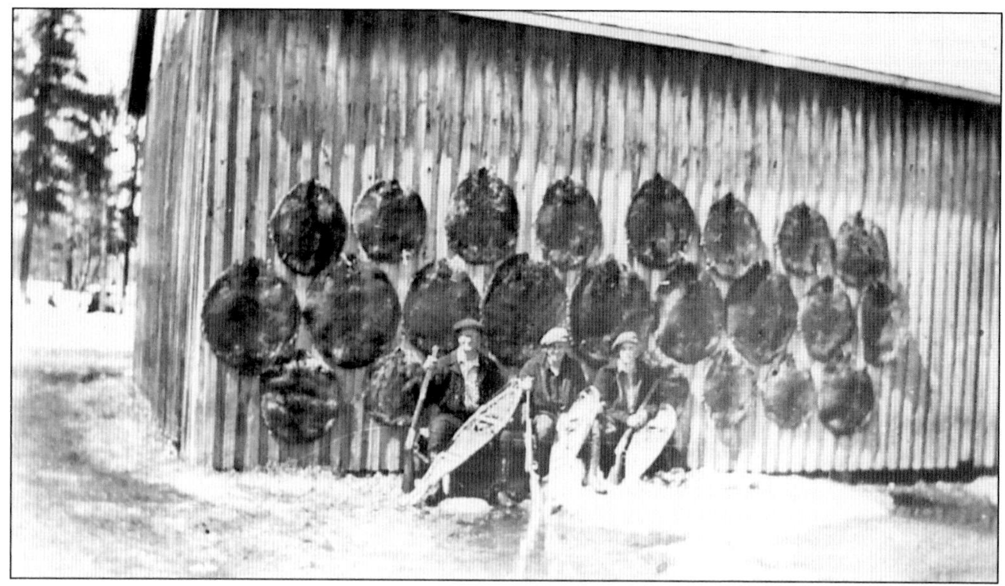

Lauri Kiviranta, son of famed poet and masseur Eelu Kiviranta of Nisula, had a banner spring trapping beaver in 1937. Not only were the pelts valuable items for immigrant trappers to sell, but the removal of these large rodents aided landowners by alleviating the animals' dams and the resulting flood problems. (James Kurtti.)

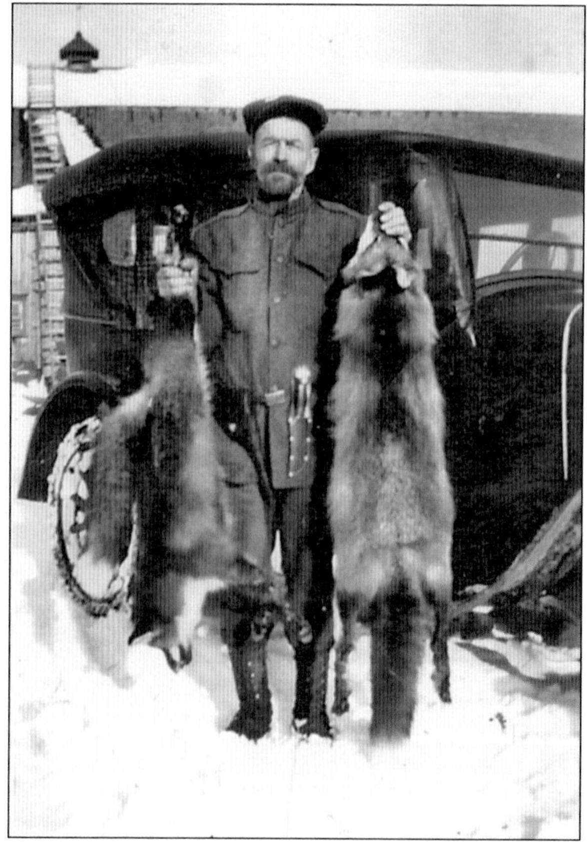

Trapping is now a hobby for many outdoorsmen, but in the early years, it was a vital way to supplement a family's meager income. The furs from animals nabbed in a trap line, such as these red fox pelts, could be sold for some much-needed extra cash. (James Kurtti.)

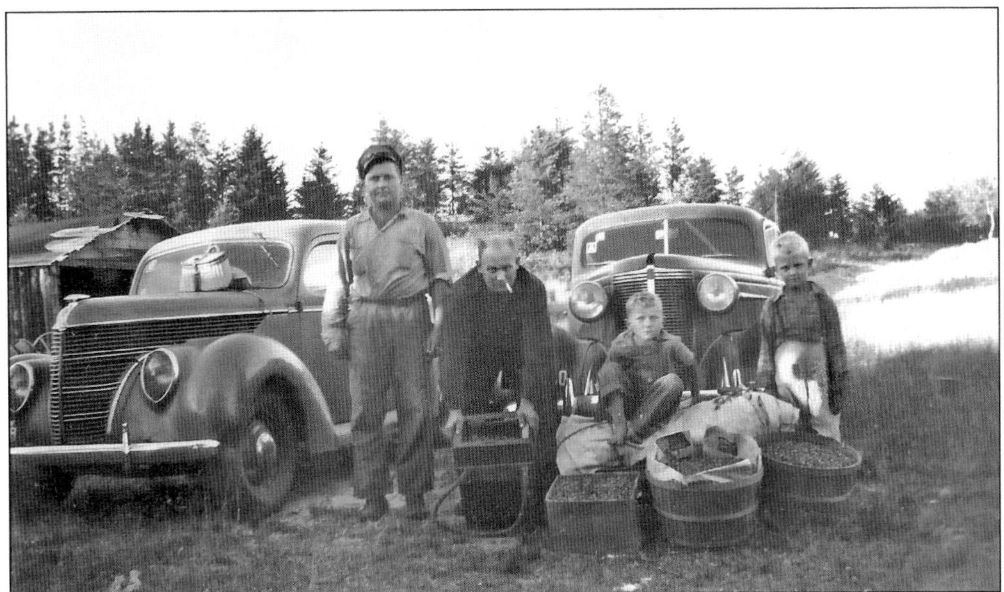

When the blueberries were ripe, families packed up and went to the forest, often staying for days, as seen here. In a weekend in 1944, the Jurmu family of Negaunee picked 174 quarts, filling every container they had. (James Kurtti.)

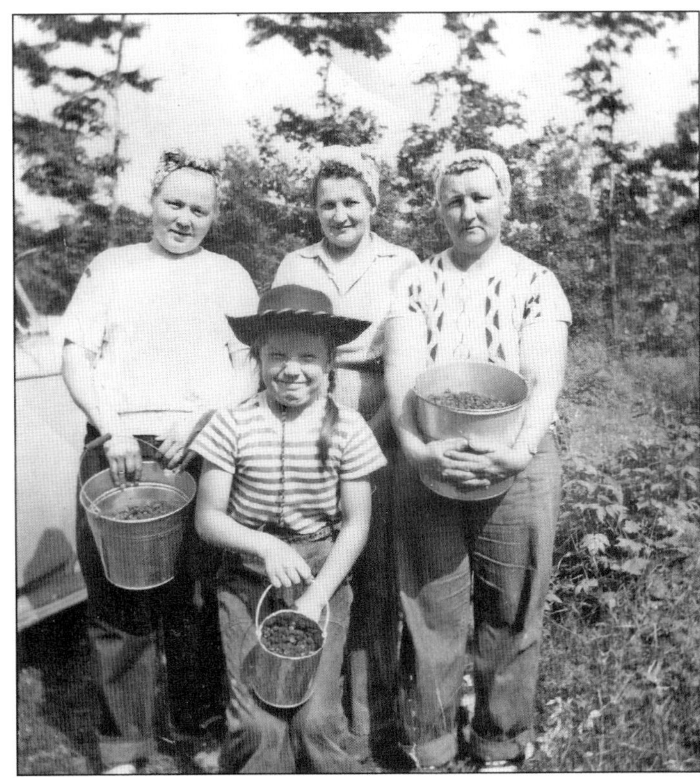

Strawberries, raspberries, blueberries, and the like—the forest provided its bounty for those who could keep their favorite patches a secret. Jams, jellies, and canned berries provided families a taste of summer over the long UP winters. (Rebecca Hoekstra.)

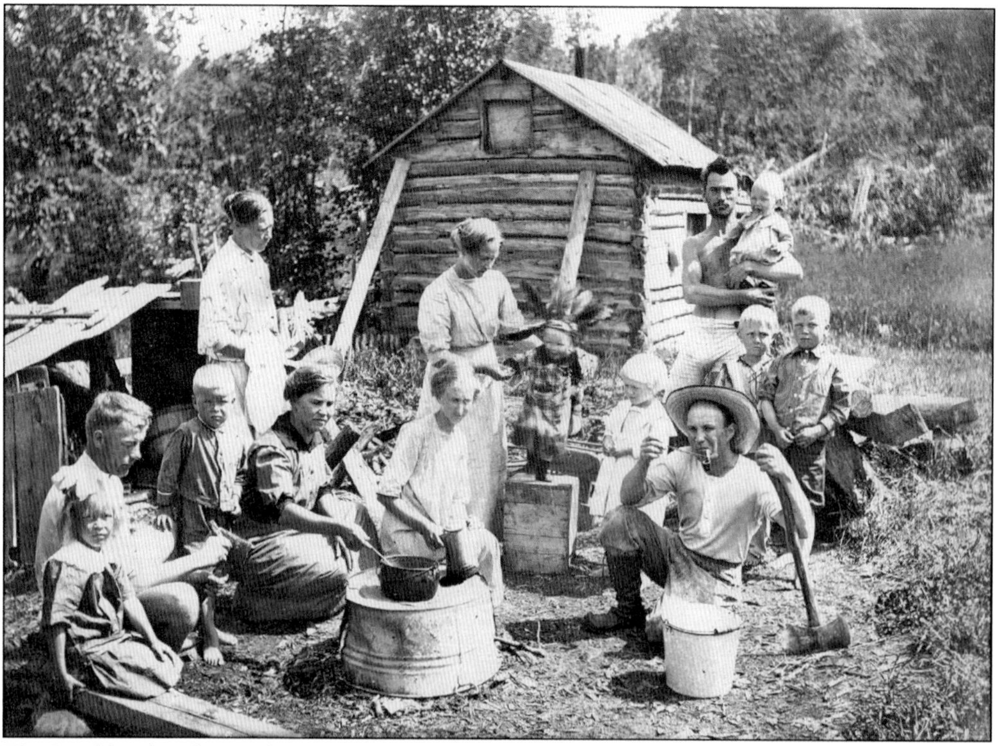

The Bjorklund and Parta families picnic at the Bjorklund home in Heinola, a farming settlement in Houghton County. Russell Parta family was the owner of Parta Printing and the editor of the conservative newspaper *Minnesotan Uutiset*, while Bjorklund was once the editor of the leftist newspaper *Työmies*.

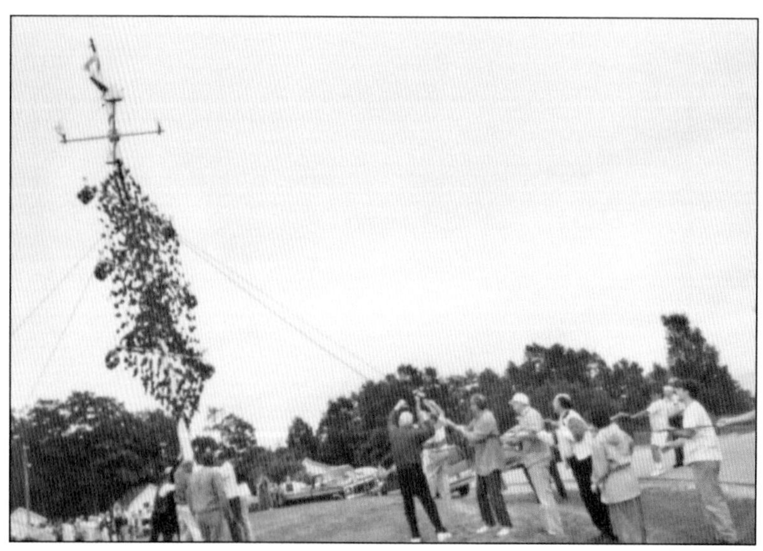

Hard work culminates with the raising of the Midsommar pole in the village of Brevort, which was largely settled by Swedish-speaking Åland Islanders, who brought the tradition of raising a pole decorated with birch boughs, wreaths, and ships on summer's longest day of the year.

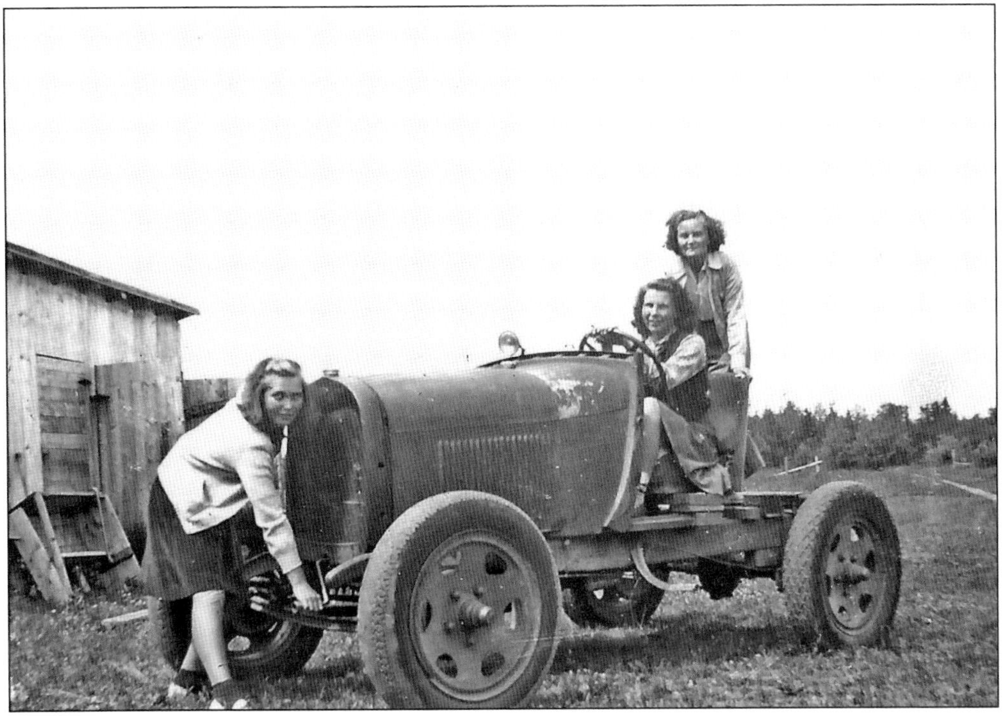

Finnish American farmers would often build their own tractors. Called *jokeri* or "joker" (among other names), they were fashioned from an old Model A or Model B Ford truck. The body and fenders would be removed and the frame shortened so the driver would be sitting almost over the rear axle. Toini and Tuovi Wiitala, with friend Lillian Lahti, showed that using the *jokeri* was an equal opportunity endeavor.

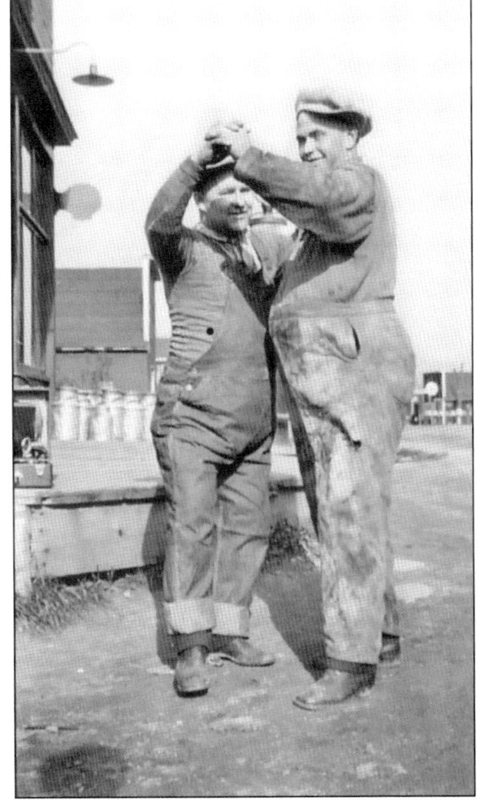

It takes two to tango . . . or waltz, or *schottische*, and as far as these good-natured buddies were concerned, it does not matter which two. These guys hammed it up for the camera during a work break near Karvakko's Market in Tapiola, a small village in Houghton County near Otter Lake. (James Kurtti.)

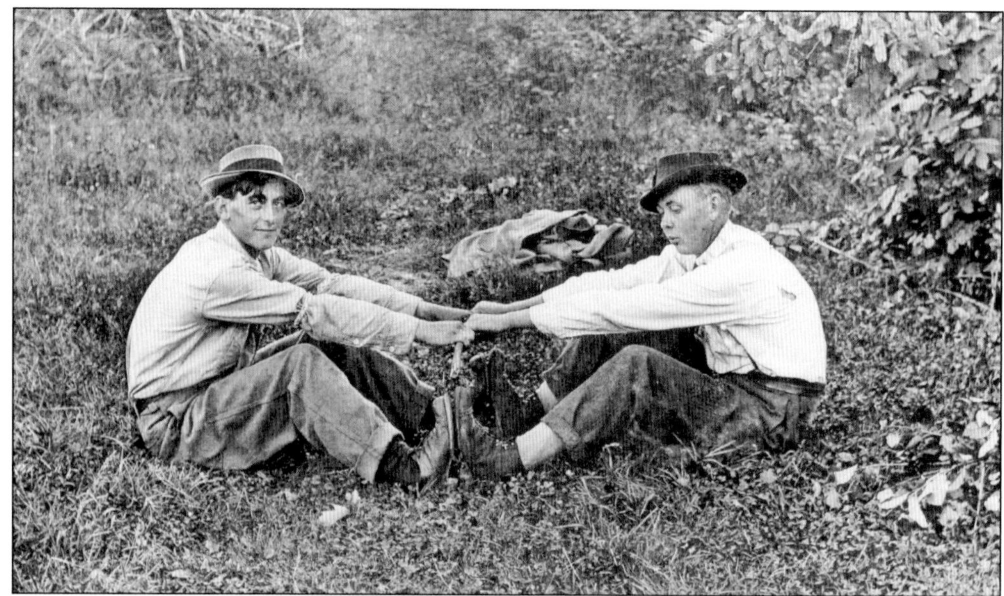

Finnish American men have been known for generations as guys who work hard and consequently play hard. Couple that with the traditional Finnish ingenuity, and most anything can become a game or contest—even the concept of pulling with all one's might on a stick to see if he could lift the other off the ground.

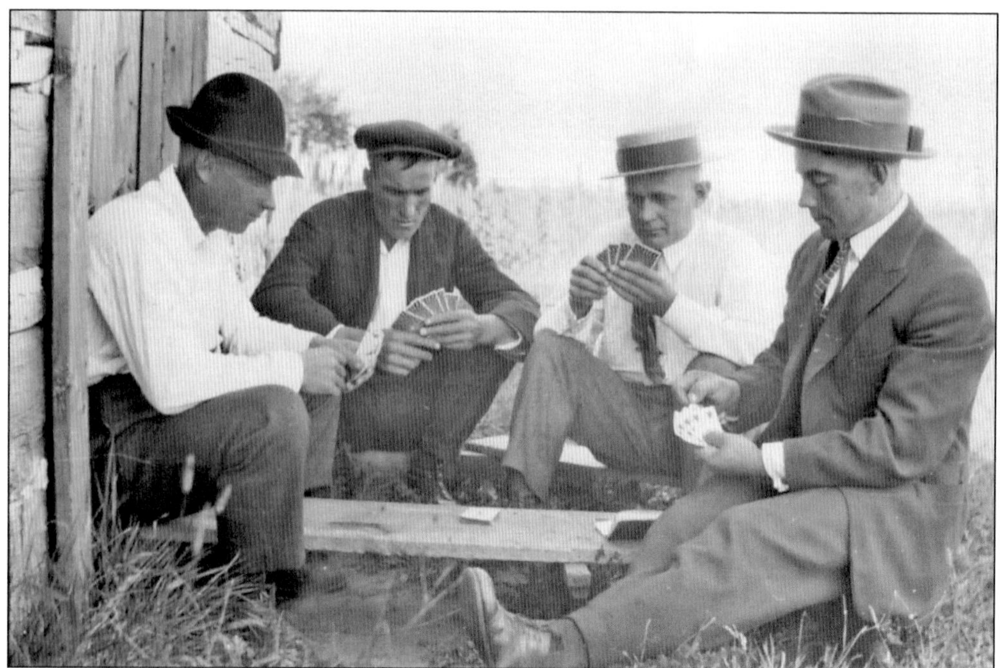

In the early 1930s, while some men spent their Sunday in church, others would opt to gather for a game of cards. Seen here from left to right are Arthur Lampinen, Charles Jarvi, Michael Haapaniemi, and Lauri Sandberg, who, while wearing their "Sunday best," enjoy the fresh air, sunshine, and camaraderie.

Seven

Famous Finn-dividuals

In every situation or crisis, someone rises to the occasion. It also was so in the early days among the Finns. They were teachers, preachers, and top-prize reachers. Some had remarkable musical ability, or were simply remarkable in their stature. While many were famous within the Upper Peninsula Finnish community, sometimes their fame reached well beyond the UP. From media personalities to women well ahead of their time, their indelible marks left on the fabric of the Finnish-American community are fondly remembered.

No doubt many of these folks would be stereotypically Finnish in their self-effacing embarrassment to be listed among the famous. Perhaps famous, used as much for its alliterative quality as for its actual definition, ought to be considered a stand-in for many words, including inspirational, lovable, and representative of that special Finnish quality called *sisu*.

Among the notable Finns who for a variety of reasons could not be included in this chapter are Suomi College faculty like founder and first college president J.K. Nikander, head of the commercial department Waino "Pops" Lehto, and music directors Martti Nisonen and Arthur Hill, who guided and educated many over the decades. Teacher and writer Mayme Sevander, whose family moved to Russian Karelia in the 1930s, and whose father was killed in the purges there, documented her experiences in several books. Rosa Lemberg, teacher, performer, and adopted daughter of Finnish missionaries, is believed to be the first black person granted Finnish citizenship. She moved to the United States as an adult and became a member of the Finnish communities in New York and Chicago, spending the last years of her life at the Finnish Rest Home in Covington. Leo Nippa was a well-known manufacturer of sauna stoves in Bruce Crossing. Eugene Sinervo of Deerton worked with Carl Pellonpää to establish the *Suomi Kutsuu* television program in 1962. Musicians like accordionist Art Moilanen and fiddler Edward Lauluma set toes-a-tapping at dances and concerts across the UP. Finally, while their husbands are mentioned in this book for their contributions to the religious heritage of the UP Finns, Lempi Heideman and Mary Mickelsen were the backbones of their spouses' ministries.

As the reader learns these stories and others, no doubt they, too, will see them as among the famous "Finn-dividuals" remembered in these pages.

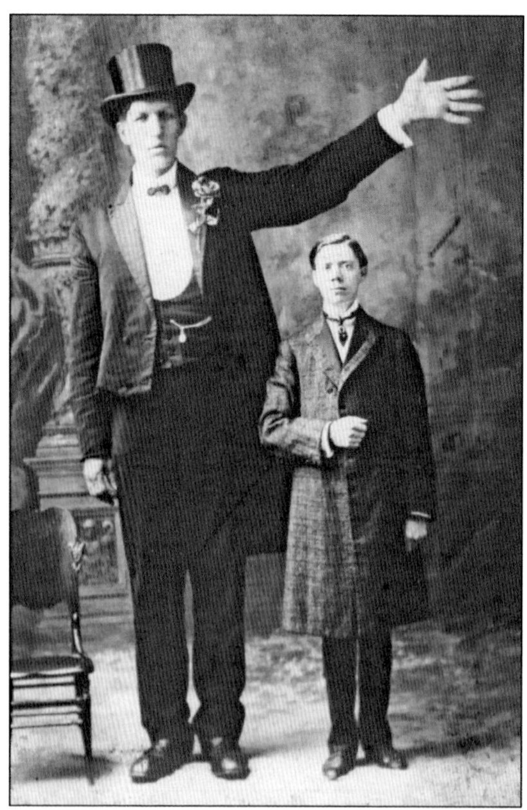

Lauri "Big Louie" Moilanen (1886–1913) was once the tallest man in the world. He stood eight feet, three inches, and was called the Copper Country Giant. He was a farmer, miner, and justice of the peace, and toured with Ringling Brothers Circus. He operated a tavern in Hancock and could reach both ends of the bar from the middle. He spent his final years on the family farm north of town.

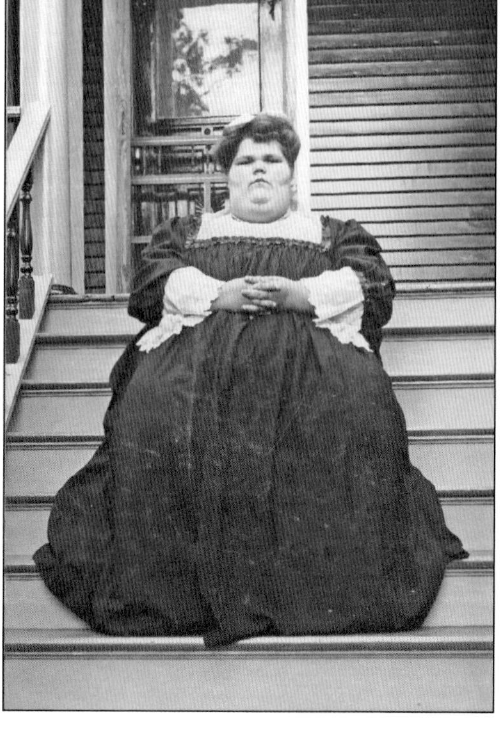

Weighing more than 660 pounds, Lydia (Veteläinen) Weidelman was known as "Big Lydia" among locals in the Calumet area. Born in 1888 in Kuusamo, Finland, Lydia's exceptional weight made her the carnival-like subject of several postcard portraits, but she reportedly handled her size with dignity. Historic reports indicate that Big Lydia (who died in 1937) sometimes appeared with Big Louie Moilanen in parades.

Arriving in Hancock in 1895, Jooseppi Riippa was to serve as an assistant to the pastor of the Finnish Evangelical Lutheran Church and as a teacher at Suomi College the following year. While there, he penned the famous tune "Kotimaani ompi Suomi" (My Homeland is Finland). In August 1895, Riippa was teaching summer school for immigrant children when he was killed by a lightning strike on the church steeple.

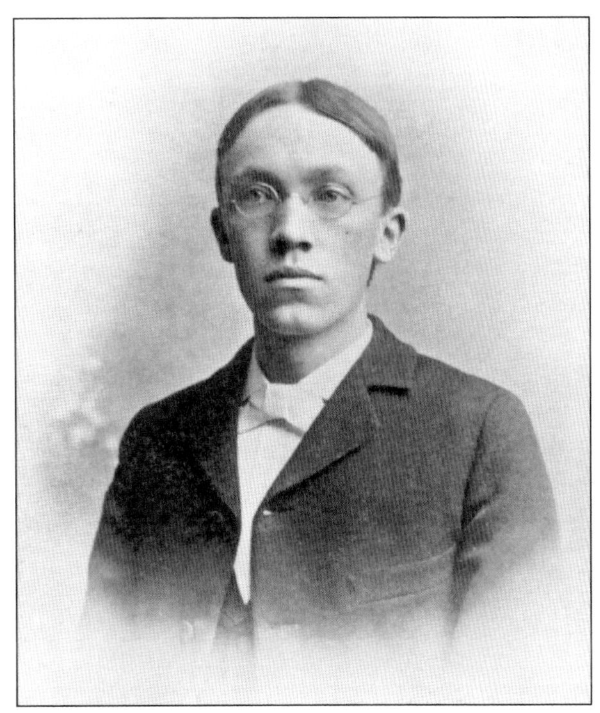

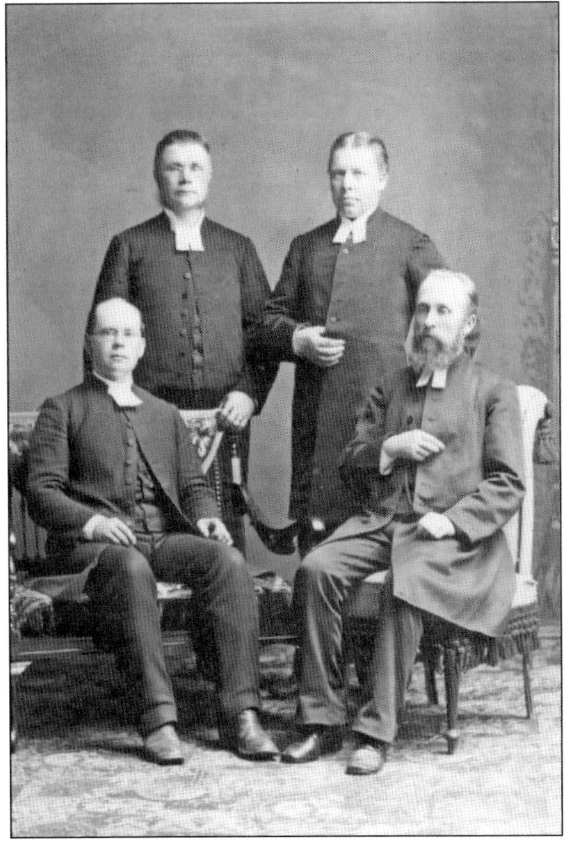

From left to right, Revs. J.K. Nikander, Kaarlo Tolonen, Heikki Tanner, and Alfred Backman, seen in this early 1900s studio portrait, were among the pioneer pastors who helped to establish the Finnish Evangelical Lutheran Church of America, also known as the Suomi Synod. These men, along with their colleagues, served numerous congregations in the UP, where many Finnish immigrants settled, and were active with the Finnish American press and religious publications.

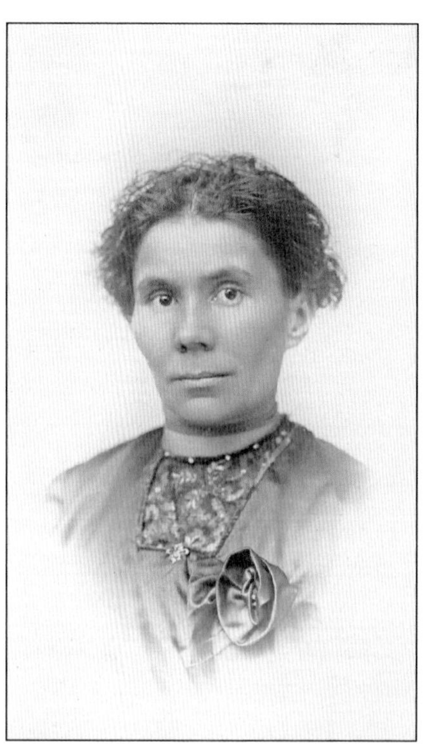

Lohtaja, Finland, native Minnie Perttula-Mäki (1880–1957) was the first, and to date only, female president of Suomi College/Finlandia University. A member of the college's first class, she graduated in 1904 and went on to continue her education in Chicago, Duluth, and at the University of Helsinki.

The Heideman brothers—Paul, Bert, and Lawrence—were the children of Apostolic Lutheran Church leader Arthur Heideman, but they each made names for themselves in the Copper Country. They are remembered for their contributions to not only area religious life but also politics. Bert was a candidate for several different state political offices during his adult life, and Paul was a leader in the First Apostolic Lutheran Church. (James Kurtti.)

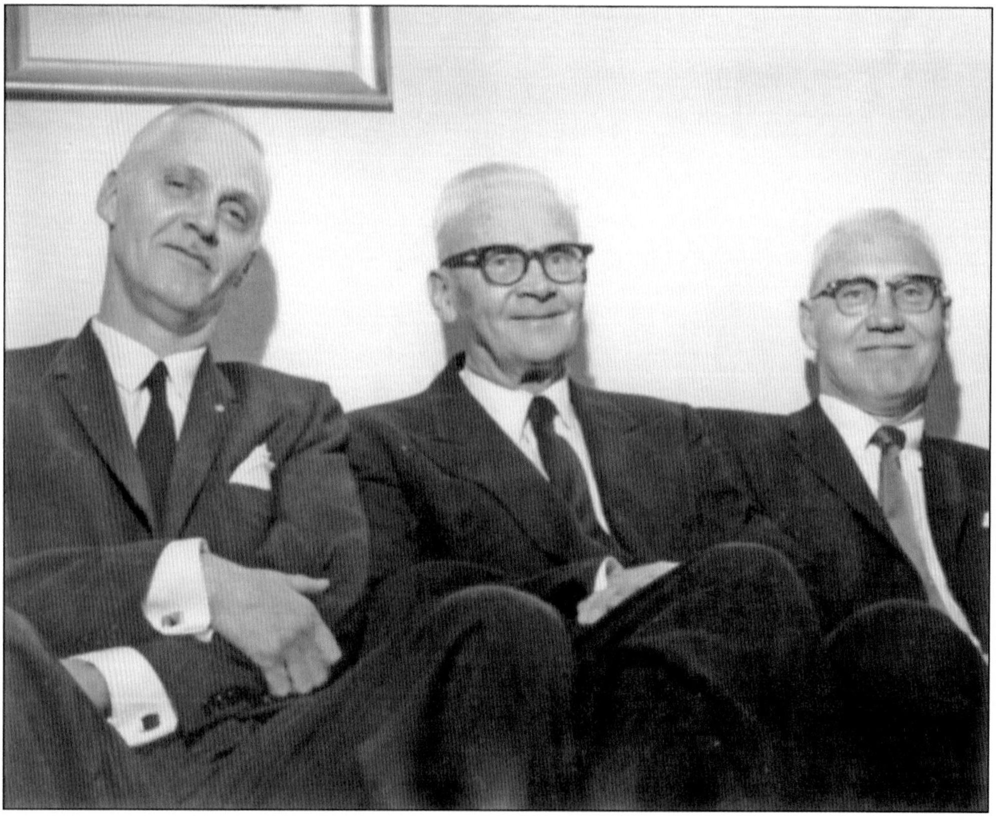

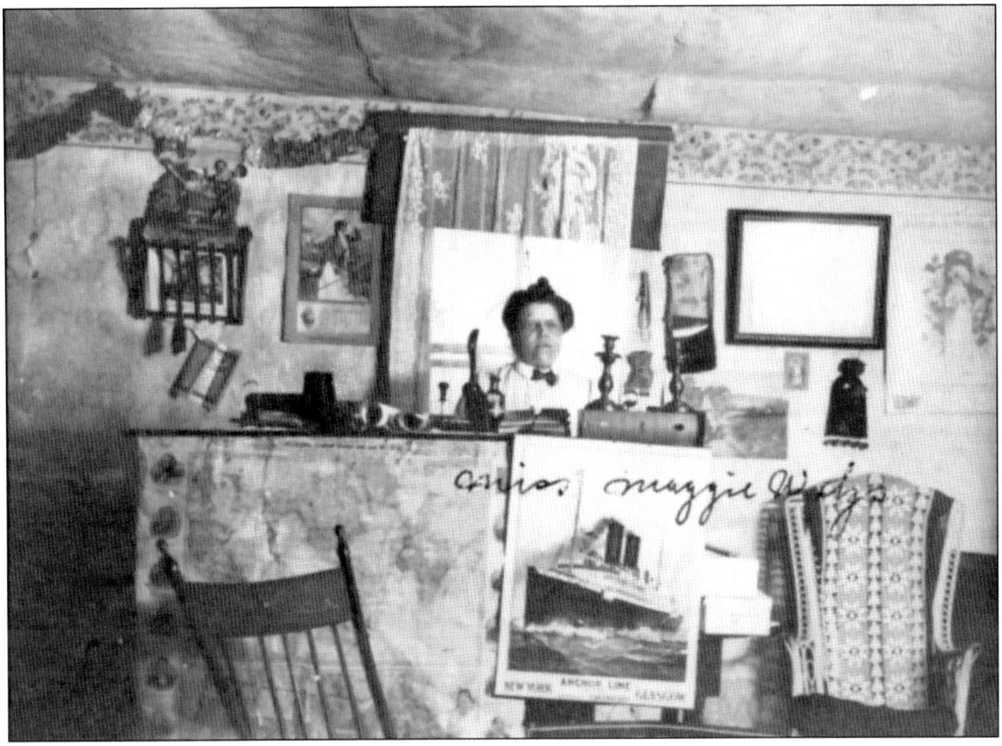

Maggie Walz was not a typical woman. She attempted to establish a women's suffrage organization in 1888; that failed, but Walz rarely did. She was editor of the *Naisten Lehti* and helped Finnish women come to the United States by underwriting their passage, teaching them English, and helping them find employment. She became a ticket agent, a notary public, and opened a currency exchange. She also provided interpretation for Finnish-speaking immigrants.

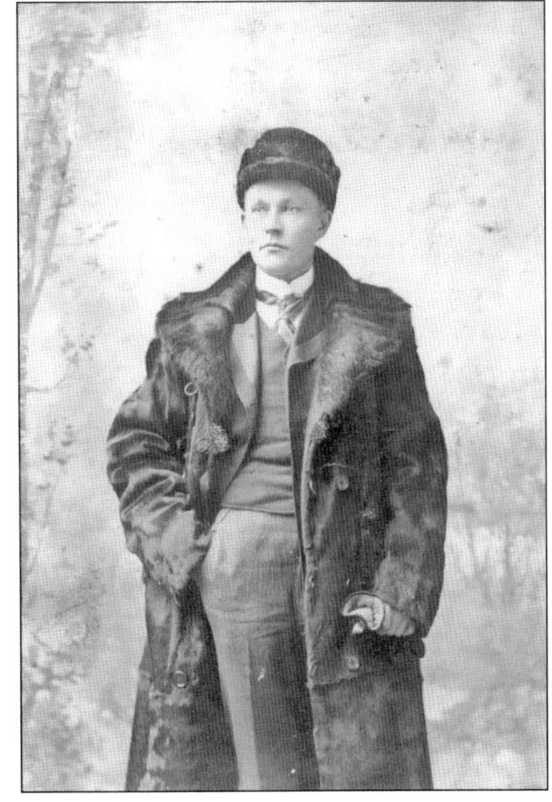

John William Närä, born in 1874 in the Tornio region of Finland, used his camera to chronicle the people and places of the Copper Country after migrating to the United States. He not only captured studio portraits, family events, and Keweenaw adventures, but also had an eye for telling the story of the copper mining industry, with many subjects featuring miners, minework, the 1913–1914 strike, and the industrial landscape.

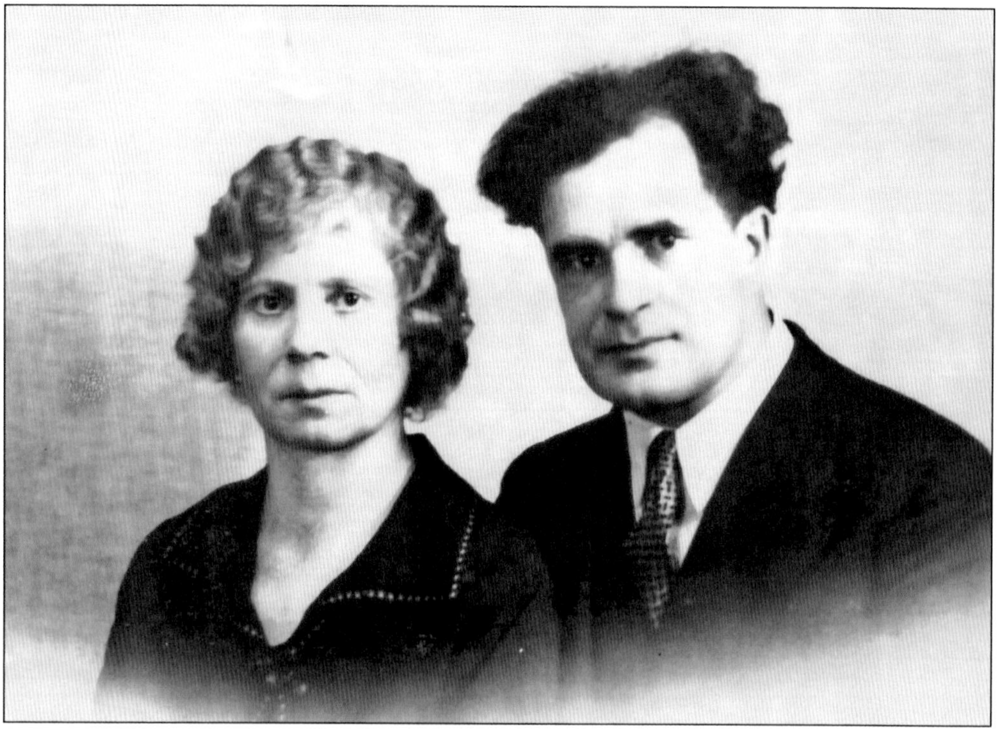

Born Hiskias Möttö in Kangasniemi, Finland, in 1891, Hiski Salomaa immigrated to Hancock in 1909, where he worked as a tailor, opening a shop in 1917 where he sang while working. He was arrested for sedition in Calumet due to his opposition to World War I. After leaving the Copper Country in 1919, he became a famous Finnish American singer/songwriter who depicted working-class immigrant life and used "Finglish" (a combination of Finnish and English) in many songs.

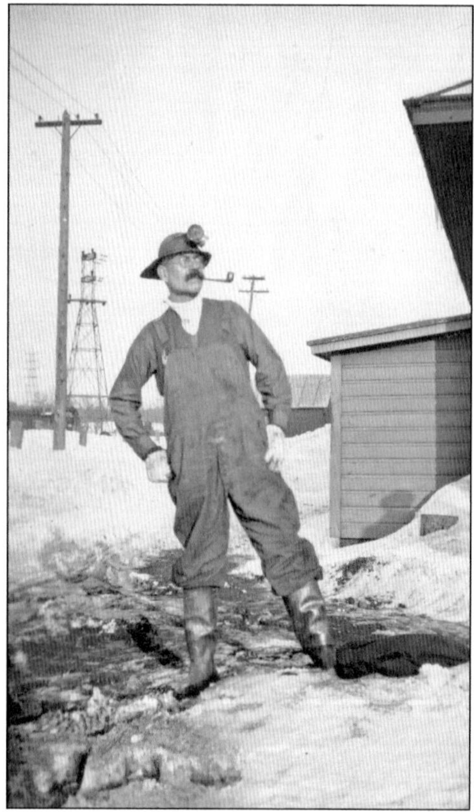

Finland's most beloved painter, Akseli Gallen-Kallela, best known for his illustrations of the epic *Kalevala*, visited the United States twice in the 1920s. His letters tell of raucous times in the wilds of the UP. Here, he is dressed as a miner in Negaunee in 1924. A painting he completed while in the UP was later gifted to Suomi College. (Gallen-Kallela Museo.)

Tauno Nurmela of Covington was a cross-country skier and an outstanding performer in track and field who won 97 first-place medals and ribbons in the 1920s and 1930s in competitions across the upper Midwest. Several of his track and field records exceeded those of Olympic decathlon greats of the time. He was inducted into the UP Sports Hall of Fame in 1973.

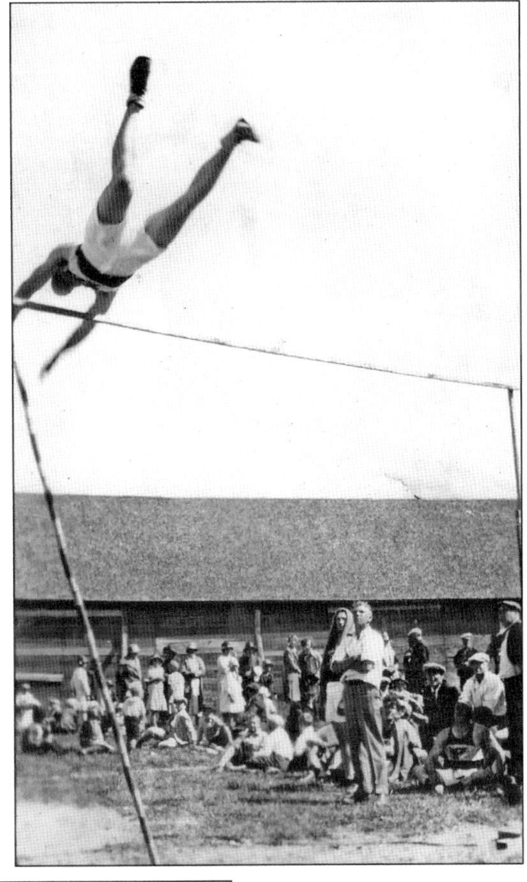

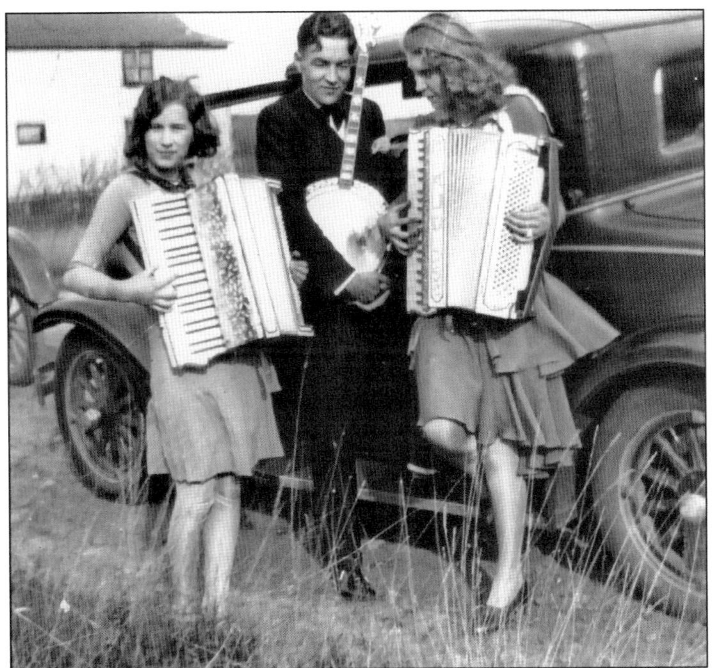

Famous Finnish American accordionists Viola Turpeinen (right) and Sylvia Polso are pictured here in the 1930s. Turpeinen was born in Champion in 1909 into a Finnish family. From a very early age, she practiced accordion and, in 1928, did her first recording for Columbia Records with Finnish-born violin and banjo player John Rosedahl (center). Her career continued until 1952 when she did her last recordings.

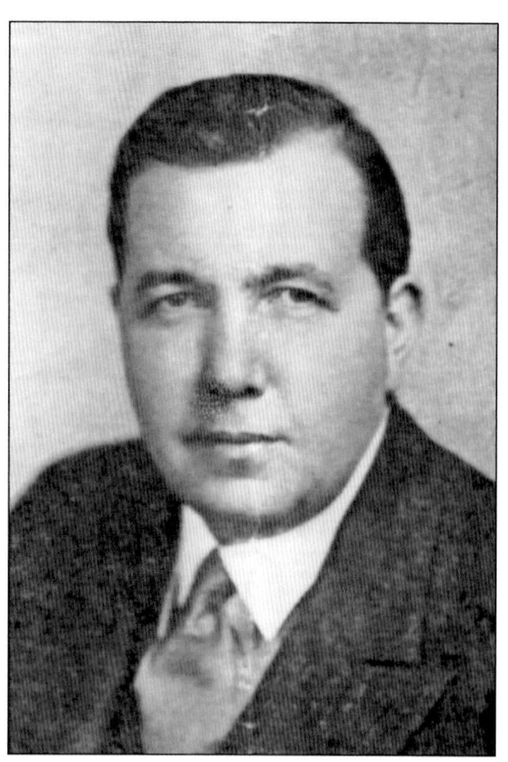

The "pioneer of political polling," Crystal Falls native Emil Hurja (1892–1953) was featured on the cover of *Time* magazine in March 1936. Hurja was Franklin Roosevelt's private pollster—the first man to systematically gather data on political behavior and use it to win elections. Some have said that Hurja helped transform American politics.

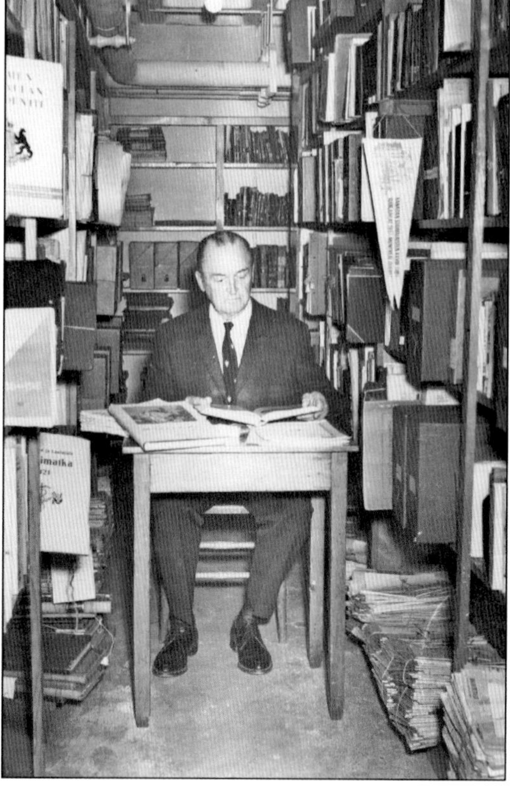

Helsinki native Armas Holmio (1897–1977) was a theology and church history professor at Suomi College who is best known as the archivist at the college. His efforts established the Finnish American Historical Archive, which grew from a basement office to a world-renowned collection housed in the Finnish American Heritage Center. He was the author of *History of the Finns in Michigan*, a go-to resource for scholars of Finnish American history.

For several decades, Finnish Americans would stop for afternoon coffee at 3:00 p.m. and tune in to WHDF radio as longtime newsman Reino Suojanen (1902–1995) provided a newscast in Finnish each day, sharing with listeners the information from Finnish-language newspapers in their native tongue. During his long career in media, Suojanen also worked for several Finnish-language newspapers.

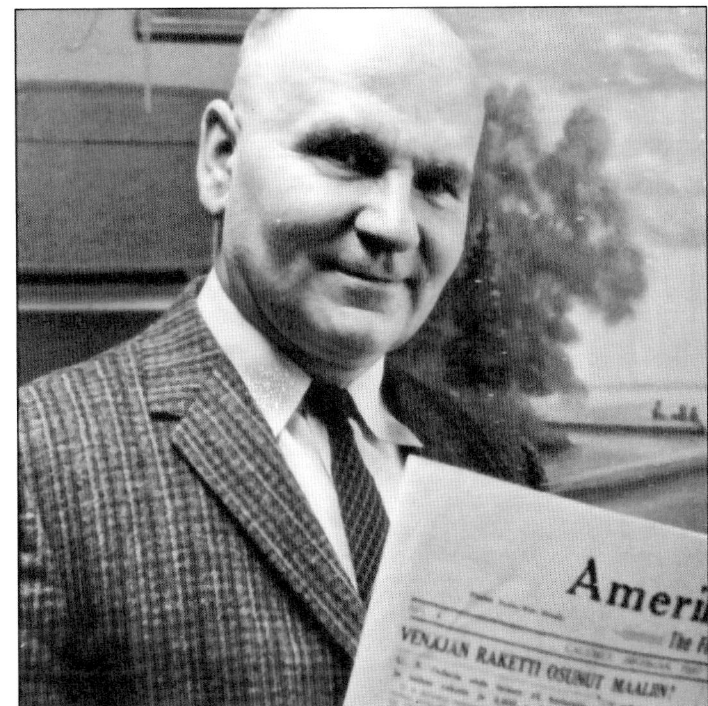

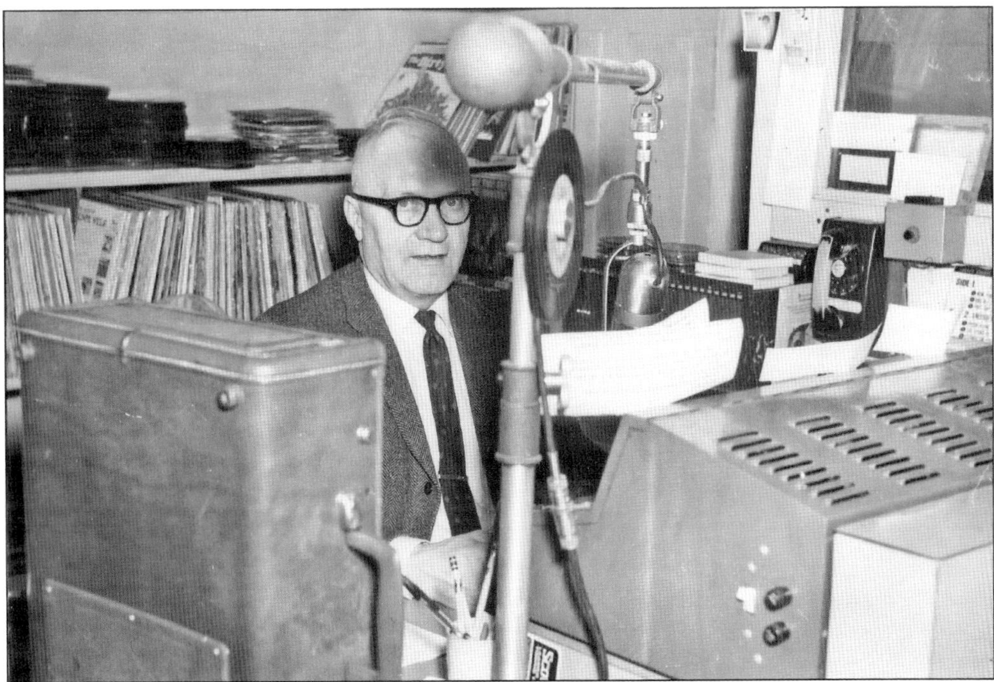

Rudolph "Rudy" Kemppa (1909–1992) began his long and storied broadcast career at Houghton-based WHDF, and over the course of several decades, became well known for bringing Finnish music to listeners in the western UP. He was so devoted to his craft that by the end of his life, he had accumulated an album collection so vast that Finnish DJs sought copies of needed recordings from him. (Kemppa-Miettinen family.)

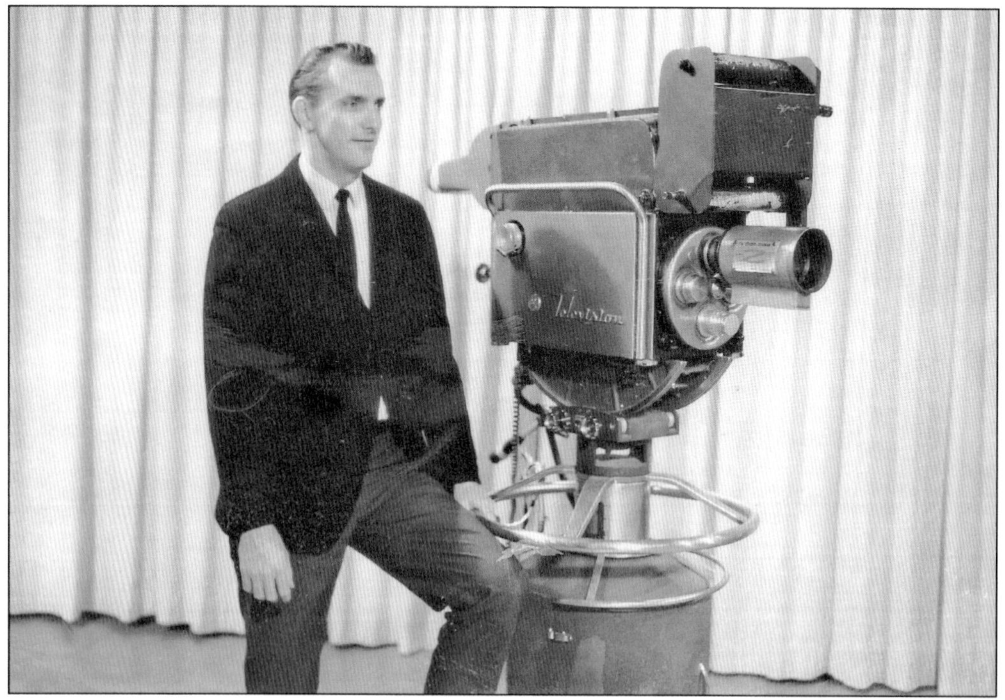

One of the longest-running shows in history, *Suomi Kutsuu* (Finland Calling) started in 1962 to increase interest in travel to Finland and was expected to last a couple years. Every Sunday morning for more than five decades, WLUC-TV6 anchorman Carl Pellonpää hosted the hour-long program, which magnified the Ishpeming native's celebrity. Sparked by the success, Pellonpää led frequent tours to Finland, and *Suomi Kutsuu* dances across the UP.

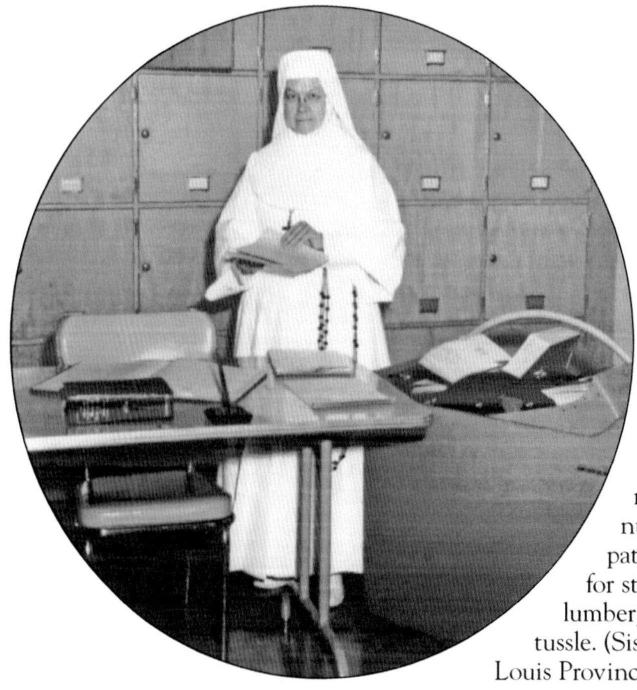

Called the "Finnish Angel of Mercy on Snowshoes," Sr. Mary Augustine (also known as Sister Mildred) served the Copper Country as a nurse, nun, and social worker to the elderly. Folks were surprised that a Catholic nun could speak Finnish. She is remembered for teaching the other nuns Finnish phrases to use with patients who struggled with English and for standing her ground with an unruly lumberjack who broke her spine during a tussle. (Sisters of St. Joseph of Carondelet, St. Louis Province.)

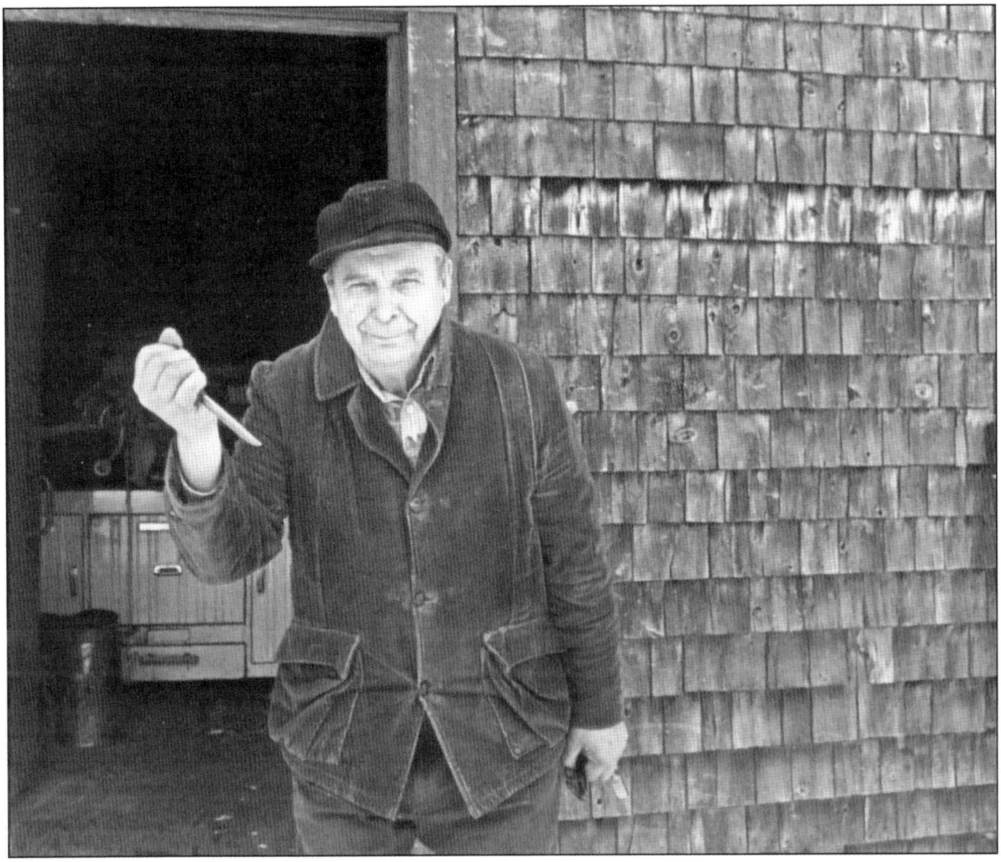

Copper Country residents might not have recognized the name Arvo Pyörälä, but they surely remember "Hotline Charlie." Pyörälä (1905–2001) was known throughout the region by his nickname, bestowed upon him for his frequent radio appearances on WMPL of Hancock during the station's daily morning programming. He educated listeners with his vast knowledge of Finnish folklore, sayings, and weather predictions.

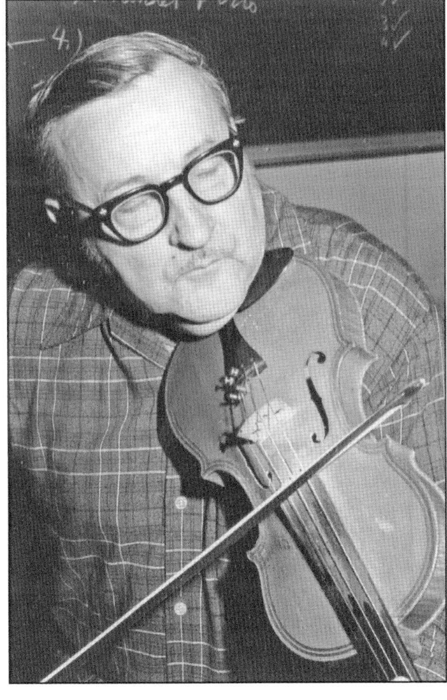

Helmer Töyräs (1926–2014) was a centerpiece of the famed Aura Jamboree, which annually draws hundreds of folk musicians to his small hometown in northeastern Baraga County. Töyräs developed his interest in the violin while in high school; that interest evolved into fiddling while he and his wife owned Hoppy's Bar in Kenton from the 1960s through the 1970s.

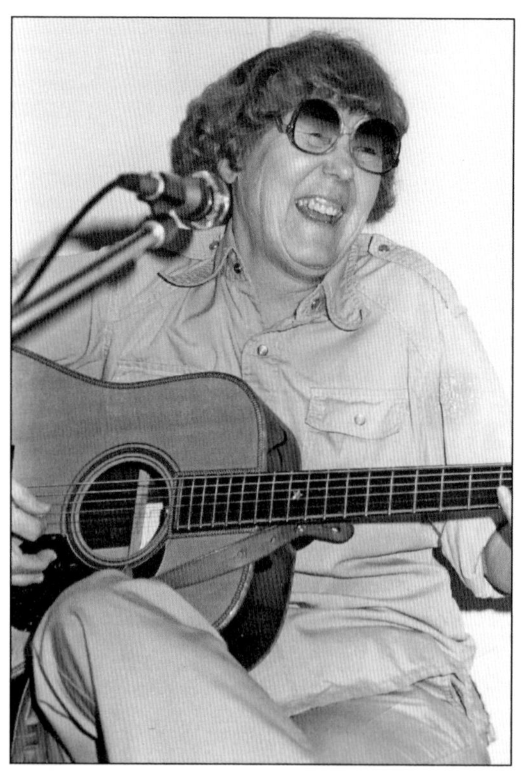

Every picture tells a story, but with Jingo Viitala Vachon (1918–2009), every story painted a picture. Jingo shared stories from her childhood in Toivola in newspapers and in books. Her works resulted in three volumes of anecdotes, written in Finglish, about growing up Finnish-American. Not limited to writing, she also played the guitar and shared folk songs from the immigrant generation.

Ralph Jalkanen (left) was president of Suomi College for 30 years, achieving many successes; the pinnacle of his career was when he hosted Finland's president Urho Kekkonen (right) in 1976 for a bicentennial celebration dubbed Finn Fest; this was the first time a Finnish president had visited Upper Michigan. Kekkonen, revered as Finland's greatest president, was in Hancock for only one day, but the significance of that visit is still remembered.

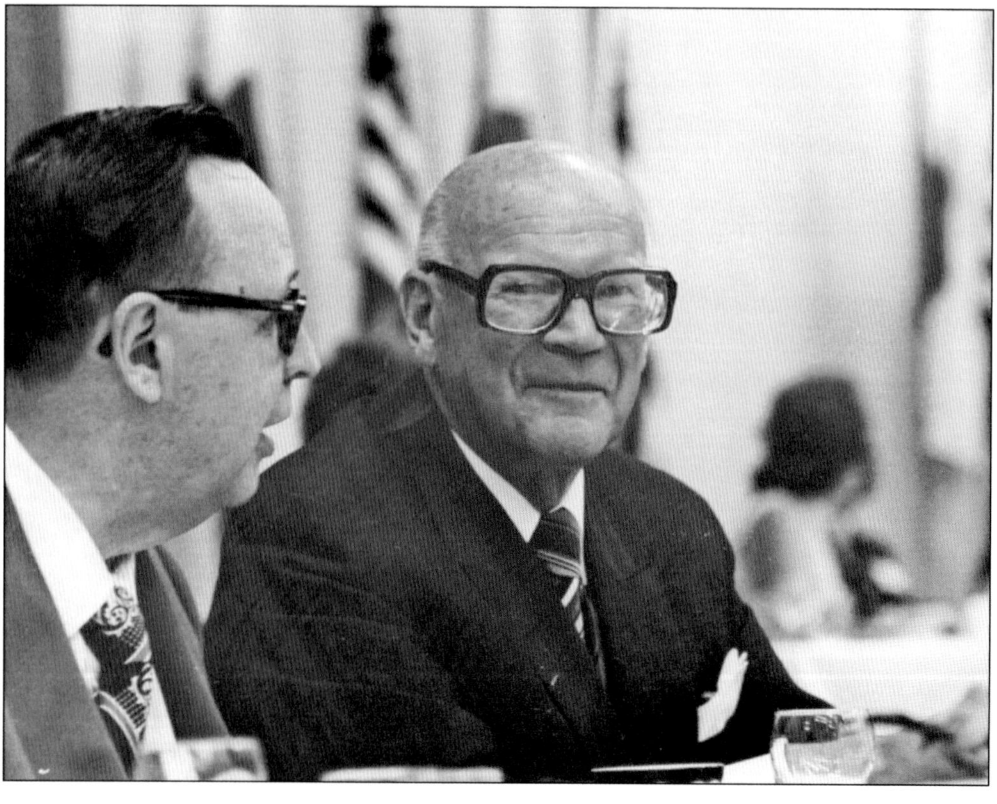

Eight

Do You Remember?

The story of Finnish Americans in Upper Michigan is filled with anecdotes, episodes, and incidents that will forever be lodged in the memory banks and photo albums of the folks who were involved in these events and pastimes, or at least heard about them. Some stories are vividly remembered, while others are looming just below the surface, waiting to be recalled. That is why the question "Do you remember?" is perhaps the greatest conversation starter—no matter the language.

Sometimes memories, stories, and facts get a bit jumbled when they are passed down from generation to generation. Sorting out anecdotes from actualities can be difficult when the immigrant generation has all but disappeared. Even today, many later-generation Finnish Americans believe their great-great-grandfather left Finland to avoid being conscripted into the czar's army, but in actuality, this was only a threat between 1901 and 1905, when the Finnish army was discontinued, and the law of compulsory military service stated that Finns should join the Russian army. Most immigrants departed Finland due to lack of land and jobs.

Similarly, the oft-repeated story of a family name being changed at Ellis Island is little more than a myth. Most name changes were made by the immigrants themselves in an effort to be more Americanized, to start their new life with a clean slate, or to fit in better in their new communities.

The reader is invited to remember the special and sometimes just curious moments in the history of Upper Michigan Finns. Of course, not every occurrence can be preserved on the pages of this book—to share them all would necessitate a volume much thicker than this. So, here is a sampling of the episodes that have helped to make the story of Upper Michigan Finns unique and unforgettable. Do you remember?

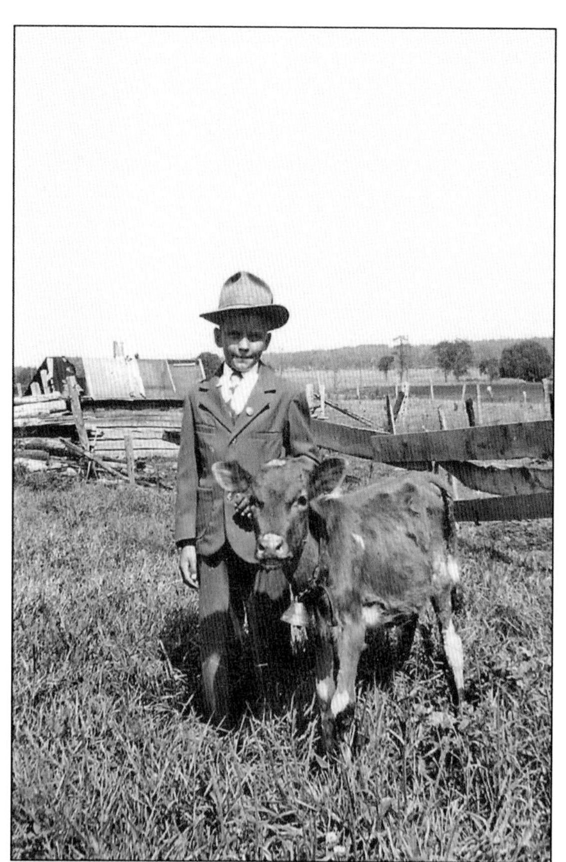

Making hay, picking berries, fishing, and taking sauna was a part of many city kids' summers when they were sent to their grandparents' farms in the UP. Young Gary Lelvis, dressed in his Sunday best, poses with his favorite calf down on the farm. (James Kurtti.)

In the rural schools of Upper Michigan, like Tapiola's Doelle School, students had instruction not only in reading, writing, and mathematics, but also delved into lessons that were quite practical for their life and family circumstances. Such was the case when the butcher from the town's Karvakko-Järvenpää store offered a first-hand demonstration of his craft. (James Kurtti.)

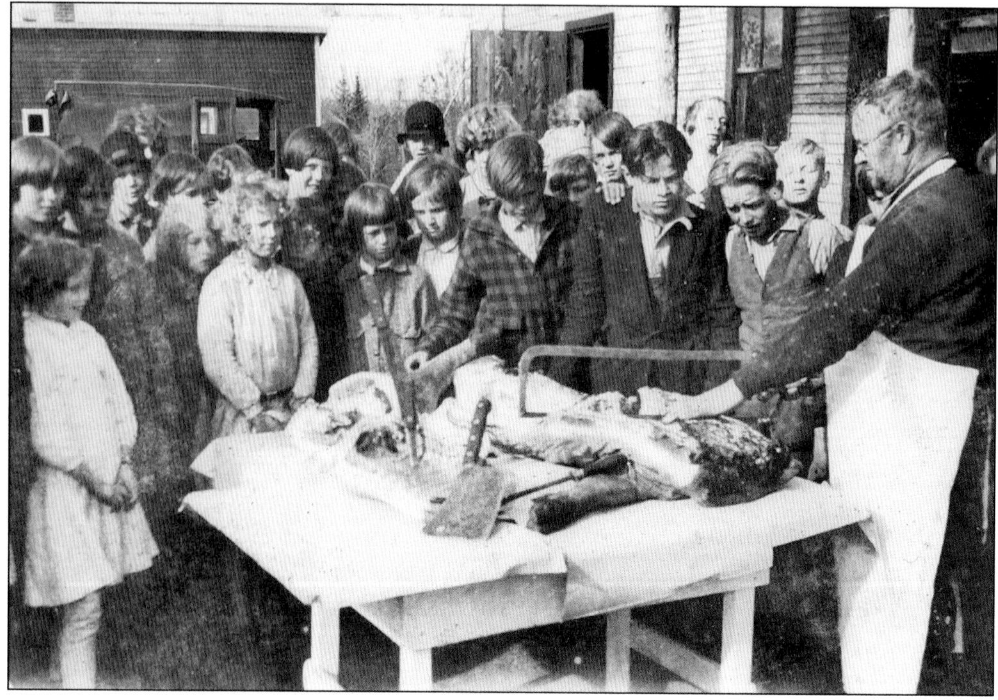

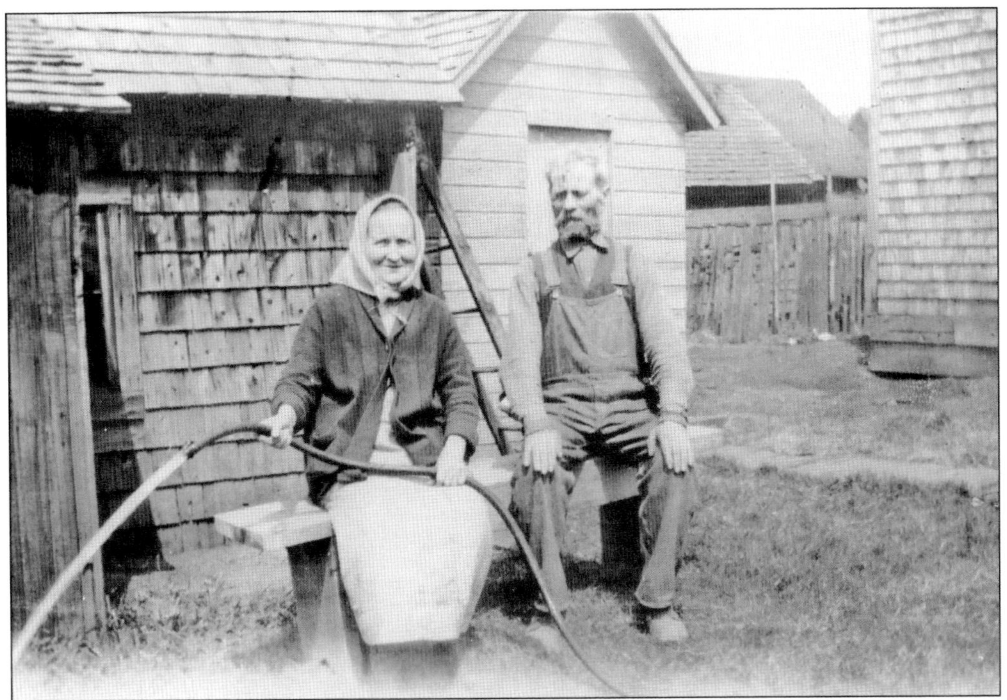

It was a great day in the Keweenaw County village of Kearsarge when Finnish American homesteaders Maria and Joonas Wahtola finally got the modern convenience of running water at their farm. Though they were not going to discard their favorite water cans as a result, they were proud to show the photographer their new garden hose. (James Kurtti.)

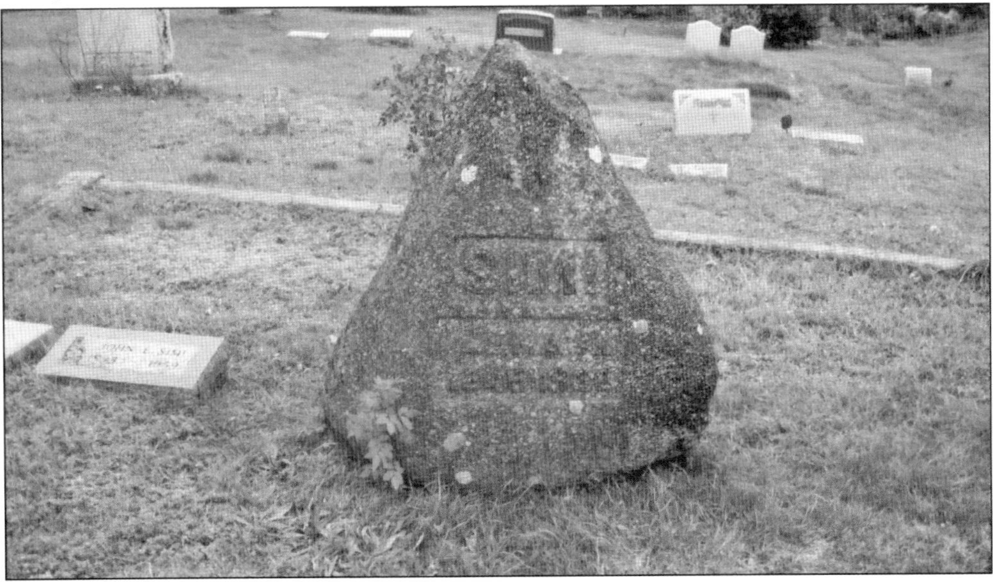

St. Henry's Lutheran Church in Nisula, named for the patron saint of Finland, is the model of traditional Finnish American churches—log construction in a Finnish farming area. But what sets this church apart from others in Upper Michigan is a meteorite that landed near the local Simi farm and was recovered by the family and preserved, eventually being engraved and used as the headstone for Lena K. Simi. (Joanna Chopp.)

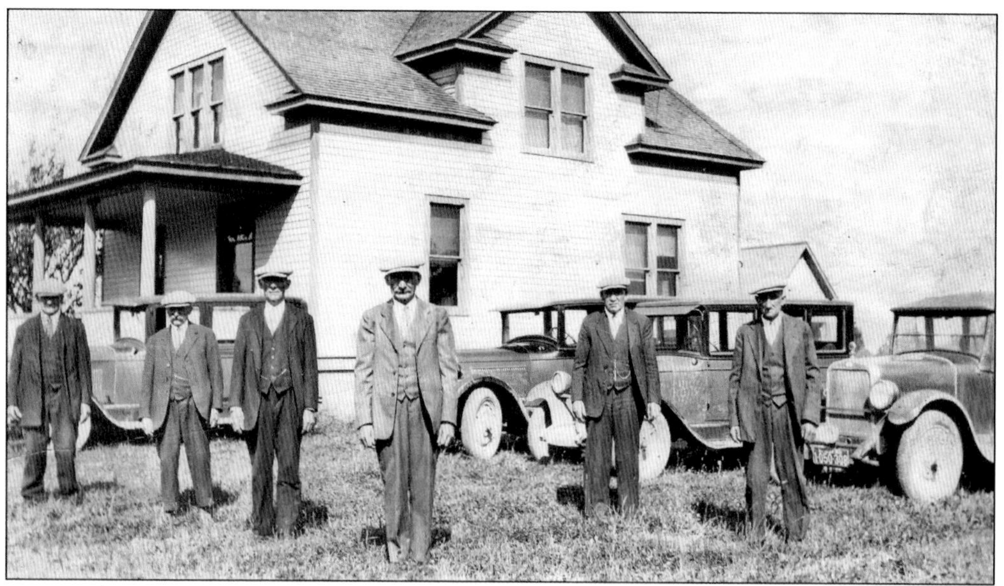

Among these six immigrant brothers who gathered at one's home in Watton were three different last names. In Finland, it was a common practice for men to take on the surname of the home where they lived, rather than to keep the name of their father.

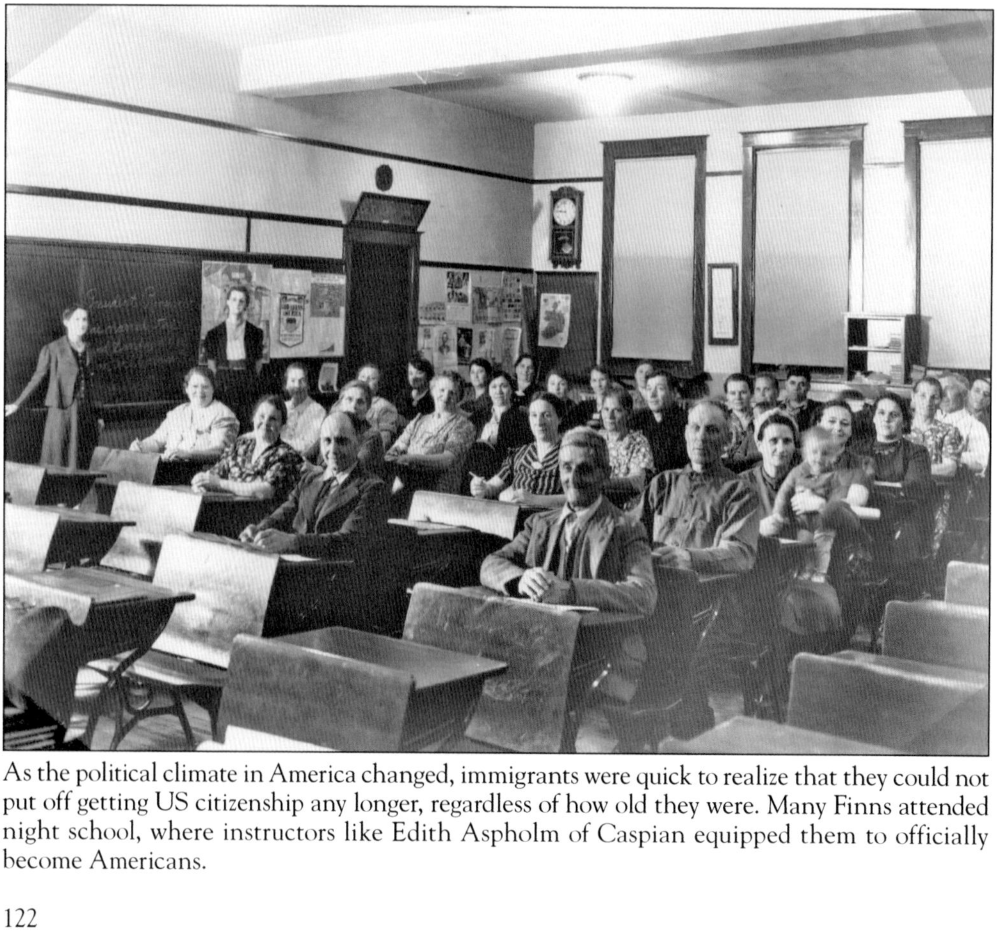

As the political climate in America changed, immigrants were quick to realize that they could not put off getting US citizenship any longer, regardless of how old they were. Many Finns attended night school, where instructors like Edith Aspholm of Caspian equipped them to officially become Americans.

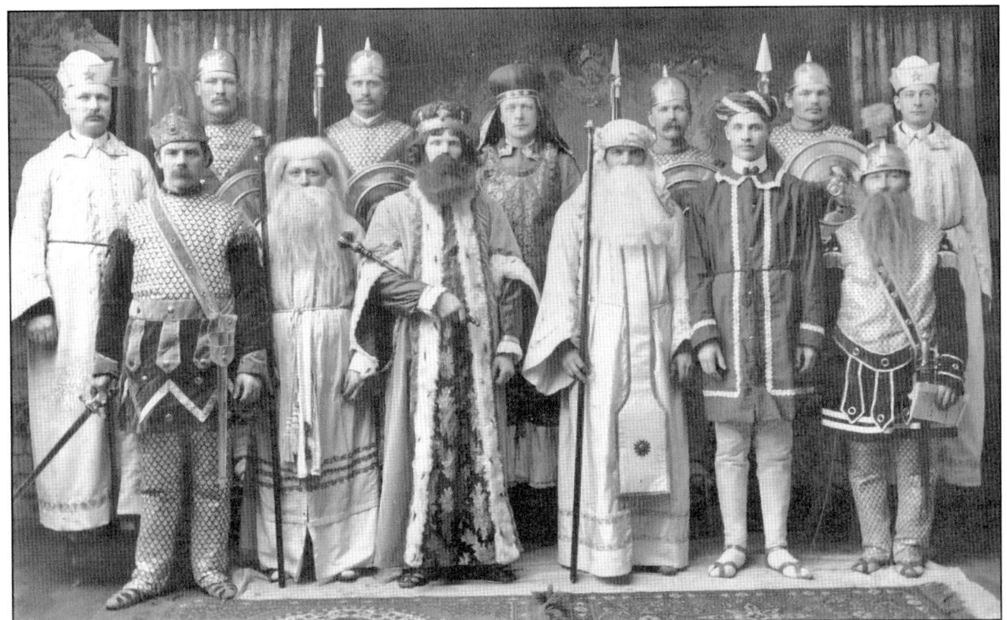

Finnish halls across the UP played host to many cultural events. Among them were plenty of theatrical performances, which drew not only capacity audiences from the local community, but also extensive involvement from the locals, both as actors and as behind-the-scenes personnel, costumers, set builders, and the like.

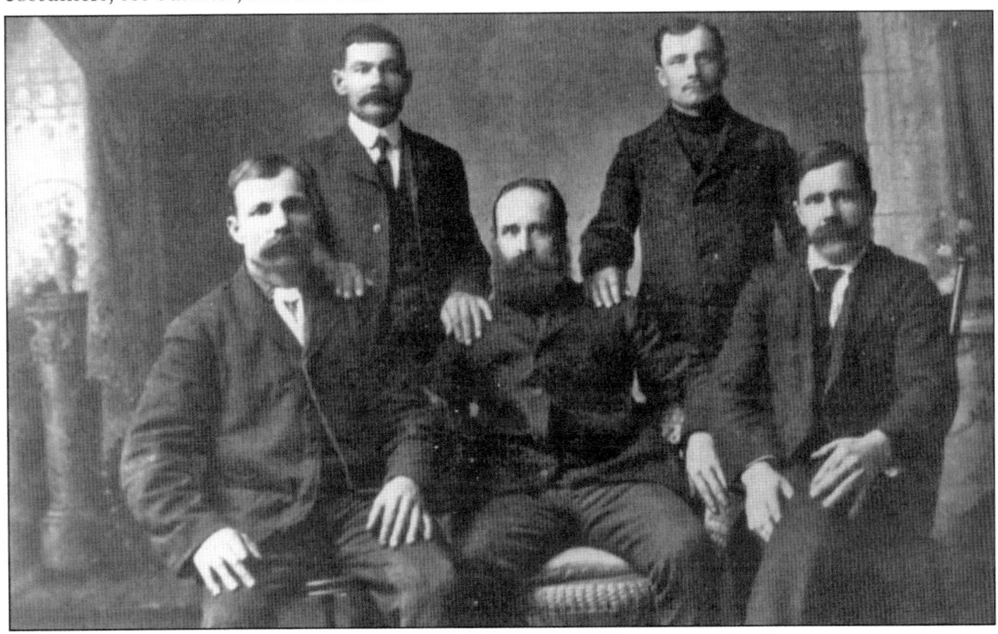

In the late 1800s, J.H. Jasberg was a Finnish businessman in Hancock. He was involved in the Finnish Mining Co., with interests in Alaska's gold rush. At that time, a US government program brought reindeer to Alaska to alleviate starvation and promote economic development among Alaska's indigenous people. A decade after the program started, Jasberg offered to recruit reindeer herders from among the newly arrived immigrants to Michigan's Copper Country. Pictured are five of the eight Finnish reindeer herders recruited from Michigan to Alaska in 1904.

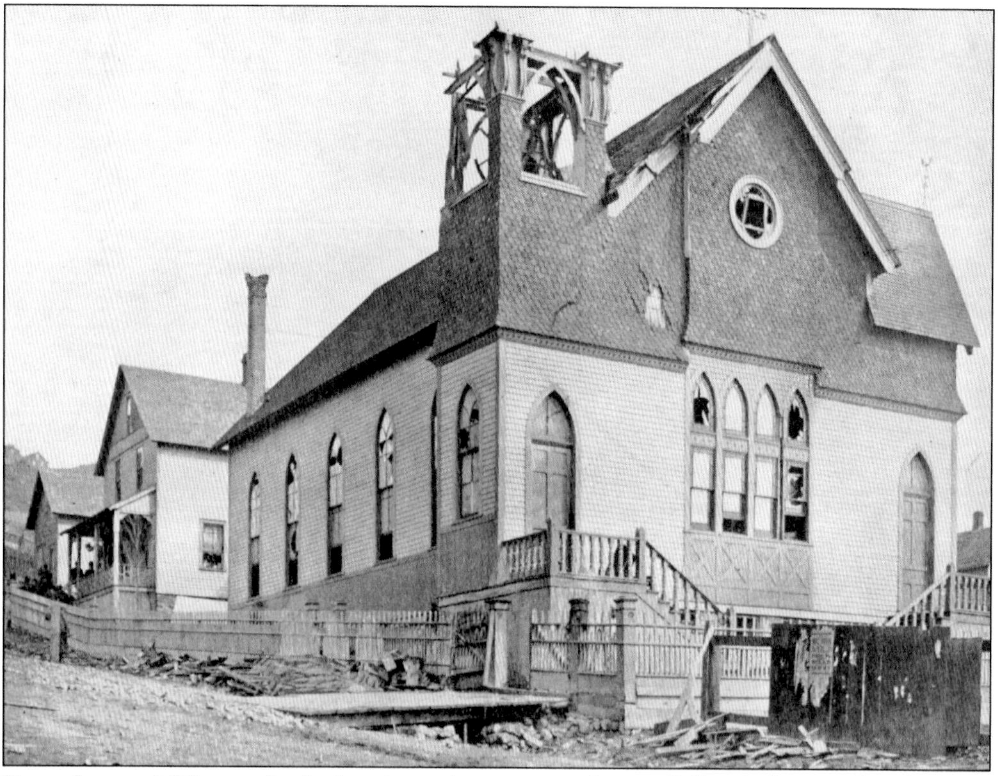

Pastor Jooseppi Riippa, who had emigrated to serve as Suomi College's first teacher, had just dismissed his Sunday school students at the Finnish Evangelical Lutheran Church he served when this picture was taken. A thunderstorm blew in, and a bolt of lightning struck the church steeple, with the resulting current killing the young clergyman. The church burned completely in 1909, and the present building was erected in 1910.

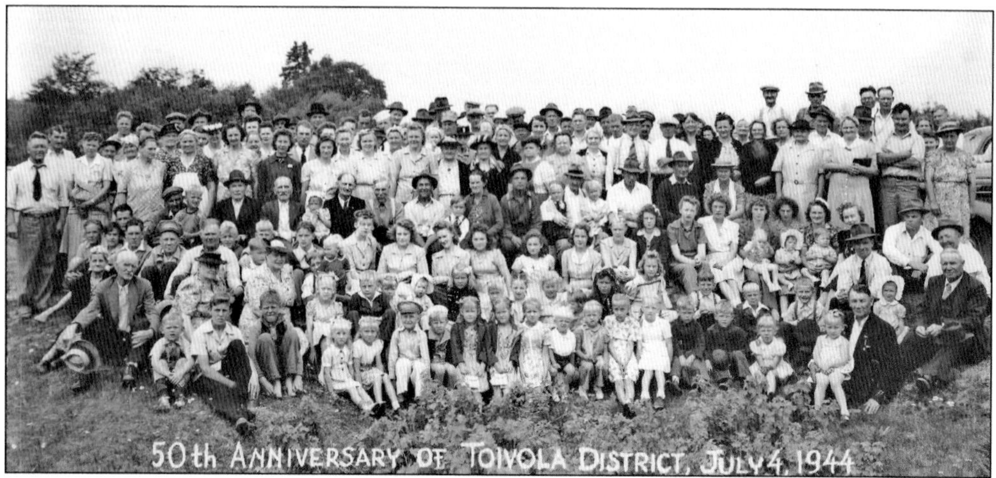

In its heyday, the Houghton County village of Toivola had enough population to support several rural schools. Named for the Finnish word meaning "Land of Hope," the residents of this small settlement never lost their sense of community; the village still celebrates Juhannus (Midsummer) annually by lighting a bonfire on the shore of Lake Superior, with hundreds coming to join the fun.

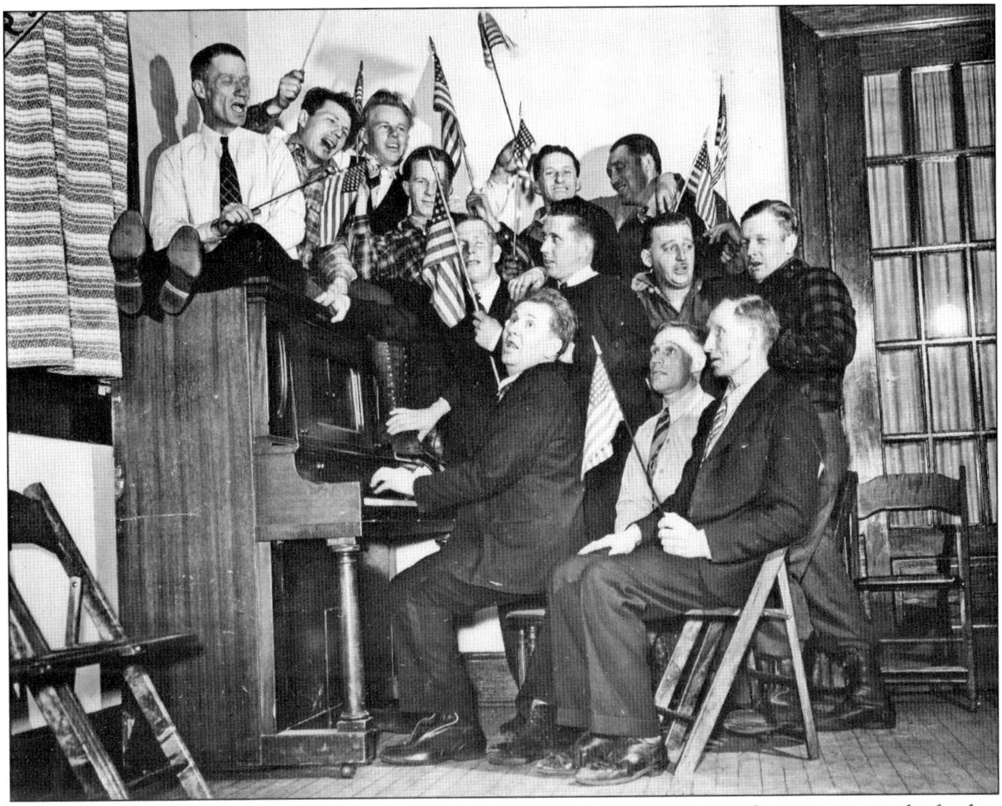

Suomi College music director Martti Nisonen (center, at piano) was known not only for his musical talents, but also his intense and unwavering patriotism for both his homeland and his adopted homeland. He recruited many Finnish American men to serve their country, whether it was Finland or the United States. Nisonen himself fought alongside famed general Mannerheim to establish Finland as an independent republic.

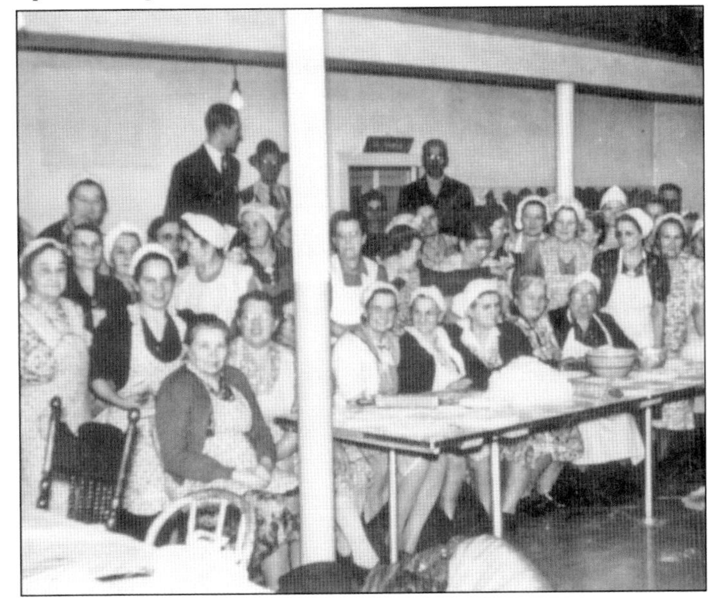

After wars decimated Finland over six years (1939–1945), the country was in shambles. Every Finn across the United States—including the women of St. Matthews Lutheran Church in Hancock, who sent profits from pasty sales—stepped up as they could to ease the suffering. These efforts, known as "Finnish Relief," began during the Winter War and were headquartered in New York. Former US president Herbert Hoover was president of the Finnish Relief Fund.

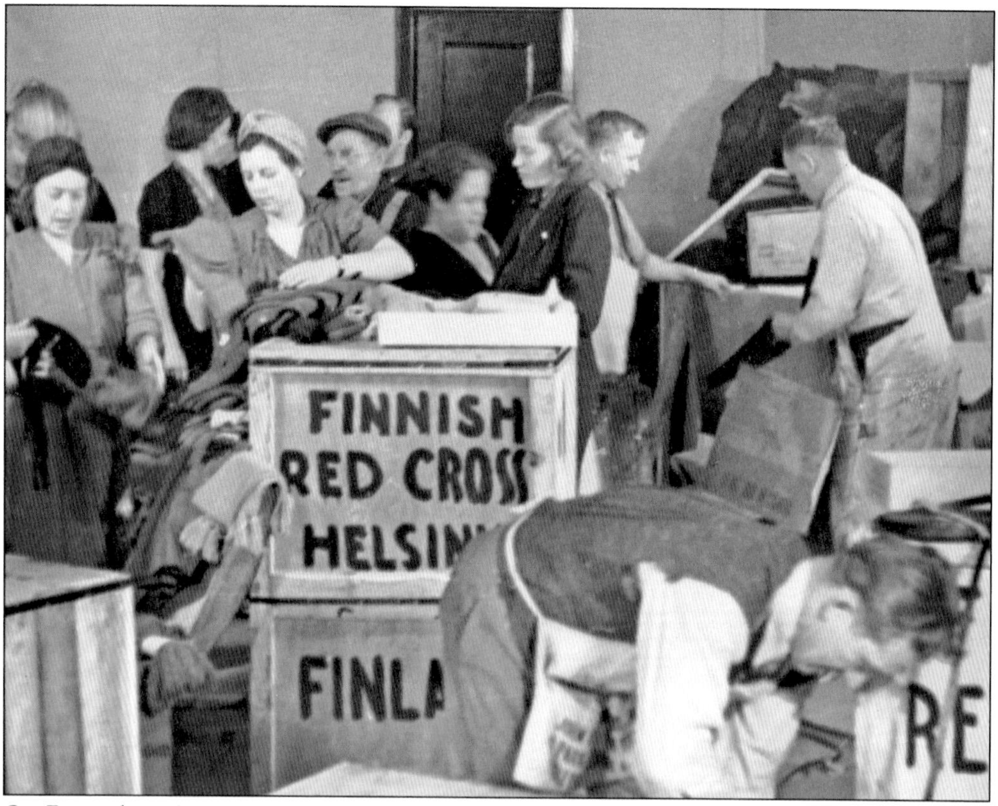

On December 12, 1944, a group known as Help Finland Inc. organized to provide Finland's citizens desperately needed packages of clothes, food, and shoes. Dr. Viljo Nikander was its president; Oskari Tokoi, Dr. John Wargelin, Rev. A. Groop, and O.J. Larson were vice presidents; Preston Davie assumed the treasurer's role; and Esther L. Hietala became the secretary and, later, executive director.

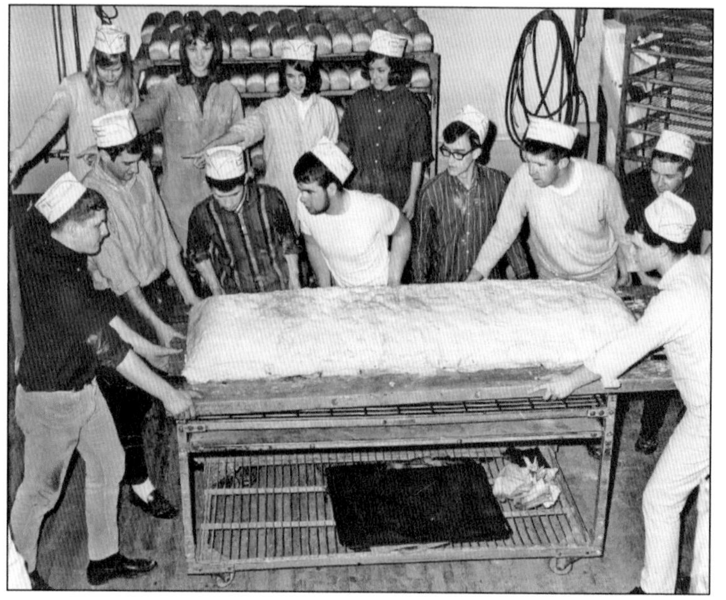

This group of 1960s Suomi College students was intent on creating and baking the world's largest pasty. Rather than serve as the lunch pail-sized meaty treat that sustained immigrant miners during the underground shifts, this pasty could have nourished an entire crew of Finnish laborers—though it would have certainly taken quite a while to bake.

These Boy Scout troop members from Redridge are all Finns, but being Finnish did not mean that they could not be part of the American culture around them. Organizations like Boy Scouts helped the youth not only to learn knot tying and other new skills, but also how to become active members in the American society.

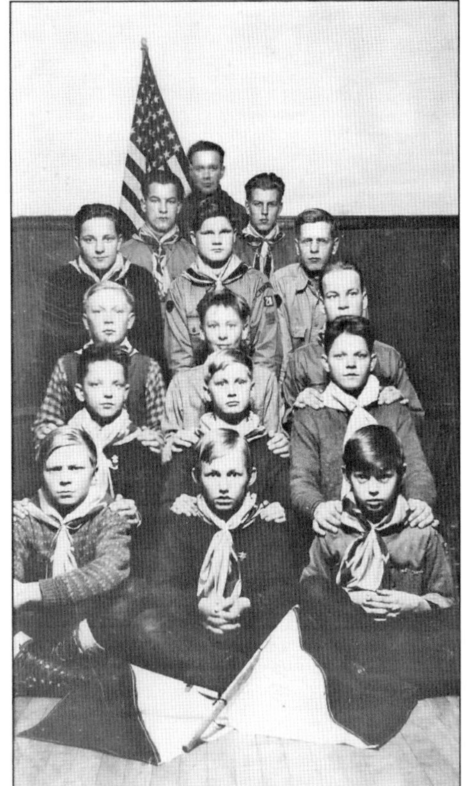

From the time it was built in 1930, through to the final performance under its roof in 1986, the Co-op Hall in Bruce Crossing was truly the center of things. Community members held a spectrum of events in the hall, ranging from weddings or funerals to fundraisers and theater performances, such as this 1955 children's program that was staged in an effort to raise funds for the hall.

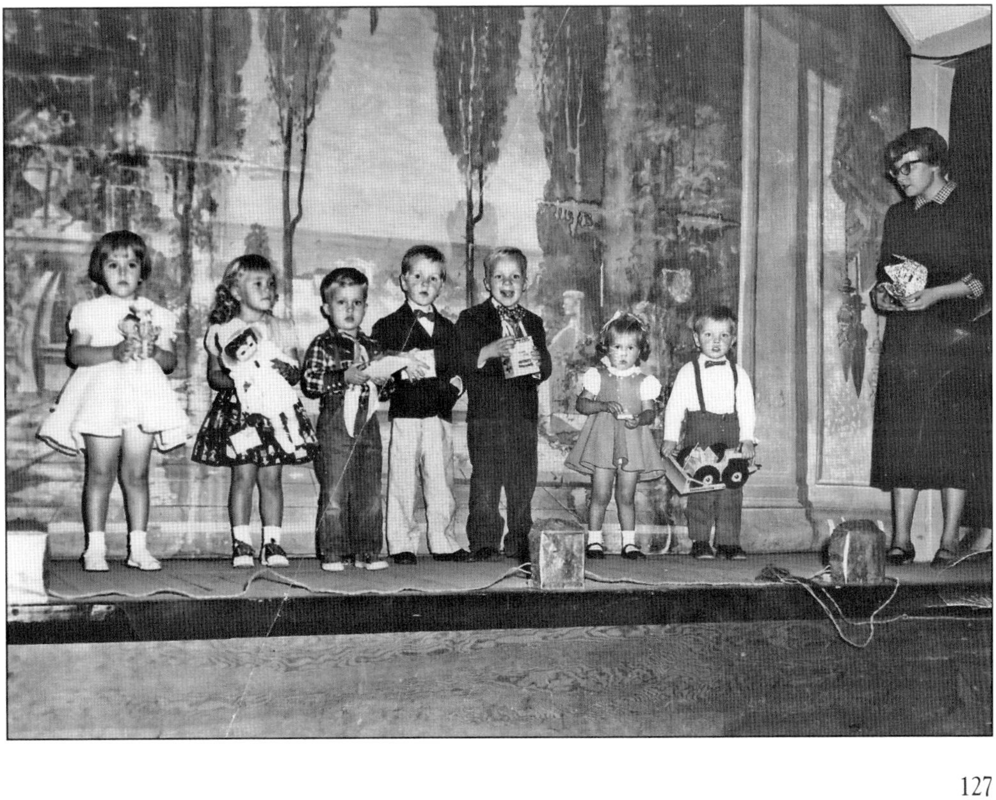

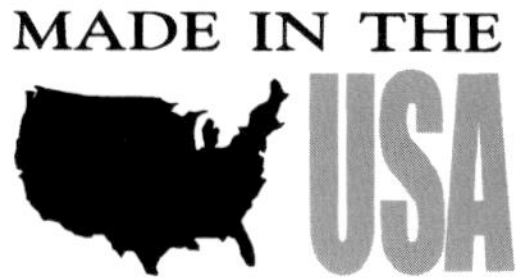
MADE IN THE
USA